THE DEVIL'S CHILDREN

A number of cases of serious child abuse have resulted from beliefs that children may be possessed by evil spirits and may then be given the power to bewitch others. Misfortune, failure, illness and even death may be blamed on them. The 'cure', nowadays called deliverance rather than exorcism, is to expel the spirits, sometimes by violent means.

This book draws together contributions on aspects of possession and witchcraft from leading academics and expert practitioners in the field. It has been put together following conferences held by Inform, a charity that provides accurate information on new religions as a public service. There is no comparable information publicly available; this book is the first of its kind. Eileen Barker, founder of Inform, introduces the subject and Inform's Deputy Director goes on to detail the requests the charity has answered in recent years on the subject of children, possession and witchcraft. This book offers an invaluable resource for readers, whether academic or practitioner – particularly those in the fields of the safeguarding of children, and their education, health and general welfare.

The Devil's Children

From Spirit Possession to Witchcraft:
New Allegations that Affect Children

Edited by

JEAN LA FONTAINE
London School of Economics, UK

ASHGATE

Published by
Ashgate Publishing Limited
Wey Court East
Union Road
Farnham
Surrey, GU9 7PT
England

Ashgate Publishing Company
Suite 420
101 Cherry Street
Burlington
VT 05401-4405
USA

www.ashgate.com

British Library Cataloguing in Publication Data
The devil's children : from spirit possession to witchcraft : new allegations that affect children.
    1. Spirit possession. 2. Child abuse–Religious aspects.
    I. La Fontaine, J. S. (Jean Sybil), 1931–
    133.4'26'083–dc22

Library of Congress Cataloging-in-Publication Data
The devil's children : from spirit possession to witchcraft : new allegations that affect children / [edited by] Jean La Fontaine.
       p. cm.
    Papers presented at two seminars held Dec. 2005 and May 2006.
    ISBN 978-0-7546-6733-9 (hardcover : alk. paper)
   1. Spirit possession–Congresses. 2. Demonic possession–Congresses. 3. Witchcraft–Congresses. 4. Exorcism–Congresses. 5. Child welfare–Congresses. 6. Child abuse–Congresses. I. La Fontaine, J. S. (Jean Sybil), 1931–

    BL482.D48 2009
    204'.2–dc22

2009019658

ISBN 9780754667339 (hbk)
ISBN 9780754697404 (ebk)

Mixed Sources
Product group from well-managed forests and other controlled sources
www.fsc.org Cert no. SA-COC-1565
© 1996 Forest Stewardship Council
FSC

Printed and bound in Great Britain by
MPG Books Group, UK

Contents

PART III Children Accused

List of Figures

List of Contributors

Amma Anane-Agyei is Ghanaian by birth but trained as a social worker in England, where she has lived for many years. She is the Coordinator for the African Families Service, London Borough Tower Hamlets, Trainer, Consultant and Registered Expert Witness Assessor.

Professor Eileen Barker Ph.D. OBE FBA is a sociologist, specialising in the Sociology of Religion in which she has become internationally known. She is Professor Emeritus, London School of Economics and the Founder, Chair and Honorary Director of Inform, an independent charity that was founded in 1988 with the support of the British Home Office and the mainstream Churches. It has the aim of obtaining and making available objective and up-to-date information about new and/or minority religious movements.

Professor Filip de Boeck is an anthropologist by training, and has worked for many years on research, both rural and urban, in the Democratic Republic of Congo. His most recent work, *Kinshasa. Tales of the Invisible City*, an internationally renowned work, reports on research undertaken with street children accused of witchcraft. He is currently the director of the Institute for Anthropological Research in Africa (IARA) at the Catholic University of Leuven, Belgium.

Dr Simon Dein Ph.D. is MRCPsych Senior Lecturer Anthropology and Medicine, Centre for Behavioural and Social Sciences in Medicine, University College London. Dr Dein has studied Bangladeshis in East London.

Dr Malcolm Gold is Associate Professor of Sociology at Malone College, Canton, Ohio, USA. He completed his Bachelor of Social Science degree in 1994 at Birmingham University and has an MA in Philosophy and Social Theory and a Ph.D. in sociology from Warwick University. His principal interests are the Pentecostal/Charismatic movements and developments within evangelicalism. His book, *The Hybridization of an Assembly of God Church: Proselytism, Retention, and Re-affiliation* was published in 2003 by the Edwin Mellen Press.

Professor Jean La Fontaine, (editor) Ph.D. Anthropology Cambridge is a Research Fellow of Inform, and Professor Emeritus at the London School of Economics. She has carried out anthropological fieldwork in eastern Uganda, Kinshasa (Democratic Republic of the Congo) and in England. She has taught anthropology at Birkbeck College London and the London School of Economics. Her most recent book

Speak of the Devil concerned allegations of devil worship in England. She is currently studying accusations of witchcraft against children in London.

Professor Roland Littlewood is Professor of Anthropology and Psychiatry at University College London and Joint Director of the UCL Centre for Medical Anthropology, London, UK. He qualified from St Bartholomew's Hospital and Oxford University. He has carried out fieldwork in Trinidad, Haiti, Italy, Lebanon and Albania and is the author of eight books and over 150 academic papers.

Mercy Magbagbeola is a senior member of the Celestial Church of Christ and is one of its prophets. Although Nigerian by birth, Mercy Magbagbeola has lived in Britain for 34 years. She is a nurse, trained originally in Nigeria, but has also trained as a psychiatric nurse in Britain. She is currently practising as a psychiatric social worker, taking part in mental health assessments of clients.

Sherrill Mulhern is an anthropologist by training, and is internationally known for her work on multiple personality, rumors of Satanism and possession. After many years at the University of Paris 7, she now divides her time between the United States and France where she continues to lecture annually at the Institut Français d'Hypnose. She also serves on the editorial board of the journal *Anthropology and Medicine*.

Dr Christina Harrington has been in the Wiccan tradition for over 15 years, and is here writing as a practitioner. Her professional background is in history, with a doctorate from University College London and her monograph was published by Oxford University Press. Currently she runs Treadwell's Bookshop in Covent Garden, which specialises in magic and occult belief.

David Pearson is Founder and Executive Director of the Churches' Child Protection Advisory Service, which is a pioneer in developing safe and effective protection policies for children for use by churches. It works closely with the police, local authorities, the probation service and churches throughout the UK.

DI Robert Pull is a Detective Inspector with 30 years police service in the Metropolitan Police, and has been working for five years in a multi-faith environment. For the 12 months preceding the Inform conference at which he spoke, he worked with Project Violet in the Child Abuse Investigation Command of the Metropolitan Police. Since the conference he has retired. Currently he is working part-time with the Churches' Child Protection Advisory Service. He is a Baptist Minister and plans to set up an organisation, Safe to Worship, which will be primarily to assist black majority churches here in the UK.

Dr Bettina Schmidt gained her MA in 1989, a PhD in 1995 and an 'habilitation' (a post-doctorate degree) in 2001. She is currently Senior Lecturer in Study of

Religions at Bangor University, Wales, and was previously at Oxford University, Philipps-University Marburg, Germany, and City University of New York, USA. She is a cultural anthropologist who has published widely in the area of Caribbean and Latin American religions, cultural theories, diaspora/migration, medical anthropology and anthropology of religions.

Eleanor Stobart was a senior ward sister specialising in infectious diseases, tropical medicine and HIV in London Teaching Hospitals before changing direction and taking an MBA at Bradford University Management Centre. For the past ten years she has worked as an independent consultant leading on various projects for government departments and large organisations. Her specialist area is safeguarding children. The research published here was undertaken for the then Department for Education and Skills on child abuse linked to accusations of 'possession' and 'witchcraft'. She continues to work on this issue as well as forced marriage and trafficking.

Dr Amanda van Eck Duymaer van Twist is Deputy Director of Inform. Her Ph.D., completed at the London School of Economics (LSE) in the Department of Sociology, examined the second generation of sectarian movements and the impact their 'segregated childhoods' have had. As part of her work at Inform she has encountered many individuals affected by alternative religious movements, and frequently writes in-depth reports on particular new and/or alternative religions, or issues pertaining to such groups.

Acknowledgements

This is an Inform book. Inform staff organised the two conferences from which it emerged; the staff have done all the hard work of copy editing, ensuring that the manuscript we submitted to Ashgate was as near perfect as we could get. For cheerfully adding this work to their normal load, Amanda van Eck Duymaer van Twist, Sarah Harvey, Suzanne Newcombe, Silke Steidinger and Charlotte Alton have my heartfelt gratitude.

The cover photograph was taken by Robin Hammond (www.robin.hammond.co.uk) for Stepping Stones Nigeria, a charity that helps rescue, care for and educate children accused of witchcraft in this part of Nigeria (www.steppingstonesnigeria.org). We are grateful to them for allowing us to use this picture which displays the hostility and fear felt by adults towards these traumatised small children whom they believe to be witches.

Jean La Fontaine

Introduction

This introductory part is opened by Professor Eileen Barker, who gives an overview of the book setting its chapters in context. It is followed by a chapter written by Inform's Deputy Director, Dr Amanda van Eck Duymaer van Twist; entitled 'Beliefs in possession'. It describes the work of Inform in answering questions asked and problems posed by the public, illustrating this by sketching some of the cases that have caused enquiries. These show that ideas of possession, black magic, the evil eye and witchcraft can be used for exploitative purposes, resulting in vulnerable believers losing money and suffering from ill health through being directed away from public services that might otherwise help them. Extortion, abuse, control through fear or ignorance on the side of the client and manipulative abuse (emotional, physical, verbal, sexual) greed and misuse of power on the part of the supplier can be perceived. However, benign possession also exists and in this chapter it is distinguished from its malign counterparts, displaying the wide range of beliefs in possession.

Chapter 1

An Introduction to *The Devil's Children*

Eileen Barker

Amongst the more distressing incidents to have hit the British headlines in the twenty-first century have been a number of revelations concerning the treatment of children who, having been accused of being possessed by demonic powers, have been 'appropriately treated' in such a way that they have ended up either severely injured or dead. This book is an attempt to address some of the issues surrounding such tragedies and to place these in a wider context than that available in the more sensationalist media.

The image of a demon or evil entity possessing a human being is both titillating and terrifying; films such as *Rosemary's Baby* and *The Exorcist* have been runaway box office successes, exciting and scaring young and old alike. Audiences have been uncertain as to whether they were merely enjoying a modern form of entertainment or were witnessing an expression of dark forces that have been battling for the souls of human beings since the time of creation. Such images were, of course, commonplace in Biblical times,[1] but throughout the contemporary world one can find societies in which talk of such phenomena is a taken-for-granted part of every-day life. Nor, as is sometimes thought, are beliefs in possession confined to what are termed the more primitive societies. The Roman Catholic baptismal rite contains prayers for the exorcism of the candidate, and similar prayers have been restored to Anglicanism through the Alternative Service Book of 1980 (Cuneo 2001: 163). In his book, *American Exorcism*, Michael Cuneo tells us how, since the mid-1970s, countless Americans have become convinced that they themselves, or perhaps a loved one, are suffering from demonic affliction and are, thus, in need

---

[1] The belief in Satan and his army of demons or devils (depending on the translation) is evident in Jewish writings from 300 BCE. Evil spirits causing mental disturbances are mentioned quite frequently in the Old Testament, but they were not all from Satan, some being sent by God (Judges 9:23; I Kings 22:23; I Samuel 16:14; 18:10; 19:9). By the first century CE, possession was a well-developed concept in Palestine, with dozens of passages in the New Testament referring to demon possession causing mental and physical illnesses (e.g. Matthew 4:24; 8:16; 8:28-34; 9:32-3), and a major feature of Jesus' ministry was the curing of people with demonic possession through exorcism (e.g. Luke 8:33; Mark 1:23-6; Matthew *loc. cit*). Furthermore, Jesus assured his followers that, so long as they believed in him, they too would be able not only to cast out demons, but also to handle snakes and drink poisons with safety (Mark 16:17-18; Mark 6:7; Matthew 10:1). See also Gold (Chapter 5) in this volume.

of exorcism. He describes how, on scores of occasions, he has witnessed Catholic priests, a variety of Protestant ministers, medical doctors and certified psychiatrists performing exorcisms for thousands of middle-class American citizens. Many of those whom Cuneo interviewed claim to have come out much the better as a result, but there have been several accounts of exorcisms in North America and Europe leading to deaths and severe trauma.[2]

In Britain, among the cases to come most prominently to public attention were those of eight-year-old Victoria Climbié, who was murdered in February 2000, and eight-year-old 'Child B' who suffered serious abuse in 2005; both had been accused of being a witch (see Chapters 10 and 14). In October 2004 there was the case of three-month-old Samira Ullah, murdered by her father who was convinced that she was possessed by a *jinn* (see Chapter 6).[3] It was cases such as these that led Inform[4] to organise the two seminars at which most of the chapters in this book were first presented.[5] The first seminar, held in December 2005, was restricted to about 30 participants who had been invited to attend a closed workshop because of their professional interest in the subject of children being accused of possession by demons/evil spirits and/or of using witchcraft. Clergy, teachers, police, social welfare workers, anthropologists, sociologists and psychiatrists were represented in this group. The second meeting to be organised was more broadly entitled 'Spirit Possession and Exorcism'. It was held in May 2006 as one of the two open seminars that Inform holds each year on a given topic when it is the practice to invite speakers from as wide a range of perspectives as possible; these typically include practitioners/believers, critics, academics and others with personal knowledge or professional expertise. The Seminars are attended by about a hundred people, with a broad spectrum of interests.

Based at the London School of Economics and supported by the British government and mainstream Churches, Inform was founded with the aim of helping enquirers by providing information that is as reliable, balanced and up-to-date as possible about minority religions, faith movements and spiritual communities (Barker, 2006). Since the start of 1988, Inform has been collecting, assessing and

---

[2]   Even the most perfunctory of searches on the worldwide web can provide the casual explorer with allegations that a vast variety of exorcisms have been and are being performed – sometimes with, it is claimed, dire consequences. See, for example, 'Exorcism'. [Online]. Available at: http://en.wikipedia.org/wiki/Exorcism#Exorcism-related_deaths_and_traumas [accessed: 28 September 2008].

[3]   Some people have claimed that 'Adam', the child whose headless torso was found in the Thames in 2001, was murdered as part of a ritual killing, but to date there is no information to say how or why he died, despite the impressive result of the police investigation that identified the child's Nigerian origins.

[4]   Further to the information given below about Inform (Information Network Focus on Religious Movements), more details can be obtained from its website, www.inform.ac.

[5]   A few other papers were subsequently commissioned to broaden the scope of the volume.

disseminating information about what now amounts to well over 3,000 different groups and movements. This has involved covering scores of different topics and issues, one of which has been spiritual possession, another the religiously sanctioned abuse of children.

Inform has always believed in the importance of collecting data from every conceivable source. This includes information from the religious believers, their opponents, the media (including the Internet), scholars and other professionals who have some contact or expertise related to the religions and any individuals who have, or believe they have, some relevant knowledge. These data are filed both in a variety of electronic forms and in hard copy such as books, articles, cuttings, videos, cassettes, and DVDs. Obviously some sources are more reliable than others. Inform relies on the methodology of the social sciences to assess the accuracy and objectivity of the data it gathers in its attempt to offer information that is more dependable than that from other sources such as sections of the media, some cult-watching groups and the movements themselves, all of which may have an agenda that tends to make them somewhat selective in their accounts (Barker, 2002).

The social sciences have to recognise their limitations, however. They have no expertise, technologies or skills that allow them to judge theological or ethical claims. But that does not mean that they cannot use their methods to understand as far as possible the theological and ethical beliefs of those whom it studies, and to understand the variety of beliefs and perspectives that can motivate the actions of individuals and organisations. A related limitation of social (indeed all) science is that it can only describe and explain empirical or natural phenomena. It has to be 'methodologically agnostic' as it has no way of testing whether or not a supernatural being is responsible for any particular happening – or, to put it another way, it cannot cite God, the Devil, angels or evil spirits as independent variables. The fact that there are no objective criteria by which we can adjudicate between different claims of supernatural causation – whether, for example, an individual is possessed by some paranormal entity – has often resulted in methodological atheism, where happenings that some claim to be the result of possession are explained away as 'nothing but' a cultural expectation, a psychological illness or a somatic malfunctioning. Such reductionist explanations may be true, but science has no more entitlement to assume that they are the only 'real' explanation than that it has to assume theories of possession are false.[6] For this reason, Inform regularly invites proponents of a wide range of views to speak at its conferences in order to try to help others understand beliefs that are different from their own,

---

[6]   There are, of course, cases in which it can be shown that certain supernatural claims are extremely unlikely, even if they cannot be conclusively shown to be false. The point being made here, however, is that empirical evidence, by its very nature, cannot be used to disprove a non-empirical belief (Popper, 1963: 33-65) and that social scientists are more justifiably engaged in trying to describe and understand who believes what, under which circumstances and with what consequences than they are in trying to judge the truth or falsity of supernatural beliefs.

rather than to reach a conclusion about whose beliefs are 'right' or whose beliefs are 'wrong'.

Sometimes alternative explanations can be seen as being in direct competition, and, indeed, it is frequently the case that if one particular belief is true, then another belief must, logically, be wrong. Alternative perspectives can, however, be accepted as complementary. For example, in South Africa I spent some time with a *Sangoma* who was explaining to me how her healing powers depended upon her close association with (and occasional possession by) her ancestral spirits.[7] What interested me even more, however, was to discover that she had also been working as a representative of her 'Union' in close cooperation with the South African Ministry of Health to draw up a rigorous code of practice for the use of medical personnel, both blacks and whites, using both traditional and Western medicine.

While social science cannot always know what The Truth is, it can be drawn upon to inform people of certain things that are *not* the case. Where minority religions and alien beliefs and practices are concerned, suspicion, fear, ignorance and misinformation are rife. Frequently mistaken opinions about the beliefs and practices of others have led to inappropriate actions. Too often, people starting from one set of assumptions respond inappropriately to a situation arising from a different set of beliefs – on the one hand those who abuse may be ignored, and on the other hand perfectly innocent, 'good' people who would be horrified at the thought of hurting a fly are tarred with the same brush as the abusers.[8]

In Chapter 2, Amanda van Eck Duymaer van Twist describes some of the cases that have come to Inform and how they have indicated ways in which concepts of possession, black magic, the evil eye and the like can be used for exploitative purposes, resulting in vulnerable believers losing money and suffering from ill health. Sufferers may be directed away from medical services that might otherwise have helped them. Fear and ignorance on the part of the client; extortion, manipulative abuse (emotional, physical, verbal, sexual) and greed for money and power on the part of 'experts' can all contribute to this unhealthy situation. It would, however, be a mistake to believe that beliefs in possession are used only for nefarious ends; benign possession is clearly distinguishable from this cluster of damaging behaviour.

Roland Littlewood, a clinical psychiatrist and a social anthropologist, has analysed the phenomenon of possession both in psychopathological terms as either illness or treatment for the individual, and from an anthropological perspective as manifestations of social tensions and group dynamics. In Chapter 3, he warns of the dual dangers for the clinician faced with possession beliefs: on the one hand, if local cultural explanations or interpretations of illnesses as manifestations of possession are ignored the clinician may misdiagnose the condition as a

---

[7]   A *Sangoma* is a South African traditional healer or diviner.

[8]   Christina Harrington (Chapter 8) mentions how saddened she is by the fact that monotheists have regarded the Pagans' inviting deities to inhabit their bodies as deliberate demonic possession, when it is, to the Pagan, nothing of the kind.

mental health problem when it is not; on the other hand, if the local culture is overemphasised serious mental conditions may be missed.

Sherrill Mulhern begins Chapter 4 by providing an historical backdrop to the development of ideas of possession and witchcraft within European Christianity, describing how medical explanations overtook purely religious explanations. Such theories included the conclusion reached by Freud's contemporary, the French psychiatrist Pierre Janet, that patients may be interacting with their sub-personalities. Moreover, Janet warned, when physicians show a fascination with their patients' secondary personalities then the latter can respond by creating more. Mulhern then recounts how, around the mid-twentieth century, the writings of the German-born Protestant theologian Kurt Koch influenced the growth of North American deliverance rituals, which functioned as 'cathartic psychotherapies' to restore psychological and emotional health as well as the participants' spiritual state. The rituals developed into mass exorcisms in which demons would be summoned from whole congregations, and those who had indulged in the free sex and psychedelic drugs of the hippy culture were encouraged to be delivered from their demons and to accept the Holy Spirit in their stead.

Taking a comparative perspective, Mulhern then directs us to the anthropological literature that illustrates the widespread function of possession to control, explore and celebrate the deviant, possession-permitting ritual expressions of normally unthinkable behaviour. Finally she returns to Western psychiatry and its changing understanding of human personality. Although there had been an increasing awareness of the individual as a multi-faceted, malleable structure, psychiatrists tended to continue to treat patients as if they had a unique and unified personal identity until the influx of traumatised veterans of the Vietnam War, and the emergent visibility and recognition of victims of rape and intra-familial sexual abuse. Towards the end of the twentieth century, there was an increasing diagnosis of Multiple Personality Disorder (MPD) based on an assumption that trauma created alternative personalities which served to shield the victims from abuse they had experienced as children. Although MPD theorists concede that the alternate personalities are not actually people, the model characterises them as relatively independent with a distinct sense of self and their own motives, desires, skills and talents. Furthermore, Mulhern tells us that when they are not 'out', 'alter personalities' are said to retire to a 'Third Reality' situated behind the multiple's consciousness threshold, where they continue to interact with other 'alters'.

Another approach to understanding possession is to focus on the detail of particular places and people, described here both by academics who have done the research and religious leaders who offer an insider's view. Malcolm Gold (Chapter 5) reminds us of the Biblical authority for Christian beliefs in possession and exorcism in the story of Jesus casting out an evil spirit that had possessed a young boy (Matthew 17:14-23; Mark 9:14-32; Luke 9:37-43). He charts the changes undergone by the City Christian Centre, an Assemblies of God congregation in Yorkshire, when it shifted, under the guidance of a new pastor, from a primary focus of strict adherence to the Bible to one of internalising the Holy Spirit or, alternatively, demonic spirits. His account shows how one minister, by introducing the practice of exorcism into a church, can radically alter its religious practices. He also demonstrates how power and authority reside in the person of the exorcist, who claims to have both doctrinal knowledge and previous experience – the exorcist is God's minister and has supernatural power to look into the spiritual realm, and it is, therefore, his interpretation of reality that must be accepted. The subject of the possession, on the other hand, is reduced to a contorting, screaming, incapable victim. The control introduced by exorcism may not, however, last indefinitely. Gold reports that those who had been delivered found themselves slipping back into their sinful ways and/or continuing to be sick. The promise of instant and complete cleansing required modification; and, with the departure of the exorcist, the church reverted to its earlier practices.

Simon Dein (Chapter 6) lays out the different ways in which Muslim immigrants from Bangladesh in London's East End account for various misfortunes. It may be that the sufferer has annoyed a *jinn* by trespassing on the spirit's space; it could be that someone has paid a specialist to employ black magic or sorcery to ensure the victim becomes ill or fails examinations; or it might not be possession that it is at work at all as the misfortune might be the result of someone, probably unconsciously, casting the evil eye on the victim. Dein points out that the fact that many of these beliefs are not accepted by orthodox Islamic theologians does not prevent their providing many of the Bangladeshi Muslims whom he studied with a persuasive way both of explaining and of doing something to overcome their everyday misfortunes.

Looking from a sociological perspective at possession as the central ritual of a religion, Bettina Schmidt (Chapter 7) presents us with a strikingly vivid description of a Puerto Rican *Vodou* ceremony.[9] Here we are introduced to a form of possession that aims to tame and control spirits that possess people so that they can be used to provide benefits to the individual and the community at large. Schmidt also elucidates the unintended benefits of the rituals, providing as they do both a focus for the community and a clear identity for Afro-Caribbean migrants.

Christina Harrington, an historian of religion, offers us in Chapter 8 the most personal account of possession when describing her own progress as a practitioner of the neo-Pagan religion known as Wicca (and in earlier stages of its history as Witchcraft) to the stage where she was ready to experience the 'drawing down the Moon' as a priestess. This phrase refers to the ritual in which the Goddess enters the body of the priestess. Although she maintains that the experience is ineffable, Dr Harrington conveys very clearly the sensations she experienced in her first possession. She is, furthermore, able to use her professional training to observe and explain some of the apparent contradictions in Pagan beliefs and practices. One of the most significant points that she makes is that when the Goddess enters into her she does not believe she is in any way diminished or 'not there' – she is, at the one time, both herself and something far, far beyond herself.

---

[9] *Vodou* is sometimes popularly known as Voodoo.

The views of insiders differ, of course, from those of outsiders who seek to understand possession. Mercy Magbagbeola is a psychiatric nurse, practising as a psychiatric social worker, but she is also a prophetess in the Celestial Church of Christ who receives the Holy Spirit when called upon to heal and help other members of the congregation. In Chapter 9, she provides an insider's account of her Church's beliefs about involuntary possession, which is attributed to the Powers of Darkness or affliction by a demonic power, and she describes the measures taken by the Church to deliver members of its congregation from such possession. Like Littlewood, Magbagbeola draws a clear distinction between, on the one hand, people who are possessed by an evil spirit and, on the other hand, those with thought disorders whose words do not make sense or who are making impossible claims and are, thus, not possessed but ill and in need of psychiatric treatment. She is also at pains to point out that her Church does not target children as witches – it is only if their abnormal behaviour coincides with misfortune in their family that children are thought of as witches. 'If the children are possessed at all, then we bring them into the Church to pray for them, using the prayer of spiritual welfare to save them … and the power of the Holy Spirit to deliver and destroy every work of Satan in their lives.' She claims that only prayer and the power of God can deliver those who are possessed. 'This is our reality', she says. 'It is not just gossip and it is not just odd ideas, it happens in people's lives.'

Jean La Fontaine, herself an anthropologist, introduces in Chapter 10 the phenomenon of the child witches in London by giving a brief introduction to the discovery by anthropologists of their arrival – or at least their increased visibility – in parts of Africa during the latter part of the twentieth century. She, like some of the other contributors, mentions the complicated relationship between (usually adult) witchcraft and Christian (particularly but not only Pentecostal) mission teaching and the subsequent syncretistic developments. Satan and his evil spirits are now seen as the original donors of the powers of witchcraft so that possession *linked* to witchcraft is characteristic of the beliefs of many small Christian churches with African founders and leaders. This transformation in beliefs has occurred predominantly in areas characterised by social upheavals and the decimation of populations, and it is then that children have taken on roles unprecedented in traditional thought, thus changing the prevalent understandings of what children may be like. This, combined with the Christian fundamentalist doctrine of evil, can, La Fontaine suggests, explain the rise of beliefs in child witches as explanations of misfortune in both Africa and the African diaspora. She stresses the point that witchcraft explains the *why* rather than the *how* of misfortune, and that it is not only children but also the adult carers who may suffer when they find themselves being punished for taking action against what they perceive as evil forces. Merely by punishing them, western society is likely to push practices such as exorcism underground and exacerbate the situation 'until we understand more and offer more to both accusers and accused'.

Filip de Boeck, a Belgian anthropologist who has spent many years in Kinshasa and other parts of the Democratic Republic of Congo (DRC) was the first to draw international attention to the recent phenomenon of child witches. It is estimated that there are between 20,000 and 50,000 street children, some as young as two or three, who have been forced onto the streets of Kinshasa after being accused of practising witchcraft and blamed for every conceivable thing that goes wrong within families. In Chapter 11, de Boeck examines the production of child witches within the wider context of the social and spiritual insecurity to which families have been exposed in the contemporary DRC. He sees it as a new phenomenon related to the breakup of the extended family with its traditional male authority and morality of gift exchange. He describes how children may be taken to a 'church of awakening' where the preacher will confirm and thereby legitimise the family's accusation of witchcraft, and how the children are then taken by the church and subjected to a period of fasting and ritual purification during which they will come to construct a standardised and stereotypical narrative about how they became witches. Following public exorcisms, reintegration into the family may occur, but all too frequently members of the kin-group remain in fear of the child, who is then left with no option but a life in the streets. It would be wrong, however, to assume that power and control is solely in the hands of the adults. De Boeck describes how some children actually choose the life of a street child because of the freedom it gives them, and how calling oneself a witch can give a child independence from parental control. De Boeck also describes how the children can implicate adults in their testimonies with disastrous consequences for the named adults. 'Children, therefore, are not only at risk, but may also constitute a real risk to those living with them.' He also warns us that Non-Governmental Organisations (NGOs) that try to ameliorate the situation for the children may not fully understand the children whom they are trying to help, because they are looked at in isolation rather than as part of a complicated, changing social scene in which one needs to take account, not only of the characters of the parents, the children and the pastors, but also of the multi-dimensional complexity of the relationships between them and the wider society.

Chapter 12 is a slightly abridged form of the report Eleanor Stobart prepared for the British Government's Department for Education and Skills.[10] It is concerned with accusations of possession and witchcraft made against children in the United Kingdom, and it provides an overview of 38 of the 74 cases of child abuse linked to accusations of 'possession' and 'witchcraft' identified there since 2000, and provides a numerical analysis of the cases, relating them to the common features of their social and economic background, rather than an attempt at explanation. Almost all the cases come from households of immigrants although not necessarily recent immigrants, and from a wide range of backgrounds, the majority of which are African. She confirms de Boeck's point that children who live as marginal members of households are particularly likely to be accused. Certain patterns emerge from her research that are similar to those found in other studies (see Chapter 11).

---

[10]   The Department has since been reorganised and the relevant section is included in the new Department for Children, Schools and Families.

Stobart concludes with a number of recommendations that could contribute to curbing such abuse in the future, including a plea for further research.

Amma Anane-Agyei is a social worker with experience of working with families where children are perceived as being possessed. In Chapter 13, she offers as an example a particular case where not only the adults but the child himself believes that he is possessed or a witch. In a culture like that of Britain, where 'beating the devil out' is a practice that has been abandoned and where exorcism of children is perceived as abuse, she is at pains to stress the importance of social workers not only understanding, but also respecting the culture from which their clients originate.

Robert Pull (Chapter 14) writes about the work of 'Project Violet', a unit that was set up by the Metropolitan Police in order to investigate child abuse that has arisen as a result of adults' religious beliefs, including beliefs about the exorcism of demons. He describes his role in establishing the 'Congolese Pastorship', an umbrella group with over 180 pastors concerned to establish and adopt policies designed to safeguard children not only in the UK but also elsewhere, especially in the Congo itself. Although well aware that it is impossible to guarantee safety for all children and that enforcement plays a crucial role in their protection, Pull is optimistically confident that community engagement, education and training have helped in reducing, if not entirely eliminating, such tragic suffering.

Finally, David Pearson (Chapter 15) describes the work of the Churches' Child Protection Advisory Services (CCPAS), emphasising that holders of Christian and other faiths who believe in possession may provide explanations for the birth of children with special needs, but they can do so in a manner that can lead to their abuse, thus exacerbating rather than helping the situation in which the children find themselves. He emphasises the importance of identifying situations which can put children at risk and then confronting the issues in a sensitive and informed manner.

Concluding Remarks

The chapters in this book clearly demonstrate that the concept of possession is not a new one, nor is it one that is confined to any particular social or geographical area or any particular religion. People in most parts of the world have made use of the idea that individuals can be and have been possessed, taken over, shared or inhabited by some alien spirit, ancestor, god or deity – and there are very many ways in which possession is recognised, induced or evaluated. It is also evident that possession is not always something to be avoided. While in some circumstances it is common to see possession as the action of evil demons or Satan himself, in other instances possession may be a much sought-after state, enabling the possessed person (who may be a spirit medium, priest of the ancestors or a diviner) to make use of supernatural beings to perform positive functions and exercise 'good powers' on behalf of individuals or the community at large. A spirit or entity may be invited to enter a particular person's body, or encouraged to do so through special techniques such as dance, divination or through imbibing special potions. Several chapters have demonstrated the very different ways in which this happens in, say, Caribbean *Vodou*, neo-pagan groups practising white witchcraft and various Christian churches that aim to induce the Holy Spirit to enter members of the congregation as a special blessing during their services.

In other situations, however, the last thing people want is to be possessed; they believe that some evil spirit can sneak its way into the innocent body to wreak havoc by causing sickness or misfortune. A variety of manifestations are thought to indicate the presence of an evil spirit, ranging from serious disabilities such as cancer or AIDS to afflictions such as miscarriages, addictions such as alcoholism or emotional conditions such as excessive lust, bouts of violence or lack of true faith. For the community, unexplained deaths, crop failure or widespread infertility in animals or people might indicate an evil spirit is at work. Sometimes such misfortunes lead a diviner or healer to expose an alleged case of spirit possession when the victims are, at least initially, unwilling to accept the diagnosis. In parts of contemporary Africa, there are Pentecostal Christians who believe that a demon can endow the person it possesses with the power to harm others by witchcraft; the Lingala term *kindoki* is often used to refer to this power,[11] the power of witchcraft. But not all those who believe in possession by evil spirits think they are able to use evil power to harm others. For example, *jinn* possession can be seen as the cause of the child's misbehaviour or illness, but it does not lead to witchcraft harming other members of the family (Chapter 6).

Wherever the possessing spirit is believed to be evil it follows that it must be ejected from the body of its victim before what is wrong can be remedied. Various forms of exorcism (or deliverance) may be practised, either by specialists, or by relatives of the possessed, to remove the unwanted invaders. Specialists may also supply rituals or charms to ward off evil spirits and protect those who are seen as vulnerable to possession. In many places children are among the categories of potential victims of demons, and in these parts of the world it is common to see protective charms round their necks. Roland Littlewood, in discussing the usefulness of possession (Chapter 3) points out how dangerous exorcism can be unless the practitioner is careful. Children can be seriously damaged and even killed when the adults they live with think they harbour an evil spirit and are practising witchcraft. Even where it is not thought that possession by an evil spirit can lead to the possessed person being given magical powers to hurt others, exorcism can be harmful and even lethal.

It is not coincidental that no attempt has been made in this book to cover the subject from a single perspective, nor is it an oversight that no attempt has been made to reach a single conclusion – there are plenty of other volumes that have tackled such tasks. On the contrary, as with Inform seminars, the aim of the book

---

[11]   Lingala is spoken as a *lingua franca* in the western part of the Democratic Republic of Congo, particularly in its capital, Kinshasa, where it is the first language of many of its inhabitants.

is to highlight some of the very many ways in which a controversial subject may be approached. The approaches here include those of the practitioner (Christian and Pagan), the anthropological and sociological observer, the concerned social worker, the law enforcer, the child protection adviser to Christian churches and the clinical psychiatrist. Some of the contributors play more than one role – combining the clinical psychiatrist with the social anthropologist, the prophetess with the psychiatric social worker and the pagan priestess with the historian of religion. The underlying motivation is a conviction that it needs to be recognised that there are many ways in which possession can be viewed – and if the book raises more questions than it answers, this will be seen not as failure but as success.

References

Barker, E. (2006). 'What Should we do about the Cults? Policies, Information and the Perspective of INFORM', in P. Côté and T.J. Gunn (eds), *The New Religious Question: State Regulation or State Interference? (La nouvelle question réligieuse: Régulation ou ingérence de l'État)*. Brussels: Peter Lang, pp. 371-95. Available online at: http://www.inform.ac/aboutInform.pdf
—— (2002). 'Watching for Violence: A Comparative Analysis of the Roles of Five Cult-Watching Groups', in D.G. Bromley and J. Gordon Melton (eds), *Cults, Religion and Violence*. Cambridge: Cambridge University Press, pp. 123-48.
Cuneo, M.W. (2001). *American Exorcism: Expelling Demons in the Land of Plenty*. New York: Doubleday.
Popper, K.R. (1963). *Conjectures and Refutations: The Growth of Scientific Knowledge*. London: Routledge and Kegan Paul, pp. 33-65.

Chapter 2

Beliefs in Possession

Amanda van Eck Duymaer van Twist

Religions around the world, including Christianity, Islam and indigenous religions, have doctrines which support beliefs in possession by supernatural beings such as gods and spirits, as well as evil spirits. A variety of practices have been instituted in these religious traditions to deal with such possession, ranging from prayer to more invasive practices. The latter have, occasionally, resulted in physical or psychological harm, or even in death – which has propelled this issue into the headlines and, consequently, into a demand for new policies to safeguard children.

But this issue is neither new, nor is it necessarily representative of a particular subsection of society. Beliefs in witchcraft and spirit possession are wide-ranging. When looking at Inform's electronic news file, reports of witchcraft and spirit possession (of which there are hundreds) originate from all over the world – with all continents represented. However, most of the enquiries to Inform concerning beliefs in possession, exorcism, and related topics refer to Christian-inspired groups. Notably, concerns regarding exorcism in Britain usually involve committed members of Christian churches considered to be Pentecostal or Charismatic in character, although not all churches might give themselves these labels. This may be for several reasons: Christianity is more concerned with 'cultism' and perceived deviations than some other religions, wherein a diversity of beliefs/practices may be more acceptable, and, by the same token, less newsworthy; also, there are likely to be many cases that Inform is not aware of – many may take their concerns to their local spiritual adviser, rather than to Inform. In this paper I will focus on the types of cases that have come to Inform's attention, and put these in a wider context. I shall begin with the context.

Concepts of Witchcraft and Possession

'Deliverance ministry' and 'exorcism' are terms used in Catholic, Pentecostal and Charismatic ministries for activities aimed at freeing people or places from alleged demonic possession. Evil spirits and even Satan can be invoked as the cause of a variety of physical, emotional, or societal problems. Islam has its *jinns* (see Chapter 6) and Hindus recognise a variety of evil spirits. It is commonly believed that exorcising the spirit or spirits in question will alleviate the problem. In Pentecostalism, phrases such as 'spiritual warfare' are often evoked to describe both the attitude necessary to overcome these evil influences in life and the activity of exorcism itself.

Various forms of exorcism and spirit possession have long played an important role in many indigenous religions and practices such as shamanism, *Vodou* and in the rites and practices of fetish priests and so-called witch doctors. They also appear in some syncretistic religions such as *Candomblé* in Brazil, as well as in segments of most traditional religious traditions and more recent traditions (such as Paganism).

It is important to remember that spirits are not necessarily always evil, and in some religious traditions there is a history of possession by spirits that is not necessarily problematic. Mediums embody selected spirits for beneficial purposes, and Wiccans invoke the Goddess in their rites.[1] In the case of the latter, Wicca, also often referred to as the Craft, and many other names, is seen positively, and generally refers to the desire/aim to influence the elements through ritual, without doing harm. In Wicca and most forms of contemporary Paganism, spells should never be used against others.

Also, the concepts of spirit possession and witchcraft have often been, and occasionally still are, confused and blended together. 'Witchcraft' as perceived in, for example, some African countries and in sixteenth-century England, connotes the practice of those who harm others by hidden (occult) or supernatural means – it can be referred to as sorcery. Sorcery is *also* a name for 'black magic', it is harmful, and can allegedly be used against others – the French use the word *sorcellerie* to connote witchcraft. There have been several periods throughout European and North American history when people (usually women) have been accused of being witches and harming others or causing misfortune, and consequently have been subjected to various forms of 'diagnoses' to verify whether they were witches, and punishment if they were considered to be witches – not infrequently resulting in their death.[2] Scenes like this are still occurring in some remote parts of the world. This is significantly different from the interpretations of many religious people today who believe in spirit possession, which spans a variety of religious traditions, and can be harmful but is not necessarily so.

The concepts of possession and exorcism have also, on occasion, merged with fears over alleged satanic abuse and 'witchcraft'. In the 1980s there was a widespread scare concerning beliefs in Satanists and satanic forces in North America (Richardson, Best and Bromley, 1991). This then spread to England, where much of this debate in the UK media was fuelled by an evangelical

---

[1]   In the fictional *The Teachings of Don Juan* (1968) Carlos Castaneda, a Shaman, described demonic predators which reportedly thrive on human energy. His books have been controversial, with Castaneda starting as an academic but eventually bridging over into fiction, yet some supporters argue that his *Don Juan* writings were based on his anthropological fieldwork, a claim rejected by Castaneda's peers.

[2]   Arthur Miller's *The Crucible* describes the witch scare in seventeenth-century New England.

cult-watching group, the Reachout Trust, whose member of staff, a Christian missionary, presented herself to the police and the social services as an expert on satanic ritual abuse.[3] There had been many allegations of child abuse resulting from satanic ritual abuse. During the early 1990s, Professor Jean La Fontaine carried out a thorough investigation, supported initially by Inform and then by the Department of Health, concluding that, although there had been cases of abuse, there was no evidence for Satanism or ritual abuse.[4]

One can distinguish between different types of beliefs and accusations/ allegations, although in practice they often overlap. Traditional African religion includes the belief in witchcraft (sometimes referred to as *kindoki*) – a belief system widely held in Africa and among African immigrant communities around the world. Today this presupposes the possibility of demonic possession and the efficacy of ritual practices to exorcise this possession. In the African context, it is common to find that beliefs in indigenous concepts of witchcraft (or other traditional African equivalents) have been influenced by the tenets of major world religions, such as Christianity or Islam.[5] Hence one may find a syncretistic blending of possession and witchcraft concepts.

Possession and Children

But of course there is variation. And we need to distinguish between accusations of adults and accusations of children, and between accusations of children as witches/ sorcerers, accusations that children are possessed by demon spirits, and accusations that children are possessed by the Devil. Being aware of variation is important, as the consequences are likely to be significantly different. Possession may be seen as having different consequences depending on whether the possessing entity is a spirit, a demon, or the Devil. The cause of possession may also be a significant variable, was it due to a lack of faith, food accepted from a stranger, or a previous defilement? These may be consequences of some sort of 'spiritual differentiation', i.e. the possessed was previously 'unclean', lacking in faith, disobedient (should not have accepted food from strangers). There is, of course, a history of spiritual differentiation, and the scapegoating of those who are deemed to be 'less' than

---

[3] For an account of exorcisms carried out by those connected with mainstream Churches who believe in satanic possession see, for example, the second half of Jenkins' (2000) paper, starting from 'The Satanism Issue'. 'The New Witch-Hunt: Evangelical Christians and the Invention of the Satanic Threat'. [Online]. Available at: http://www.ull. es/congresos/conmirel/JENKINS.htm [accessed: 26 March 2008].

[4] The research findings were published by HMSO in 1994, entitled 'The Extent and Nature of Organised and Ritual Abuse'.

[5] For more detailed information on African Independent Churches, Steve Hayes (2009). 'African Initiated Churches'. [Online]. Available at: http://www.geocities.com/ missionalia/aic.htm [accessed: 10 September 2009].

others in some way or other. There are comparable ideas of spiritual differentiation between individuals and groups, in some cases especially children, when looking through the wider religious spectrum.

Numerous religious groups believe that a lack of faith may 'open the door' to the Devil or other evil spirits, which may lead not only to possession but also perhaps to illness, misfortune, and impure thoughts. Mary Baker Eddy of The Church of Christ Scientist wrote many books about the ways in which lack of faith could affect health. The Bruderhof believe that children can be easily tainted and need to be raised with a 'firm hand'. In the past frequent 'clearings' (interrogations by ministers to unearth impure thoughts) reportedly ensured the cleansing of children's alleged (sexually) impure minds. In some cases children were put in exclusion, and shunned, for extended periods of time.

In the Family Federation for World Peace and Unification (also known as the Unification Church), for example, a distinction is made between children who are 'blessed' as opposed to those who are 'not blessed', which leads to a hierarchy within the membership – internalised differentiation between members on a spiritual level. The leader, Revd Sun Myung Moon, 'blesses' couples into marriage, before and after which they go through rituals that allegedly 'purify' their bloodlines (the 'blessing' is part of a complicated five-stage ritual). This enables them to have 'blessed children', who reportedly are not tainted by the sins of their ancestors and who are, consequently, in a position to create a foundation for Heaven on earth. The children who are not 'blessed' are tainted by their forebears' sins and consequently have to pay 'indemnity' through work. Former members have described a system of apartheid where the 'blessed children' were favoured over the 'non-blessed children'. When one African member of the Church claimed to be possessed by the spirit of Moon's dead son (a blessed child), he became a prominent member and was asked to travel around the world to address other congregations.

The Family International had no such hierarchy among their children. All those born within the movement were seen as the harbingers of the end-time, and eventually they would be Jesus' helpers during the Millennium. But eventually the reality proved that not all children in the movement were equally good missionaries, and the leaders instituted special training camps for troubled children and teenagers where it was hoped they would again find their enthusiasm for their missionary tasks. An added benefit was to keep these 'bad apples' from the rest of the bunch. In some cases children were identified as suffering from spiritual troubles, or even to be possessed by spirits. In contrast to the Unification Church, this was neither beneficial nor an honour. In one instance a prominent member, the leader's granddaughter, Mene Berg, was accused of being possessed. *The Last State? – The Dangers of Demonism!* (1987), describes the exorcism of Mene Berg at the age of 14 in great detail. In this publication Berg scolds her saying she was, as his granddaughter, supposed to be saved, yet she allowed the devil and demons in. Her exorcism involved enforced fasting, physical abuse (beatings and caning) and confinement during which she was tied to the bed. Another former member who I have interviewed reported to have been exorcised as a child – he had been ill for an extended period of time, and leaders concluded this was a result of demonic possession. He was prayed over, spent significant amounts of time in isolation, and had to fast, which did not assist his healing process.

Exorcism in the UK

The topic of witchcraft, possession and exorcism has hit the UK headlines in the last few years particularly as a result of a few very sad cases where children were harmed or died as a result of alleged deliverance. In particular, in 2005 there was a case of the eight-year-old Angolan girl ('Child B') who suffered beatings, starvation, and had chilli powder rubbed in her eyes. In 2001 there was also the well-publicised case of Victoria Climbié, who died as a result of serious abuse and neglect related to a belief by her carers that she was possessed. Around this time, the torso of a boy, known as 'Adam', was found in the Thames, leading to speculation that his murder and the removal of his limbs had been due to beliefs in witchcraft and/or possession.

These cases were within the African immigrant communities in the UK, consequently the discussion has focused on beliefs and practices within African Initiated Churches. These tend to be amalgamations of Christianity (mostly Pentecostalism) and indigenous beliefs and practices.[6] Recently, publicised demonic possession beliefs in African initiated religions feature the alleged possession of children – evil spirits are thought to target children either while still in the womb or in early childhood. Causes and results, including ideas that possession results from accepting food from strangers and the belief that, once possessed, the children are able to change shape and/or fly, suggest a mixing of witchcraft and possession beliefs.

These publicised accounts, of course, do not indicate the extent to which these beliefs are normative, and we have to be critical of media reporting that does not necessarily reflect reality. Famously (and erroneously) in The Cook Report, the 'professional exorcist' Revd Kevin Logan claimed that over 80 per cent of children had been affected by the occult, and reportedly exorcised a group of young children

---

[6]   Pentecostalism is the one of the fastest growing forms of Christianity, particularly in Latin America, Asia and Africa. Peter Brierley has estimated that there were 4,467 Pentecostal congregations in Britain in 2000 (UK Christian Handbook, 2001). The most recent estimates for the number of black majority churches in Britain were made in 1995. At this point in time the UK African and Caribbean Evangelical Alliance estimated that there were over 3,000 churches with over 300,000 members in Britain. These statistics include all churches with a majority of the membership being of African or African-Caribbean heritage across all spectrums of Christian belief, not just Pentecostal/Charismatic. It also claimed that in London a majority of church attendees are either Black or Asian (Black Majority Churches UK Directory, 2003/4).

(some below school age) behind closed doors in his Blackburn church in front of cameras.[7] Logan said 'Some of these youngsters have been victims of child abuse and Satanism is at the root', another mixing of concepts.

Techniques used to exorcise reported spirits or demons are extremely varied. In many churches deliverance ministries are held on a weekly basis, and prayer suffices – including remote prayer. In other cases rituals may be the norm, including music, dance, food offerings, and so on. But there have been publicised cases where exorcisms have been more invasive. Violent means of exorcising children in Africa have featured prominently in the media over the past few years and have exposed practices of induced vomiting, beatings, and murder to exorcise children believed to be possessed.

The Role of the Church

Although the guardians of Victoria Climbié and Child B did indeed contact their churches (The Church of Spiritual Combat in the case of the 8-year-old Angolan girl and the Universal Church of the Kingdom of God in the case of Victoria Climbié) with regard to the possessions, pastors of these churches reportedly did not suggest the means of exorcism used by the relatives (which amounted to abuse). The Church officials did, however, confirm that the children were possibly (and probably) possessed.

Considering that probably hundreds of deliverance services are performed in Britain every week without incident or complaint, physical violence does not necessarily follow from a diagnosis of possession.[8] In both the Victoria Climbié case as well as the more recent abuse of the Angolan girl, the abuse was perpetrated by relatives rather than other members of the church. The abuse also happened at home, rather than on church property. For example, the official in the UCKG church (where the relatives of Victoria Climbié scheduled an exorcism) reportedly urged her carer to take her to hospital. Considering this, a direct causal connection with the church or pastor is tenuous. On the other hand, Angus Stickler argued in his 2006 Newsnight documentary that the Congolese pastor Dieudonne Tukala of a Tottenham church in North London diagnosed possession in children and allegedly suggested they be sent back to Africa for exorcism (although he had no evidence of the latter). The pastor was arrested on charges of child cruelty but not charged due to lack of evidence (after the main witnesses withdrew their evidence). Also, Inform has encountered sermons where it was claimed that certain children may come from 'demon seed', and are consequently irredeemable. It is unclear

---

[7]   See, for example, *The Daily Mirror*, 5 May 1989.

[8]   Although one aspect of this may be that those who are exorcised may not feel in a position to complain, perhaps because they do not question the 'diagnosis', dare not, or cannot complain or minors may not know where to go to complain about such practices.

how this church would behave towards children it labelled as 'irredeemable', but it is a label that causes those interested in child welfare serious concerns.

Inform's Data

Since 1996 Inform has received 68 enquiries specifically about possession and/or exorcism, the majority of these from the media after the well-publicised cases of Victoria Climbié and Child B. (The media enquiries were largely concerned about issues of child abuse in exorcism.) Interestingly, a significant number of enquiries came from people concerned about possession and/or exorcism. It is important to keep in mind that these are not representative of belief in possession, exorcism and related concepts. Those who believe in possession and exorcisms would probably find little need to contact Inform, finding their needs addressed by those offering deliverance ministries. (However, some enquirers who contacted Inform were concerned that the Roman Catholic Church was not doing enough to exorcise the demons reportedly possessing them or their relatives.) Inform has also received enquiries requesting assistance for what enquirers felt were problematic curses, allegations of witchcraft, and similar themes. Frequently such cases had a similarity to others where the terminology of possession was used rather than that of witchcraft, curses or spells. When looking beyond the terminology used since Victoria Climbié, and analysing Inform's database of enquiries along other themes that may be related, a wider trend came to light. As I described earlier, a number of different culturally relevant terms can be used to describe similar phenomena – either resulting from different uses of language or from a blending of concepts others consider to be distinct. (Inform has frequently received complaints from Pagan organisations with regard to other cult watching groups who, they felt, did not make a distinction between Paganism and Satanism.) When searching for enquiries logged under the headings Magic (as opposed to 'magick', which is associated with Crowley's vision of ritual magic), *Vodou* (although people tend to use the term 'Voodoo'), Curse, and Witch in addition to Possession, Exorcism and Witchcraft, many more interesting cases with similar elements arose from the archives (182 cases). Some of these described possession in different terms, and could be cross-referenced with files on Shamanism, Paganism, Spiritualism (in particular Mediums), and others. There was also a significant overlap between the different terms; cases could show up under two headings. Yet others describe similar themes and point to a wider and complicated picture of beliefs in possession and witchcraft, and similar beliefs by a different name.

Many of these enquirers were referred to Inform by Church House, the Home Office, the police, Citizens' Advice Bureau (CAB) or other advice centres – institutions and centres who did not know how to address the questions posed to them. Inform was well-placed to help, but, being a research and information centre, had to develop its network quickly in response to more therapeutic requests that went beyond its remit. Someone who claims to be suffering from a curse is not necessarily eager to receive information about what a curse is, or about different types of curses and their definitions. Hence Inform developed, and still nurtures, a network of individuals and organisations to help enquirers beyond providing information. But it took a close look at developing trends to analyse that there was an area where existing institutions were not equipped to address these issues – and a lot of work still needs to be done.[9]

The Wider Context of Allegations of Supernatural Agency in Britain

Inform receives enquiries and allegations of harm and harassment from supernatural sources in general. These enquiries contain difficulties on several levels; Inform can neither comment nor advise on the acts of supernatural entities, but, at times, the supernatural claim brought to Inform might be part of a larger problem that is easier to identify. A man whose conviction that he was cursed led him to a 'healer' who offered to help him, only then to state that he had created a more evil curse that could only be lifted if the man paid him a significant amount of money, could go to the police and file a complaint for financial extortion. Perhaps less straightforward are cases where people's descriptions of 'supernatural harassment' closely mirror some of the diagnostics for mental illness.[10] Often, the supernatural description is a result of language, ethnic and/or cultural differences that might warrant further exploration before a reasonable understanding of the situation can be reached. Particularly in communities which are marginalised and poorly connected to (and with little trust of) the local authorities/social services, material and psychological problems might be given a supernatural explanation that spiritual leaders in the community offer support for, as well as possible redress, which can be very attractive. It should be emphasised that these allegations of supernatural harm are by no means limited to African or Afro-Caribbean ethnic groups. Other immigrant groups have voiced their problems with perceived supernatural agency, and those of traditional British decent have also articulated a belief in supernatural agency. A young man once phoned in a panic; he had been playing with an Ouija board with a friend but had not expected anything to happen. When the cup did move they instantly stopped out of fear. He then remembered reading that if the 'game'

---

[9]   In 2003 I wrote a report for a Metropolitan Police department describing a trend in enquiries where magic was reportedly being used for the purposes of financial extortion and fraud.

[10]   In these cases, complaints to authorities have often been met with scepticism. While this scepticism on the part of authorities is understandable (differences in terminology may lead them to speak at cross-purposes), these people are often in real fear and distress. In the face of what is often experienced as a hostile and disbelieving response from law enforcement and/or social workers (as it occasionally was before the Victoria Climbié inquest), the appeal of those claiming the ability to intervene on the supernatural plane is obvious.

is interrupted prematurely, the 'players' are cursed. He wanted to know how to undo this curse.

Inform is well aware that conversion to a new religion often comes paired with a change of world-view, a shift in priorities, and a turning away from old friends and family in favour of new friends and a newly found (spiritual) family. But occasionally different language is used. On two occasions young women, after joining a Pentecostal African-initiated church, argued that they did not want to see their family again and accused them of being witches.

Magic and Finances

Many of the enquiries that mentioned curses, spells, or magic (usually referred to as black magic) also involved money. In one case, a woman lent money to someone and was threatened with 'black magic' when she asked for the money to be repaid. This is apparently not that uncommon. A man, L, contacted a 'magician' who advertises in a Pakistani paper (claiming that he combines 'black and white magic' to solve all your problems – and offers a free consultation). After the consultation the magician demanded £140 and upon payment, the magician announced that he had put 'a spell' on L and that 'no one can save him now'. L believed this, and when his health and career suffered he blamed this on the spell. When he contacted the 'magician' again asking for help, the latter demanded more money. Ms X contacted an 'occult organisation' through an advertisement and paid them £80 to perform rituals on her for good luck, but she has had bad luck since. Another occult practitioner then told Ms X she was under a 'black spell', and offered to lift the curse for £100. Ms X couldn't afford this and felt she was doomed to a life of bad luck as a result. In other cases amassing 'good luck' is used as a motivator rather than avoiding 'bad luck'. Mr Z's mother had been giving large sums of money to a man; the mother had been told there was going to be a 'financial paradigm shift' that would significantly change the global financial situation. She was receiving emails urging her to pay into a pool of money that would be invested – great returns were guaranteed. After the financial paradigm shift, she was told, she would be very rich. The mother was donating £250 at a time. The founders of this operation are in prison in the USA for financial fraud. (The individuals in the UK were not directly associated with the American operation.) In another example of attempting to harness 'good luck', a man reportedly argued that having sexual relations with his third daughter would bring him prosperity, riches and luck.

Magic and Health

Although financial 'luck' is important, health and well-being can be more immediate and powerful motivators. One young man (in his late teens) felt he needed to borrow money and pay for a certain practice that would, reportedly, virtually make his body immune to disease and depression, and would also guarantee wealth. He worked full-time for the organisation and was incurring debts of tens of thousands of pounds. In another case a Vietnamese woman believed a Chinese woman in her neighbourhood had put a 'spell' on her and her family. She blamed the problems in her family and all her misfortunes on this neighbour's 'spell'. Her son is severely learning disabled, which was causing problems at school, but rather than following the advice of the care worker, the mother sought to undo the 'spell'. D, who had recently lost her husband in a road accident, received a letter accusing her family of having done 'bad things' to people. The letter then explained the sender had been paid to 'curse' the woman's family which would eventually result in death, unless she paid the demanded sum (which was large). J reported being sexually abused and verbally harassed in her home by her ex husband whom she had not seen in years. She thought he was doing this from a distance using 'black magic'. She had reported this to the police, the local council, as well as social services and the National Society for the Prevention of Cruelty to Children (NSPCC) (she also feared the safety of her son), but reported that no one would help. (Apparently the police suggested she get the building 'exorcised', which she thought was 'rubbish'.) Interestingly, rather than seeking help to undo a spell or curse, one woman requested help in finding a 'Voodoo' expert – she had trouble with speaking and wanted to try 'Voodoo cures' to overcome this. Another enquirer was already receiving aid from a 'practitioner' to counter a 'Voodoo curse', but this practitioner was reportedly asking extraordinary sums.

Magic and Control

Financial and health issues aside, magic is ultimately about control – the control of elements. Hence for enquirers, their concerns are frequently about lack of control over key issues in their lives. Mrs A, a Muslim woman, entered an arranged marriage at the age of 17. Since then she had not been alone with friends or family; there was always a member of her husband's family with her. Mrs A's friends and family were fearful of approaching her, believing the husband might use 'black magic' on Mrs A in reprisal. A friend believes Mrs A is living in fear of her husband's 'magical powers'. (The story was told in the language of 'magic' rather than threats and/or abuse – words that were not used once.)

In another case, a man told women he could teach them how to 'self-actualise'; he claimed to be in control of energy. But if they left him, 'their worst nightmares will become true'. He told one woman she would die of cancer if she ever left him. Another woman believed she would go insane if she ever left. In order to 'clear their karma', the women offered him money and bought him expensive gifts. Many of the women worked as erotic dancers and lived sexually promiscuous lifestyles, which (according to this man) fits into Buddhist teachings of eliminating all attachments. In another movement, followers did not contact those who had left, as they were, according to the leader, possessed by evil spirits, and communication with such former members could affect the followers as well. Similarly, a woman left a new religious movement but was suffering from severe abdominal pains because, she was convinced, her erstwhile guru was punishing her. She eventually moved abroad to escape from the 'negative vibrations' that she believed were being 'sent out' by the guru.

In some cases 'magicians' are believed to exercise control by visiting individuals in their dreams. One man believed he had been 'cursed' by a 'High Priestess' and that his life was at stake – a group of 'occultists' reportedly supported the diagnosis that he was 'cursed'. The perpetrators were currently 'invading his dreams', and the man believed strongly that they would assault or even kill him. In another case, K briefly joined a church the previous year, but since he stopped attending, the man from the church was 'coming to him in spirit in his dreams'. In the dream the man touched K's shoulder and neck, and he had had aches there since those dreams. The church sent letters asking him to come back to church, and wrote that they had a handkerchief and bottle of oil for him that they prayed over so he would not suffer from 'curses'. K reported that a friend dreamt that the leader of the church injected her knees with something, and the following morning she was limping. One solicitor contacted us for advice regarding a case where a mother believed that she was under attack by three 'Voodoo practitioners' who raped her children in their sleep and terrorised them by putting snakes in their stomachs and appearing in their home in the form of a giant rodent. The way to stop these attacks, according to her spiritual adviser, included methods abusive and harmful to the children. The youngest child had already been sent to her home country in Africa, possibly for 'treatment'.

Possession

This last case is reminiscent of other cases that have been publicised in the media as well as the Stobart report (see Chapter 12) where treatment to alleviate reported witchcraft or possession is potentially harmful to those believed to be possessed or under a spell. One enquirer was worried because her friend had convinced members of her church (including 'priests') that a child in that church was possessed. Another enquirer called on behalf of a 16-year-old teenager who was subjected to a 'deliverance ministry' at a Christian conference, without her consent. In another enquiry, from abroad, we were alerted to a murder resulting from an exorcism in a Congolese community. This created concerns for other children in that community. Another concerned caller, a mother (from Ghana), claimed that her teenage daughter was possessed. And Inform was also contacted in a missing person enquiry; there were concerns because the associated church practiced exorcisms.[11] One woman, from Africa but living in the UK, reported that she had been back to Africa for 'black magic healing' because her son was unwell, but since then, she claimed, she has been possessed. She received 'minor exorcisms' from the Roman Catholic Church, but now wanted a 'full exorcism', which they were not offering to her. The woman claimed that she was touched and raped by demons at night. On another continent altogether, an American university student joined a new religion with his twin brother, upon whom he inflicted severe physical abuse as his guru told him that his brother was 'possessed by evil spirits'. A woman contacted us after she had escaped from her home and her mother, who she accused of 'invasive hypnosis' and 'spirit possession' through her 'psychic powers'. A man alleged that his friend had been affected by 'witchcraft' for the past seven years, and wanted treatment. Neighbours 'did witchcraft' on his friend, and since then the friend could hear them all the time 'in his head', and 'they were looking through his eyes'. He reported there were six people involved; but somehow the witchcraft had 'separated his friend' and 'mixed him up with all these people'.

Terminology and Conceptual Boundaries

As mentioned before, language is significant, as it may lead people to categorise one type of act or abuse while ignoring similar cases. There is also a cross-over of concepts and language. One woman complained that her neighbour, who reportedly was 'into black magic and Satanism', had put a curse on her. She had approached an Anglican Vicar for help, but he turned her away after he found out that she worked as a spiritualist medium. He urged her to stop, but she refused, arguing it was a 'gift'. One man called to report a spiritualist medium who he thought was falsely reporting messages from the spirit world, and breaking up marriages (including his). He also accused the medium's boyfriend of performing 'black magic'. This is interesting, as spiritualism can also be a form of possession, and mediums reportedly have contact with the spirit world. But clearly this man distinguished between a spiritualist medium who abused her skill/position to harm others and her boyfriend, who also used his skills to harm others – yet the latter he referred to as 'black magic'. Similarly, the former medium considered her own skills as a 'gift' but was scared of her neighbour's skills ('black magic' and 'Satanism'), while the Anglican Vicar was worried about her 'gift' as a medium. They each set the boundaries of what they considered safe and appropriate in a different place. Within spiritualist movements boundaries are drawn as well, and

---

[11]   Interestingly, now that the authorities are taking accusations of witchcraft and/or possession of children very seriously, we have heard of one case where a father argued that another family member (with whom his child was living) accused his child of being a witch. Such accusations could potentially jeopardise existing custody arrangements.

mediums are taught to be aware of the harm that can come from 'undisciplined' or 'uncontrolled' possessions.

Another blurring of boundaries occurs between spiritual/religious concepts and mental illness. Our archive makes painfully clear that many of these earlier enquirers came to us after having been ridiculed by other organisations who did not take their claims seriously. And, in some cases, language that is considered normal in some cultures and belief systems is considered a-typical and possibly pathological in this culture. But this is not a straightforward distinction, and often the two spheres do overlap. Once an elderly woman walked into my office and lifted her skirt above her knee to show me a lump on her leg, which she argued was filled with the spirit of Cardinal Hume. She said she had alerted Westminster Cathedral, but they were unwilling to do anything about this. She urged me to help her because he was keeping her up at night. In another case a woman believed she had been 'bewitched'; she heard voices in her head regularly and had chest pain when she heard the voices. She appeared to know the person who was talking to her, but was unsure whether this person was the one speaking to her or whether she was possessed by the spirit of a dead person. She had been to the hospital, and had been diagnosed with paranoid schizophrenia, but would not accept their diagnosis and was reluctant to return to the doctors.[12]

Conclusion

The variety of enquiries described above and the range of terminologies used suggests a blurring of boundaries on several levels – linguistically, conceptually, culturally, and perhaps also between what is 'different' and what may be a symptom of a mental health issue. Inform, being an information centre, is well equipped to deal with some of these blurred boundaries. Inform's methodological approach is helpful; the comparative and contextualising approach allows us to make connections and unearth trends. Also, the methodological agnosticism of staff members means that these beliefs are taken seriously and at least accepted as being held deeply by those who are afflicted. Enquirers, after receiving information from staff, frequently request further support. Hence over time a large network of practitioners and experts has been developed which can be helpful in case enquirers also want therapeutic support.

At the moment the debate on possession in Britain is focused on African initiated Pentecostal Churches, but general beliefs in witchcraft and possession and the practice of exorcism is by no means restricted to these churches. Enquiries to Inform suggest that these and related beliefs and practices may be more widespread and varied. Seeking to generalise at this point is unhelpful – we could

---

[12] Inform in many cases suggests people seek support from their GP, and has worked together with Spektra National Health Service (NHS) South Lambeth and Maudsley on several cases.

be closing our eyes to other potentially problematic or even abusive beliefs and practices. Hence Inform will continue to analyse regularly its cases, question the use of terminology and culturally relevant descriptions, and keep an eye open for new trends. In this endeavour, staff will continue to liaise with and seek to expand Inform's network of experts who feed back knowledge and information.

References

Berg, D. (1987). *The Last State? The Dangers of Demonism!* The Family, private publication.

Brierley, P. (2001). *UK Christian Handbook: Religious Trends No. 3.* (2002/2003 Edition). London: Christian Research.

Castaneda, C. (1968). *The Teachings of Don Juan: A Yaqui Way of Knowledge.* Berkeley: University of California Press.

Eddy, M.B. (1875) (regular revisions to 1910). *Science and Health with Key to the Scriptures.* Plain Label Books USA.

Evangelical Alliance and Churches Together in Britain and Ireland. 2004. *Black Majority Churches UK Directory 2003/4.* London: African and Caribbean.

Hayes, S. (2009). 'African Initiated Churches'. [Online]. Available at: http://www. geocities.com/missionalia/aic.htm [accessed: 10 September 2009].

Jenkins, P. (2000). 'The New Witch-Hunt: Evangelical Christians and the Invention of the Satanic Threat'. [Online]. Available at: http://www.ull.es/congresos/conmirel/JENKINS.htm [accesssed: 26 March 2008].

La Fontaine, J.S. (1994). *The Extent and Nature of Organised and Ritual Abuse: Research Findings.* London: HMSO.

Miller, A. (1992). *The Crucible.* Pearson Education, Oxford: Heinemann Educational Publishers.

Richardson, J.T., J. Best and D. Bromley (1991). *The Satanism Scare.* New York: Aldine de Gruyter.

Stickler, A. (2006). *Newsnight*, BBC 2, 12 January.

The Daily Mirror, 5 May 1989. Inform archive.

PART I
The Meaning of Possession

The next five chapters show how beliefs in possession may have different meanings and effects in different religious contexts. It makes clear that to say that a person's family believe him or her to be possessed is not enough to ensure that their beliefs are really understood. These chapters are written by anthropologists who have studied possession in different places and at different times. Professor Littlewood's 'Possession states',[1] (Chapter 3) gives an overview of different types of possession with some case histories to illustrate the different forms. As a clinical psychiatrist as well as an anthropologist, he has analysed the phenomenon in psychopathological terms as both illness and treatment for the individual and as manifestations of social tensions and group dynamics at the societal level. His paper warns of the dual dangers for the clinician faced with possession beliefs of, on the one hand ignoring and, on the other hand, over-emphasising local cultural explanations of diagnoses or interpretations of illnesses as manifestations of possession. The article was originally written as an aid for psychologists and psychotherapists who encounter claims from the family that a patient is possessed, and is included here as an introduction to the subject. Such information may also be useful to others who may have similar dealings with people who believe that spirits may enter a person and cause harm to others by doing so.

Sherrill Mulhern, in Chapter 4, 'Embodied alternative identities: Spiritual possession, psychiatric disorder or socio/political stratagem?',[2] traces the history of Western notions of possession and their link with other ideas about the functioning of the human being that led, ultimately, to the discipline of psychiatry. She shows how the Western conviction that there can only be one entity in one body is modified in various ways until, for some people, it has reached the opposite and controversial position: that the 'person' can split into a number of different entities within one body: that is, there emerges the concept of a Multiple Personality, now known as Dissociative Identity Disorder. The disorder is believed to be the result of traumatic events in childhood and by circular reasoning, manifestation of the disorder is seen as evidence that trauma has occurred.

Malcolm Gold (Chapter 5) reminds us of the story of Jesus casting out an evil spirit that had possessed a young boy (Matthew 17:14-23; Mark 9:14-32;

---

[1]   Originally published in *Psychiatry* 3/8 (2004), this article was given as a paper at an Inform conference. It is reprinted here by permission of the author and publisher.

[2]   This is a modified version of the paper given at the Inform conference of 2005.

Luke 9:37-43), and he charts the changes undergone by the City Christian Centre, a Yorkshire Assemblies of God congregation, when it shifted under the guidance of a new pastor from a primary focus of strict adherence to the Bible to one of internalising the Holy Spirit or, alternatively, demonic spirits. His chapter, 'Possession and deliverance in a British Pentecostal Church', shows how one minister can introduce the practice of exorcism into a church and in so doing alter its religious practices. He demonstrates however, that although the members of this church were encouraged to hunt out the evil spirits that might possess people, there was no indication that children might be singled out for attack.

Dr Simon Dein's (Chapter 6), 'The *jinn*, black magic and evil eye among East London Bangladeshis', explores the meaning of beliefs about possession among Muslims who, he says, have blended their Islam with some beliefs from their area of origin. He records that such ideas are disapproved by some spiritual leaders who have studied Islamic doctrine. Among these Bangladeshis, children are considered particularly vulnerable to possession by evil spirits, but they are not believed to be dangerous to others while in this condition. It is they who are damaged by the spirit's possession of their body. Exorcism of the spirits is to cure the children, not to protect others from harm.

The final chapter in Part I, 'The practice of spirit possession in Haitian *Vodou*', by Bettina E. Schmidt (Chapter 7), describes a religion, whose name, *Vodou* is often inaccurately used to mean any belief in possession by spirits, or to denigrate a religious practice of which the speaker knows nothing and disapproves. The real meaning of the term is explained by Dr Schmidt, who shows how possession can be a religious technique for making contact with the divine. The spiritual entities display the cultural mix that has formed this religion over the course of its history. While she writes of a religion in the Afro-Caribbean diaspora in New York, practitioners of *Vodou* in Britain probably follow similar practices. The chapter is included here to distinguish this established religion from witchcraft, black magic or worshipping Satan.

Chapter 3

Possession States[1]

Roland Littlewood

Forget the drama of a succession of Hollywood films with their rather specific idiom of demonic possession. 'Possession' is arguably the most common culture-bound psychiatric syndrome, and the experience of its converse, 'soul loss', perhaps more common internationally than depression (Shweder, 1985). The term possession denotes a local belief that an individual has been entered by an alien spirit or other parahuman force, which then controls the person or at least significantly alters their actions and identity to a greater or lesser extent. This would usually be manifest to the observer as an altered state of consciousness.

'Possession states' proper refer to this altered consciousness backed by the belief in possession, and they can be divided into these two components according to Bourguignon (1973) – see Figure 3.1 below.

In Figure 3.1, 'PT' refers to an altered state of consciousness backed by the acceptance of the reality of an intrusive spirit; 'P' refers to the acceptance of a possession (explanation) alone, while 'T' is trance or other altered state of consciousness by itself. Thus a shamanic vision quest is likely to be T, and the possession cults of Brazil or the Caribbean to be PT. A possession belief alone (P) can be fairly unobtrusive and hardly affect daily life at all; the fisherman's wife with whom the current author boarded while doing fieldwork in Trinidad in the 1970s used to complain frequently of another villager attacking and entering her as a spirit at night, causing a painful leg, but this assertion never affected her daily domestic routine, still less any counter-attack on the supposed witch.

Possession which is involuntary can be distinguished from the sought possession typical of Africa (*sar* in East Africa, *bori* in West Africa), the African-Caribbean (Cuban *santeria*, Trinidadian *shango*, Haitian *Vodou*) and the Afro-Brazilian cults (*Candomblé* and *umbanda*) (Figure 3.2). Each has its own characteristic pattern and associated beliefs and practices, such as zombification in Haiti (Littlewood and Douyon, 1997). Something very similar is found in the newer African evangelical churches, particularly Aladura in Nigeria, and in Pentecostalism more generally. By contrast, involuntary possession is less socially standardised and the experience is that the spirit enters a person in the course of everyday life and causes illness, madness or other altered behaviour.

---

[1]   This article was originally published in Littlewood, R. (2004). 'Possession States', *Psychiatry*, 3/8: 8–10, Copyright Elsevier.

Figure 3.1   Bourguignon's typology

> **P**   Acceptance of possession alone
> **T**   Trance or other altered state of consciousness
> **PT** Both together

Figure 3.2   Types of possession states

- Involuntary possession state

- Sought possession state

Figure 3.3   Clinical cases

1. A 45-year-old Angolan refugee reunited in London with her adopted daughter (then aged four years, now six) believes the girl is possessed by spirits because she has nightmares, sleepwalks and speaks to absent people. (The biological mother's own sister, when looking after the girl, does not notice any of this.) The adoptive mother, worried that the girl is possessed by spirits sent by the deceased biological mother's family in Angola, thinks that the spirit is dangerous to the girl and to the others, and wants to return to Angola for a healing ceremony. The local social worker, who is not aware of what is involved, goes to court to prevent this, and a lawyer refers the pair to me for medico-legal advice.

2. A 20-year-old Bangladeshi woman, recently married, becomes depressed after a spontaneous miscarriage and gets into disputes with her mother-in-law. The husband and his brothers suspect that she is possessed by a spirit and, although prepared to accept psychiatric help, also want her to wear a *tawiz*, or amulet. The clinical team do both.

3. A 54-year-old Moroccan woman, divorced and isolated, is referred to me via a colleague by her adult daughter for 'hysterical behaviour', as the doctor puts it. Every time she sees a medic, she immediately starts acting strangely: eyes glazed, she motions with her arms, and speaks in a strange voice, and runs about the room. I see her and she does the expected actions while her daughter, who is accompanying her, anxiously asks me if I accept the existence of spirits. I address the *jinn* in a loud voice (luckily he speaks English!) and he replies

through the woman that he is the husband of one spirit I named and that he has now been married to his human victim for five years. While he is possessing her she moves strangely around my office but does not upset the glass of water I gave her earlier. The spirit eventually leaves and I discuss with the woman and her daughter the chances of her obtaining appropriate therapy in Morocco (Crapanzano, 1973) – for, alas, I am no exorcist.

Sought possession can itself be divided socially into the central (for the society's religious culture, typically male, and peripheral cults (more marginal and female) (see Figure 3.2), but this is a distinction more useful for the anthropologist than the clinician (Lewis, 1996). Clinical presentation is most likely to be involuntary PT or P for which an individual presents as patient. They are commonly seen in clinical settings around the world, and in Britain are most likely to be seen among migrants from Pakistan, Bangladesh, the Middle East or North Africa (where the spirit is a *jinn*), and occasionally among evangelical European Christians, though here the presentation is more likely to be P (possession belief alone) (see cases 1 and 2 in Figure 3.3).

The Social Context of Sought and Involuntary Possession

Saka

The experience of *saka* was once not uncommon among the Waitata of Kenya (Harris, 1957). *Saka* occurs when women are denied a request made to their husbands, typically for something which men consider their prerogative. Half of the women in the community developed *saka* at some time during their lives. In a situation where women were expected to provide not only the food for their families but also domestic utensils and household objects, they did not have access to the necessary money for these things since this was generated through the sale of land and livestock and these were the concern of men alone as women were said to have 'no head for land or cattle transactions'.

The pattern of *saka*, which was described by Western observers as hysteria, provides a social caricature of women as uncontrollable consumers, as vulnerable, emotional and out of control; 'They are shown as contrasting in every way with men and the contrast is symbolised as a personal malady' (Harris, 1957). The therapy? The husband sponsors a large public ceremony in which his wife wears items of male dress or new clothes; this constitutes an inversion of normal behaviour which, from the outside, we might see as a resolution of domestic conflict. Described baldly like this, *saka* seems a transparently adaptive device, hardly to be considered an illness. From the local perspective, at least from that of the men, *saka* may indeed be understood as an illness but also as the undesirable attack of malign spirits, and as the simple expression of women's social position and personality. Nor do we find that all the men in the society always see the reaction in the same way. All the patterns of distress and misfortune are flexible – sometimes tentatively performed, sometimes hinted at – and they exist not just through discrete and dramatic patterns like *saka* but as part of everyday conversations and conflict.

If this brief account serves to make the pattern transparently functional for individual women, local men would argue that the whole thing may be simulated. Its other-worldly power nevertheless compels the community to action through the obligations inherent in 'illness' or 'possession'. In the UK, we might remark on the parallels with overdoses. Both the woman who takes the overdose, and her family and the medical staff in the casualty department make distinctions between the overdose as the symptomatic expression of an underlying despair or as a transparently instrumental manipulative action. To what extent are the psychological experiences in overdoses and *saka* identical? The answer lies not in some state abstracted from context, deprived of social meaning, but in the sort of 'fit' with available models which we may identify, if we choose, with isolation and despair or even rebellion. To note the social consequences is not to label the protagonist/patient as a callous actor, but to affirm the cultural meaning of suffering of any type. If the whole pattern (context, precipitating episode, 'symptoms', resolution) may be said to work for the individual and her community, then it only works through the power that compels us to respond to the threat of illness or possession. Nor can we argue that the pattern is always adaptive. *Saka*, like the overdose, may at times be ridiculed or ignored, or indeed become part of a continuing pattern not easily seen as adaptive for the individual woman herself.

Sar

A similar pattern, *sar*, occurs among the nomadic Somali. Here, the possessing power is clearly identified as female and jealous of men's authority (Lewis, 1966). Women are normally excluded from public decision-making and power, except in the resolution of *sar*. The members of the community who are accepted as able to recognise and treat *sar* attacks are people who have previously been victims themselves; indeed, they comprise the only public organisation in which women play a dominant part. The participation of women in such healing groups where they become voluntarily possessed has been argued to 'allow the voice of women to be heard in a male dominated society, and occasionally enable participants to enjoy benefits to which their status would not normally entitle them' (Corin and Bibeau, 1980).

Here, the representation within the illness itself of what we might feel is its aetiology – gender inequality – extends also to the healing group. While there are parallels with psychoanalysis and shamanism, in both of which transcending one's own difficulties confers the ability to help others, a closer analogy is perhaps that of self-help organisations such as Alcoholics Anonymous, or perhaps contemporary women's therapy groups. No social institution need remain restricted to its original rationale, and, just as the anti-narcotics groups Synanon and the American Mental Health Movement each transformed themselves from a self-help group into something that may be regarded as a politico-religious sect, so have the 'hernia societies' of the Congo moved beyond mutual support to adopt a powerful social role, including rights over tax collection (Janzen, 1978). Self-help groups of this type, in the industrialised West or elsewhere, seem to share a similar ideology in which the problem is recognised to be a continuing vulnerability rather than something for which the group can claim to effect a radical cure. Thus such groups are associated with many chronic disorders in medicine such as alcoholism, vitiligo, epilepsy and cystitis.

Gender Politics

Saka and *sar* appear to articulate and resolve, at least temporarily and for the individual, gender oppositions which become manifest as something we might call tensions. Men appear to be less subject to such psychopathology, either because as the dominant group they have less access to such patterns than do women who are already identified as vulnerable to sickness or possession, or else because they are less 'stressed', having access to everyday mechanisms of power to adjust their difficulties.

The distinction may be difficult to draw. As with overdoses, when do 'symptoms' become 'strategies'? Much seems to depend on the local meanings. In certain situations men, of course, become depressed or possessed: situations in which, it could be argued, they have lost access to everyday male power. This may occur, for example, when young men, in order to marry, are forced into dependence on their fathers-in-law or their kin, as in the New Guinea Highlands (Littlewood, 2002); or in Britain, where they might take an overdose when unemployed. At times they may be hoist with their own petard of male authority, as are those young men in Morocco who are unable to live up to the ideal of male virility through suffering impotence, physical weakness or deafness (Crapanzano, 1973). Again, the disabling power – the *jinn* – is conceived of as female and jealous of men: here, she is placed to achieve a cure and is explicitly involved in treatment. The resolution is achieved by her transformation from 'a force disruptive to the social and moral order into a force to preserve that order. So long as her follower obeys ... his society's moral code, she enables him to live up to the idea of male dominance, superiority and virility' (Crapanzano, 1973).

Clinical Diagnosis and Treatment

Possession belief being an explanatory model, it can be used locally to interpret almost any illness but especially epilepsy and psychiatric illness. Possession states proper are likely to attract a diagnosis of hysteria, dissociative state or multiple personality disorder although clinicians may well feel a more significant psychiatric problem, such as depression, lies behind them. Schizophrenia is unlikely to be mistaken for a possession state as its pattern is more idiosyncratic and less standardised by culture, and organic states are likely to have fixed organic symptoms and signs.

While treating the underlying major psychiatric condition, if any, the physician must remain sensitive to the cultural issues, couched as they may be in a totally alien medium. It is unwise to directly contradict a patient's or relative's statements about the reality of spirit possession (Figure 3.4 below), but instead to offer any psychiatric treatment (including pharmaceutical drugs) as something which experience has taught the doctor will protect against spirit attack.

In the case of an involuntary possession state (as in the Moroccan woman described in Figure 3.3, case 3), there may be a chance to involve culturally sensitive psychotherapists (as at the Nafsiyat International Therapy Centre in London). A 'culture broker', an imam or a health or social worker from the particular community may be able to advise on what are locally culturally appropriate beliefs and practices. One problem is that these workers are often too likely to support a biomedical approach and to dismiss the local practice as superstition. At the other extreme, the 'local healing' may well be fairly idiosyncratic and cobbled together from a number of local and Christian (or other major religious) idioms. It is easy for the family to move from a view that their relative is afflicted by a spirit to accepting that the patient him- or herself is a witch or other malign being. Particularly where physical exorcism of the spirit is locally attempted, it may be dangerous to the individual, and the clinician should not easily concede matters to the supposed local culture. Traditional modes of dealing with spirit possession states normally include gently cajoling the spirit or accommodating it, rather than brutally expelling it, but the treatment practised in Britain may be less confident and culturally validated.

Figure 3.4   Sensitivity to local culture

Dangers of Ignoring Local Culture

- Lose patient's (or relative's) support for biomedical treatment.
- Ignore patient's own interpretation.
- Thus fail to prevent recurrence or lose the patient.

Dangers of Over-Emphasizing Local Culture

- Physical (or psychological) danger to the patient.
- Abdication of responsibility and thus leave patient unsupported.
- Local healing may not be culturally standardized, and be idiosyncratic and 'do-it-yourself' at best.

References

Bourguignon, E. (ed.) (1973). *Religion, Altered States of Consciousness and Social Change*. Columbus: Ohio State University Press.

Corin, E. and G. Bibeau (1980). 'Psychiatric Perspectives in Africa', *Transcultural Psychiatric Research Review*, 16: 147-78.

Crapanzano, V. (1973). *The Hamadsha: A Study in Moroccan Ethno-Psychiatry*. Berkeley: University of California Press.

Harris, G. (1957). 'Possession "Hysteria" in a Kenyan Tribe', *Am Anthropol*, 59: 1046-66.

Janzen, J.M. (1978). *The Quest for Therapy: Medical Pluralism in Lower Zaire*. Berkeley: University of California Press.

Lewis, I.M. (1966). 'Spirit Possession and Deprivation Cults', *Man*, 1: 307-29.

Littlewood, R. (2002). *Pathologies of the West*. London: Continuum Press/Cornell University Press.

Littlewood, R. and C. Douyon (1997). 'Clinical Findings in Three Cases of Zombification', *Lancet*, 350: 1094-6.

Shweder, R. (1985). 'Menstrual Pollution, Soul Loss and the Comparative Study of Emotions', in A. Kleinman and B. Good (eds), *Culture and Depression*. Berkeley: University of California Press.

Chapter 4

Embodied Alternative Identities: Spiritual Possession, Psychiatric Disorder or Socio/Political Stratagem?

Sherrill Mulhern

Introduction

Comparative cross-cultural analyses of spirit possession are always fraught with ambiguities and exceptions because around the globe different societies use different languages to discuss spiritual entities and their interactions with the human world. Moreover, the how, when, why, and where of possession by spirits can vary dramatically both from one culture to another as well as within a given culture, from one historical period to another. This said, whether it is socially sanctioned or proscribed, spirit possession is always to some extent an organised public event during which consensually agreed upon local beliefs about the natural and the supernatural worlds, as well as the nature of the human person are embodied and acted out. It habitually involves some form of public acknowledgment that the normal state of consciousness of a given individual has been fundamentally transformed and that his/her body and mind have been taken over by an autonomous, disembodied, volitional entity, that is to say, a nonphysical being or spirit that is perceived as possessing almost all of the criteria that are used locally to define a human person. These include individuality, a sense of self and identity that persists through time, and an acknowledged capacity for moral action.

Spirit possession implies the purposeful mobilisation of a recognisable, psycho-physiological state that is, by definition, out of the control of the individual who is being possessed (Levy, Mageo and Howard, 1996). This state is rarely immediately discerned. Before they are recognised as possessed, individuals must exhibit a specific set of communicative behaviours that, in a given culture, at a certain time are defined, sanctioned and successfully promulgated – as eloquent and involuntary – by an accredited cultural elite. Once the presence of the possessing entity has been confirmed by representatives of this elite, possessed individuals function as morally competent persons within the established social networks of their respective cultures, that is to say, they are not considered to be mentally defective. Instead, the possessed individual is assigned a new social role in which he/she is accepted as being and as acting as if another 'person' – that is radically different and discontinuous with his/her psychological 'self' – has momentarily taken over executive control of his/her body. These two people, the 'possessed person' and the 'possessing person', both function as competent social actors, endowed with communicative expertise, and intentions.

Possession in Western European Societies: Satan and the Witches

Throughout most of recorded history, in European Christian societies, theologians and religionists have held that during his/her lifetime a human person can have only one body. In addition to a body, what distinguishes one person from all others is an independent, immortal soul – invested with a free will – that manifests itself though a unique cluster of emotional and psychological characteristics that constitute his/her personality or identity (Douglas, 1995). Consequently, although in these societies prophets, saints and mystics are believed to engage in intimate relationships with benevolent spiritual entities, even when experiencing ecstasy, these exceptional individuals are expected to maintain their personal identities. For example, the Holy Spirit – who is traditionally defined as one of three coeternal, coequal, uncreated and omnipotent Persons that constitute the triune Christian God – is habitually described as 'filling' or 'dwelling in' the souls of mystics, saints and those who have received 'baptism of the Holy Spirit'. In other words, there is no radical displacement of the mystic's psycho/social identity. Moreover, even in Christian societies where this state is actually designated 'Holy Spirit Possession', the 'possessed' person's identity is never absorbed by the spiritual entity (Zane, 1995; Sanders, 1996; Miller, 2000). On the contrary, however, spiritual entities that manifest their presence by overpowering, absorbing and/or displacing an individual's personal identity are invariably considered, by definition, to be malevolent or demonic and their sustained 'embodiment' is vigorously discouraged.

Up until the fifteenth century, Christian religious authorities generally distinguished between individuals who succumbed to demonic possession and those who were accused of, or claimed to be conjurors, healers or witches. Whereas the former were understood to be in the throes of authentic, albeit maleficent, spiritual crises, the latter were dismissed as deluded. Persons accused of witchcraft were usually socially isolated individuals who were accused by disgruntled members of their entourage of having used magical power to cause ill fortune – such as crop failure, impotence, malady, the death of children and/or livestock – which confounded rational explanation. When they were brought before tribunals, their accusers sought reparation for the damages that they believed they had suffered, often at the risk of finding themselves penalised when their allegations prove to be fraudulent (Jacques-Chaquin, 1987). It was only after witch hunts had been sanctioned by the institutional, religious elite that the village sorceress was transformed into a conspiring incarnation of absolute evil, possessed by the devil (Henningsen, 1980; Ginzburg, 1991).

One of the most perplexing questions surrounding the construction of the Inquisitions of the High Middle Ages is why the ecclesiastical authorities of the late fourteenth century reversed the Catholic Church's position on the intrinsic power of witchcraft and approved the manuals of the inquisitors in which witches were described as actually being able to change themselves at night into totally different persons capable of flying through the air or assuming the bodies of animals (Kramer and Sprenger, 1971). In 1991, historian Alain Boureau argued that the roots of this decisive conceptual shift can be traced to the medical, legal and theological debates of the late twelfth and thirteenth centuries concerning the essential nature of the human person, the phenomenon of sleepwalking (noctambulism or somnambulism) and the splitting of the personality exhibited by individuals suffering from this condition. According to the savants of the period, the sleepwalker can be distinguished from the dreamer in so far as none of the faculties which ensure the mastery of the soul over the body – the will, memory and intelligence – are manifested in the former. Whereas the dreamer remains intimately tied to the meanders of his expanding soul, the sleepwalker is characterised by a radical split between his conscious awareness and the violent, often criminal actions of his body; he has to rely on outside witnesses to tell him what he has done (Boureau, 1991).

At the beginning of the fourteenth century, after prolonged medical and legal study, sleepwalkers were accorded a formal judicial status by Pope Clement V, that is to say, they were absolved of moral responsibility for the reprehensible acts that their bodies might commit when they were in their somnambulistic state. Boureau maintains that it is the early thirteenth-century hypothesis of the plurality of the substantial forms of man – that had been censured by the official power of Thomism – that reemerged and crystallised into the late fourteenth-century demonologies. The split in the personality of the sleepwalker made it possible to postulate a real, albeit partial diabolising of human beings by placing the acts of their bodies under the direct control of an independent, malignant, supernatural entity. Within this conceptual framework witch possession and witch cults – to which heretofore undetected sexual orgies and blasphemous ritual murders could be ascribed – were conceivable (Boureau, 1993).

Early critics of the witch hunts demonstrated the pivotal role played by persons exhibiting somnambulistic or dissociated states of consciousness in the construction of the persona of the possessed witch and the stories of the Demonic Sabbath (Weyer, 1991). Unlike the many normal people who were accused of malevolent and evil magic (maleficium), these were the requisite participant observers at the Devil's nocturnal debaucheries. Popular accounts of the witch trials usually depict accused witches as only confessing to their reprehensible acts under torture. However, the historical record shows that some of the most lurid descriptions of the demonic Sabbath were produced by individuals who had either fallen into what appeared to be a deep state of trance – after rubbing their bodies with mysterious salves created from plants – or had simply been psychologically broken down by incarceration and repeated questioning. Convinced that their salvation was contingent on confession, somnambulistic accused witches began confabulating; incorporating their dreams, beliefs, personal experiences and mental visions into the stories of absolute evil that their interrogators expected them to tell (Henningsen, 1980; Ginzburg, 1991). Although, in some cases, these individuals exhibited unusual marks on their bodies or – when subjected to torture – developed stigmata that were interpreted as substantiating the presence of the devil, in most cases, the only evidence that was produced to corroborate their extravagant confessions was the purported eyewitness testimony of other accused witches (Kramer and Sprenger, 1971; Ferber, 1993; Hansen, 1970; Delpech, 1993; Soman, 1993).

From Demonology to Hysteria

Towards the end of the fifteenth century, in the antechambers of the witchcraft trials, medical doctors began speculating about the underlying physical and mental health of accused, ostensibly possessed witches. During the next two centuries, frustrated by the increasingly conspiratorial theories and social power of the religious elite, they began elaborating alternative, secular theories to explain the social and legal psychodrama of demonic possession. Where the representatives of religious authority discerned diabolical machinations, physicians increasingly diagnosed excesses of imagination, morbid psycho/physiological conditions, nervous predispositions, compromising socio/cultural environments and mysterious anatomo-pathological processes that demanded clarification.

However, their differing theories about the fundamental causes of accused witches' behaviours notwithstanding, religious experts and physicians generally agreed that demonic possession was a bounded phenomenon, located in and limited to the possessed individual, and that they, as authoritative experts, were examining it objectively. In other words, they discounted the possibility that their attitudes towards the individuals that they were ministering to might actually be structuring the latter's overt behaviours. Rather, they both assumed that possession is the functional equivalent of a disease from which an individual should be delivered either by a spiritual intervention that would liberate the oppressed soul or by a medical intervention that would heal the sick psyche. The goal of the intervening expert was the same: to restore the psychic and physical unity of the possessed individual in a manner that would allow him or her to recover the social individuality that is axiomatic in western culture.

Throughout Europe, during the late seventeenth, eighteenth and early nineteenth centuries, ostensibly possessed individuals shuttled back and forth between religious and medical institutions. However, over time, as social behaviours and religious preoccupations evolved, and the practice of medicine became increasingly scientific – particularly in urban centres of learning – public and professional interest in demonic beings and the manner in which they manifested their presence waned. Ultimately, the theories of the inquisitors were not so much defeated as they were rendered irrelevant by the emergence of the scientific perspective. In a rational world that could be explained by ordered, mechanical laws, belief in demonically possessed witches was dismissed as superstition (Russell, 1980). Although religious experts occasionally resorted to exorcism, increasingly people who claimed to be possessed were perceived as mentally deranged and treated accordingly.

In France, for example, doctors identified mental disorders – demonomania, defined as a form of madness in which a person conceives of himself as possessed of devils, and demonopathie, which included the ensemble of delirious pathologies in which a person believes that he is inhabited by one or more demons – to describe and classify these patients. These scientific labels reflected both medical practitioners' understanding of possession as well as their treatment techniques. This is to say, although individuals complaining of demon possession continued to haunt the halls of European mental hospitals and to receive various forms of medical treatment, since by definition their purportedly supernatural tormentors were only imaginary, they were generally ignored. It was not until the end of the nineteenth century, when French psychiatrists began using hypnosis to probe the minds of patients suffering from hysteria, that the question of the ontological status of independent possessing mental entities began to emerge as a serious clinical issue.

The evolution of Western European medical understanding of possession phenomena is particularly well illustrated in the work of one of the principal psychological theorists of the late nineteenth century, Dr Pierre Janet. In 1889, early in his career, Janet evoked the question of 'Les Possessions' (Possessions) in his philosophy dissertation 'Automatisme Psychologique' (Psychological Automatism). In that text, he drew a parallel between possessed individuals' accounts of their experiences and naive hysterical patients' efforts to understand and describe their own conversion symptoms. He concluded that 'belief in possession is nothing but a colloquial translation of a psychological fact' (Janet, 1889/1989: 414), that is to say, a form of mental illness.

Over the next 30 years, Janet diagnosed and treated dozens of patients for hysteria as well as a handful of patients who claimed to be possessed by demons. However, during this period, he apparently revised his initial appreciation of the underlying interrelationship between the two phenomena. In 1929, at the height of his career, he discussed both possession and hysteria in a series of public lectures on the psychological evolution of the personality. Significantly, however, although he defined hysteria as a form of mental 'desagregation' (disassociation) characterised by a tendency towards a permanent and complete 'doubling of the personality', he treated hysteria and possession in different lectures as if they were distinct, basically unrelated pathologies. Moreover, although he intimated that he was evaluating each subject from an objective, scientific perspective, his description of spirit possession was tinged by the anti-clerical perspective that characterised most post-inquisition medical discussions of the subject.

For example, in January 1929, in a conference on the psychopathology of possession, Janet makes it clear that he considers that all individuals who claim to be possessed are delusional, that is to say, suffering from a 'pathology of belief' (Janet, 1929/1984). He subdivides the phenomena into three basic categories: Demonic Possession – which he illustrates by summarising the reports of medieval theologians, whom he dismisses as hopelessly naive, Possession Delirium – which he illustrates by referencing clinical descriptions produced by psychiatrists whom he admires, who generally portray possessed individuals as victims of excesses of the imagination, who are 'easily persuaded to believe in anything that comes along' (Esquirol, 1838) and Exotic Possession – under which he subsumes descriptions drawn from classical Greek manuscripts, field reports published by ethnologists working in Africa, the diary of a New York tourist (who described witnessing possession in China), and the practices of mediums, who were in vogue at the time among the Parisian bourgeoisie.

Janet exhibits a distinct antipathy for this last category, particularly disapproving of the fact that in the relevant literature, this 'Black, Non-Christian' possession was usually depicted as socially condoned, actively solicited and experienced by those who practised it as a positive, healthy experience. He retorts that the main thing that distinguished these exotic cases from clinical, psychiatric cases is that the later are more agreeable, less intense than the former (Janet, 1929/1984: 158). Moreover, he maintains that the defining characteristic of all categories of possession is the manner in which the purported possessing entities apparently attack the physical integrity of their hosts, that is to say, seemingly forcing them to either adopt demeaning postures, or perform violent, albeit non-lethal acts of self mutilation. He notes that 'these individuals try to show that they are actually possessed by adopting a variety of recognisable attitudes, gestures, and expressions, exhibiting tattoos, putting on costumes and always by signalling the arrival of their spirits with a typical greeting' (Janet, 1929/1984: 155). In sum, Janet reduces possession to an ensemble of more or less dramatic postures that are performed by delusional individuals who suffer from a relatively superficial pathology of belief. He concludes that, essentially, it is the stereotypical embodiment of a struggle between opposites that suggests to observers that they are in the presence of two distinct persons (Janet, 1929/1984: 155).

In contrast to this description of possession as contrived performance, two months later in his lecture on hysteria, Janet portrays hysterics' secondary personalities as authentic psychological manifestations. Although he concedes that 'when one considers hysterics' personalities from the subjective point of view, the divisions of their personalities inevitably raise the question of possession', he reminds his listeners that although 'the possessed complain that they are under the control of secondary personalities, they don't demonstrate them very well. They take on attitudes that appear forced and somewhat comical, first imagining their possessing personalities, then talking about them' (Janet, 1929/1984: 272).

Hysterics, on the other hand, are described as never identifying or referring to their own secondary personalities. Janet asserts that it is only after hysterics have interacted with their doctors over a period of time that they inadvertently exhibit sharp and often quite brutal hiatuses of memory that seem to divide them (Janet, 1929/1984: 272). He maintains that the split that physicians observe, between hysterics' physical and emotional attitudes and their verbalisations is genuine because it is due to an underlying pathology of memory. He hypothesises that these individuals suffer from an inherited nervous weakness that renders them incapable of processing traumatic experiences in their normal cognitive state of awareness. He observes that when they change personalities, they appear to access those parts of their memories that are hidden from normal consciousness. Moreover, when they embody their secondary personalities some of their somatic symptoms temporarily disappear.

At first glance, Janet's description of secondary personalities appears to raise the same moral and legal questions that were posed by sleepwalkers during the High Middle Ages. In fact, during the late nineteenth century, his clinical studies of hypnotically induced somnambulism and hysteria suggest that he was initially fascinated with these patients' fluctuating personality states. This said, in the 1920s he ultimately concludes that, although they are occasionally very dramatic, in practice, secondary personalities are more a distraction than a key to understanding hysterics' psychological disorder. Although he continues to allow that physicians can access emotionally significant information that these individuals have dissociated from their normal state of conscious awareness by interacting with their sub-personalities, he cautions that when hypnosis is employed, particular care must be taken to maintain the asymmetrical relationship between doctor and patient that he believes defines and ensures the efficacy of the therapeutic endeavour. Furthermore, although he holds that hysterics' initial personality splits are elaborated before they enter psychiatric treatment and directly correlated with their underlying pathology of memory, he also maintains that these patients are extremely suggestible and sensitive to the expectations of their doctors. In other words, when physicians become infatuated with their secondary personalities, hysterics can easily respond by creating more.

Janet effectively circumvents the problem of the moral status of secondary personalities by distinguishing between the person of the hysteric and the symptom of his/her psychological illness. He vigorously rejects the concept of 'polyzoïsme', that is to say, multiple souls that had been proposed by his contemporary, the hypnotist (*magnétiseur*), Durand Le Gros (Ellenberger, 1970), insisting that human personality is not the reflection of any underlying material or spiritual, metaphysical entity (Janet, 1929/1984: 282). He describes secondary personalities as relatively superficial, albeit authentic psychological manifestations that do not compromise a hysteric's internal sense of physical identity (*cénesthésie*). Although he asserts that they are distinctive enough to be readily identified by a physician, he cautions that 'the individuals who present them don't actually change very much. Those who observe secondary personalities 'see one face and body, with the same weakness and strengths; they interact with the one mind, with the same knowledge and the same ignorance ... There are no marvellous faculties that appear in a particular (personality) state' (Janet, 1929/1984: 285).

Demons as Illness Entities: Deliverance and Christian Therapy in North America

By the beginning of the twentieth century, most of the major Christian denominations had begun to concede that when viewed from the perspective of scientific psychiatry, many reports of ecstatic, mystical experiences and cases of demonic possession appeared to reflect as much psychopathology as spiritual crisis. Given the rational climate of the times, religious authorities made concerted efforts to align Christian religious tradition with the findings of natural science. The spiritual 'Gifts of the Holy Spirit' such as prophesy, glossolalia and ritual healing were generally construed as having disappeared with the apostles whereas the demonic sabbaths that had bewitched the inquisitors were dismissed as myths. And although demon possession continued to be recognised as a theoretical possibility, individual cases were greeted with increasing scepticism. Most religious authorities insisted that all logical, psychological explanations and therapeutic options had to be explored before any case could be referred for exorcism.

As the century wore on, and the industrialised world struggled with the technological, economic and social changes that had been produced by science, colonialism and two world wars, social justice began to replace extraordinary spiritual manifestations as the central theme of the Christian gospel. Notwithstanding this, official church policy and the rational theories of medical scientists had little effect on a resurgence of popular interest in the supernatural, particularly all forms of occultism which, by mid-century, actually achieved a measure of official recognition in Nazi Germany. In the mid-1950s, faced with what appeared to be a pervasive occult threat against the foundations of Christian civilization, a group of German Protestant theologians and physicians began organising a spiritual counter-attack against what they perceived to be the forces of Satan. One of the principal theoreticians of the new demonology was German-born minister and theologian, Dr Kurt Koch, who specialised in the diagnosis and treatment of mental problems that he claimed were brought on by occult oppression, that is to say, the invisible influence of demons who could torment or even take over the personalities of persons seeking religious revival (Ellis, 1995, 2000).

Koch argued that over and above the esoteric practices of avowed occultists, virtually all folk-magic practices, including divination, the creation and use of protective amulets, spell casting and magical-healing rituals constituted devil worship and exposed both the practitioners and their descendants to demonically induced mental illness (Koch, 1972, 1973). Beginning in the1960s, as English translations of his numerous books became available, Koch became a much-demanded lecturer in Protestant seminaries across Europe and particularly in North America, where a heterogeneous Christian minority continued to practise the charismatic gifts of the Holy Spirit and to actively struggle with Satan and his minions during their religious services. Although they had been marginalised by the American cultural mainstream since the infamous legal battles over the teaching of evolution in 1925, in many parts of the United States, Charismatic/ Pentecostal/Evangelical Christian congregations persisted as influential social institutions. Steadfastly puritanical and politically conservative, many of these groups dismissed the optimistic promises of science, including psychology, as part of a subversive anti-Christian plot that was being orchestrated directly by Satan. Inevitably, Koch's message that emotional distress and behavioural problems could be interpreted as symptoms of demonic possession received their endorsement. Deliverance rituals were developed and incorporated into many Charismatic/ Pentecostal/Evangelical congregations' accepted religious practice – as well as their national and international missionary efforts (Cuneo, 2001).

With the introduction of deliverance rituals, these groups' traditional theories and techniques of spiritual warfare with demonic entities took on an increasingly therapeutic character (Peck, 2005). Nonbelievers, who had customarily been understood to be suffering the wages of their own personal sins, were progressively redefined as victims of the actions of occult, unwanted possessing/oppressing demons who needed spiritual treatment. And although deliverance ministers considered themselves spiritual practitioners, their ostensibly Christian religious rituals functioned increasingly like cathartic psychotherapies that appeared to be designed as much to restore possessed individuals' psychological and emotional health as they were to rectify their compromised spiritual state. Unlike Catholic priests, who subjected people who claimed to be possessed to extended periods of careful observation and who restricted the private ritual of exorcism to those rare individuals who exhibited a significant number of historically defined spiritual indicators, Protestant deliverance ministers generally accepted individuals' suspicions that they were possessed or oppressed by demons at face value. Moreover, many of these ritual specialists proposed proactive, public group deliverance services. On these occasions, congregants were advised that feelings of nausea or the urge to cry were signs that heretofore clandestine demons were emerging. Subsequently, during the service, when individuals began to exhibit these suggested symptoms, they would be approached by the minister and/or his assistants who in turn would engage the emerging demons directly.

The revival of interest in possession and demonic entities precipitated a significant broadening of many Christian pastors' and itinerant preachers' understanding of the parameters of their heretofore spiritual ministerial duties to include the diagnosis and treatment of psychological trauma, such as sexual abuse as well as behavioural disorders, like alcohol abuse and drug addiction. For example, in the late 1960s, in the United States, a loosely affiliated cohort of independent, nonprofit-making deliverance ministries caught mainstream Christian churches by surprise when they launched a much publicised national missionary effort aimed at disaffected, urban, middle-class adolescents and young adults for whom the spiritual euphoria promised by hallucinogenic drugs, and 'free love' had proven to be much more appealing than the rigors of the social gospel. Although deliverance ministers shared in the youthful counterculture's enthusiasm for the supernatural and confirmed that psychedelics had enabled the 'dropped out' generation to connect with supernatural entities, they abhorred the neo-pagan, far eastern and new-age religious and sexual practices that it championed. Furthermore they insisted that the disintegrating, increasingly violent social world of the North American urban youth commune movement was proof that the spiritual quest of the 'hippie flower children' had ended in demonic enslavement.

Young people who responded to deliverance ministers' missionary efforts were initially required to confess to their drug induced visions and depraved sexual behaviours, after which they were ritually delivered from these oppressing demons and baptised in the Holy Spirit. However, often deliverance was only the first step. Frequently, converts to what soon came to be called 'The Jesus Movement' were immediately shepherded into Christian residential groups, associated with established churches, where in addition to daily prayer meetings – that often included speaking in tongues and additional spiritual healing rituals – they were required to follow gender-specific dress codes, and social roles as well as strict rules of sexual abstinence. In the final analysis, individuals who were swept up in this movement were as much being delivered back to the puritanical, middle-class lifestyle as they were being delivered from demons.

The apparent success of deliverance ministries with disaffected youth presaged a shift in the attitudes of a broad spectrum of the American churchgoing public about the reality of demons as well as the pervasive psychological threat of demonic possession and how it should be treated (Peck, 2005). Ironically, whereas historically the excesses of Catholic inquisitors and exorcists had paved the way for the development of scientific psychiatry and the concomitant medicalisation of demonic possession, towards the end of the twentieth century, the practice of demon deliverance in the United States became the wellspring of what would become a powerful, nondenominational, albeit Christian therapy movement that effectively reintroduced spiritual beliefs and healing techniques into the heretofore ostensibly secular clinical milieu.

Ritualised Spirit Possession as an Individual and Cultural Idiom

In 1967, in a review of ethnographic descriptions of 488 different societies from all parts of the world, Erica Bourguignon reported that 437 or 90 per cent of the sample practised one or more forms of institutionalised, culturally patterned altered states of consciousness. Although the scope of her seminal research was not limited to the phenomenon of 'spirit possession' it provides a useful theoretical framework for relatively objective, cross-cultural discussion of the subject. Bourguignon found that most societies assume as an axiom the existence of a non-human, parallel spiritual universe that is populated by both benign and malevolent disembodied entities (Bourguignon, 1967). However, although like European Christian societies, non-western cultures generally eschew sustained contact and interaction with the latter, in over half of them, regular public intercourse between beneficent 'embodied' spiritual entities, their possessed hosts and members of the local community in which they appear constitute a positive, meaningful form of social experience that is encouraged or at least tolerated. In other words, in non-Christian cultures when it takes the form of ritualised spirit embodiment, the phenomenon of possession is much more than a perilous spiritual state. It is a complex, culturally specific institution that is inextricably entwined with other institutions that deal with major social concerns such as health, the settlement of personal disputes, unexplained economic catastrophes as well as customary religious practice.

In every society, individuals must learn to contend with the place that the accident of birth has allotted them. Consequently, throughout their lives, they must manipulate the symbolic systems and cultural categories that they share with other members of their social group in order to understand and influence the course of their everyday experiences. When individuals find themselves trapped in a social system where life is characterised by extreme social and/or economic disparities, or chronic abuse and where any fundamental alteration of their situation is perceived as impossible, an idiom is often developed through which they can simultaneously express and obtain some form of public validation of their shared distress. Ritual possession is just such an expressive idiom (Crapanzano, 1977).

The term 'ritual' is often used to designate sanctioned behaviours and agreed upon symbols that individuals in a given culture may use to examine the appropriateness of their lot in the ongoing flow of 'just how things are'. On the one hand, rituals are the privileged conduits through which powerful individuals propagate their message of domination by enforcing and reinforcing the socio-economic and political status quo. On the other hand, rituals can be used for subversion because they constitute a 'controlled environment where the accidents of ordinary life can be displaced precisely because they are felt to be so overwhelmingly present and powerful' (Smith, 1982). For example, in many societies, because the embodiment of spirits is a ritual action rather than an everyday action, possession is an effective technique for illustrating the radical incongruence of everyday lived experience. Within the ritual space, defined by the community of initiated believers, distressed individuals can publicly acknowledge their awareness that things could have been different by embodying the way that things might have been in conscious tension to the way things are. Once it has been embodied, the ritualised, alternative reality can later be recollected in the ordinary course of events over which the possessed individual habitually has no control (Smith, 1982).

Spirits are ritual components *par excellence* in so far as they can never be reduced to their hosts. It is their culturally sanctioned factuality that guarantees the integrity of the ritual space in which the possessed unmask the inequities of the established social order. Behind the inviolable shroud of the spirits, the possessed body can stand oppressive authority on its head with impunity. Men can behave like women, the accepted language and behaviour of power relationships can be mocked, deeply embedded social taboos can be flaunted and information that is normally suppressed can be publicly revealed (Lambek, 1989, 1996; Mageo and Howard, 1996). Notwithstanding this, whether they have turned to the spirits seeking relief from subjective distress or misfortune, or have chosen – or have been chosen – to be initiated into possession as a means of communing more intimately with approved spiritual entities, inevitably individuals who ultimately fail to exhibit locally accepted possession behaviours are either suspected of falling victim to an evil spirit or demon and subjected to rituals designed to expel the malignant entity or accused of malingering or feigning possession, in which case they are generally either treated for illness or shunned as self serving frauds (Littlewood and Lipsedge, 1985).

According to anthropologist Michael Lambek, ritual spirit possession provides an instance in which the collective and personal interpenetrate. Collectively endorsed patterns of embodiment are internalised by individuals and become self-transforming. Likewise individual intentions are externalised and given form through the voice and acts of the spirits and the career of their hosts (Lambek 1989: 238). Although spirit possession is not described as a theatrical role or mystification either by those who are possessed or by their social entourage, it defines a social arena in which possessed individuals are accorded special moral privileges that are not unlike those enjoyed by actors. The possessed are absolved of any blame for the behaviours that they exhibit both during the period of time that spirits are in executive control of their bodies as well as after the possession is terminated (Levy, Mageo and Howard, 1996).

Paradoxically, it is through this loss of control that spirit hosts achieve a measure of social authority (Lambek, 1989, 1996). For a moment in time, these individuals are granted the power to probe the established social organisation of life in their respective communities. In other words, ritual spirit possession functions as both a personal and a cultural idiom that simultaneously afford a limited cohort of individuals an intelligible means of externalising personal desires and/or suffering even as it allows societies to recall heretofore censored information and conflicts and to experiment with novel social strategies and configurations. Paradoxically, ritual spirit possession simultaneously foreshadows and forestalls social change by defining a phenomenological sphere in which subversive material can be examined in a manner that does not immediately undermine established cultural and institutional fabric (Connerton, 1989; Mulhern, 1991a; Stoler, 1995; Strathern, 1996; Mageo and Howard, 1996; Lipsedge and Littlewood, 1997).

Psychiatry, Secular Possession and the Politics of Sexual Abuse

During the first half of the twentieth century, the hypothesised traumatic/ neurological aetiology of hysteria – that had been proposed by Janet and his French contemporaries – was superseded by the Freudian theorem that the disorder is the result of intra-psychic conflict between unacknowledged, instinctual sexual drives and the constraints of external social reality. Although the psychiatric establishment adopted Freud's theory of repression, it continued to endorse Janet's basic description of hysterical symptomatology. This said, following Freud's lead, most psychiatrists eschewed the use of hypnosis with this type of patient. By the mid-1920s the new theoretical and treatment consensus had practically eliminated secondary personalities from the Western clinical milieu. In addition, the incorporation of the work of Freud, Jung and Adler, among others, as well as the findings of biological research, into psychological theorising had transformed psychiatrists' understanding of the unity of human personality. The psychological self was increasingly described as a complex, malleable structure that is continually shaped and modified by an individual's ongoing interactions with his/her environment.

Although most psychiatrists endorsed the concept of a multifaceted psychological self, they continued to interact with their patients as if they each harboured a unique personal identity until the 1970s when the arrival in the North American clinical milieu of two cohorts of severely traumatised individuals triggered a theoretical paradigm shift. The first group consisted of traumatised veterans of the Vietnam War who had returned from combat exhibiting debilitating psychosomatic symptoms. Doctors discovered that like many veterans of the World Wars in Europe, when these patients were unresponsive to traditional analytic treatment techniques, it was possible to relieve their physical and psychological symptoms with hypnosis and/or narco-analysis followed up with cathartic psychotherapy. They concluded that the link between experienced, overwhelming trauma and psychopathology that had been minimised by Freud needed to be re-examined.

The refocusing of American psychological theory and clinical practice on what came to be labelled Post Traumatic Stress Disorder (PTSD) occurred at time when another heretofore overlooked cohort of trauma victims was beginning to emerge and demand social, political and legal recognition: victims of rape and intra-familial sexual abuse. Members of this group had come together largely because of the efforts of feminist activists who, throughout the 1970s, had been organising shelters for victims of rape and domestic violence. Initially, these activists defined incestuous sexual abuse as a political issue, arguing that the intra-familial rape of female children by males was the lynchpin of male power. They contended that historically, the reality of women's experiences had been deformed by psychoanalytically informed psychiatric practice that dismissed the disclosures of female victims – who dared to denounce their aggressors – as hysterical fantasies, by liberally citing the Freudian myth of repressed sexual desire (Rush, 1971, 1980). Feminists drew a parallel between the heretofore unrecognised victims of incest and childhood sexual abuse and the survivors of the Nazi concentration camps. They demanded that members of this newly emergent class of 'survivors' of the secret horrors of intra-familial sexual violence, who filed criminal complaints, be treated as credible witnesses to their own experiences and that their accused aggressors be arrested, tried before a court of law, convicted, and jailed (Armstrong, 1994).

However, although the feminist initiative effectively raised public awareness about the prevalence of incest, their demand that the courts act on survivors' straightforward, unmediated narratives of early childhood sexual victimisation suffered from a critical lack of political acumen. Adult survivors who attempted to obtain reparation for crimes that had been perpetrated when they were children, soon discovered that the paucity of available corroborative evidence as well as the prevailing statutes of limitations often prevented them from successfully filing suit against their alleged aggressors. When it became evident that the established legal system not only offered little relief but often actually silenced complaining survivors, some feminist theorists began to reconsider their original animosity towards the psychotherapeutic establishment.

In 1980, in their Diagnostic and Statistical Manual of Mental Disorders III (DSM III), the American Psychiatric Association, in response to vigorous lobbying by feminist clinicians, confirmed a growing rapprochement between the therapeutic perspective – that implied that healing from the psychological sequellae of experienced trauma was a necessary prerequisite to political change – and feminist social theory. To wit, the notoriously vague diagnosis of hysterical neurosis – that had been used to discredit the testimonies of adult survivors of childhood incest – was dismantled (APA, 1980). Furthermore, because they were perceived as misogynistic, the attitudes of dissimulation, that is to say, suggestibility and the tendency to confabulate, that had been defining symptoms of hysteria, were split off and reclassified independently as Factitious Disorders, whereas the most dramatic psychological symptom associated with the syndrome was retained as an autonomous diagnostic entity: Multiple Personality Disorder (MPD). Once the underlying, polymorphous syndrome had been eliminated, many patients, who might have been diagnosed as hysterics according to the older diagnostic system were metamorphosed into 'multiples' and their enigmatic 'alter' personalities rapidly became the focus of clinical and mass-media attention.

The core symptoms of MPD were inspired by Janet's general theory of hysteria. However, unlike hysterics, whom he had described as suffering from a chronic psycho/physiological memory disorder that left them unable to consciously process traumatic experiences and singularly vulnerable to suggestion (Janet 1889/1989: 20), late twentieth-century 'multiples' were depicted as psychological virtuosos who, beginning in early childhood, had used their extraordinary auto-hypnotic skills to create alternate personalities to shield themselves both from the experience and subsequent memories of the unspeakable trauma of sexual abuse (Wilbur, 1984a; Gil, 1990). Significantly, whereas hysterics had typically exhibited mature secondary personalities, the overwhelming majority of alter personalities embodied by multiples were terrified young children (Kluft, 1985). Moreover, although MPD experts claimed to be the theoretical disciples of Pierre Janet, perfunctorily conceding that alternate personalities are not actually people, they proposed a radically different psycho-physiological description of these mental entities that portrayed multiples as having several mental systems in continuous, fully simultaneous and often unconscious operation, much like a computer.

This structural model characterised alter personalities as enduring, relatively independent, mind-bearing entities that satisfy nearly all conventional defining criteria of personhood, that is to say, a distinct sense of self and a first person perspective on the world. Like persons, they are purportedly capable of rational thought and differentiated by distinct sets of intentional predicates. Each alter has its own beliefs, motives and desires as well as skills and talents (APA, 1980). Moreover, alters perceive fellow alter personalities, domiciled within the same multiple, as separate people. Strong adult alters generally function either as protectors, who regularly assume executive control of 'the body' when weaker child alters feel threatened or as persecutors, capable of attacking, dominating and tormenting submissive alters either by exerting their influence without assuming executive control of 'the body' or by seizing executive control and placing 'the body' in compromising or dangerous situations in order to upset the more fragile members of a multiple's internal personality system (Kluft, 1991a, 1991b). When they are not 'out' in a multiple's body, alter personalities are said to retire to a 'Third Reality' situated behind the multiple's consciousness threshold (Kluft, 2005: 634). In other words, although they may go dormant for a period of time, as a rule when one alter is 'out in the body' the others continue to pursue their relationships, alliances and enmities within the multiple's unconscious mind.

Given its ostensibly scientific character, descriptions of the disorders listed in the DSM III were usually limited to observable symptoms and did not mention aetiology. However, in the case of MPD, 'child abuse and other forms of severe emotional trauma in childhood' were singled out as predisposing factors. Although a few experts maintained that almost any form of overwhelming childhood trauma could trigger the creation of alter personalities, most concurred with National Institute of Mental Health researcher, Dr Frank Putnam's observation that 'multiple personality is in fact a psychiatric disorder that has a relatively specific precipitant, incestuous sexual abuse, and begins in childhood'. (Elliot, 1982). In a society bent on eradicating child sexual abuse, the apparent consensus among medical professionals that individuals who either exhibit or who come to exhibit alter personalities as a result of psychotherapy are typically crime victims and that the narratives that these embodied entities produce are factual and could plausibly constitute corroborative criminal evidence that might be admissible in a court of law had far reaching ramifications.

Although the introduction to the DSM III cautioned clinicians that: 'a common misconception is that a classification of mental disorders classifies people, when actually what are being classified are disorders that people have' the description of MPD proposed by the American psychiatric establishment intimated that in fact multiples did constitute a unique class of individuals and that their alter personalities conceivably merited both social and legal recognition (Gil, 1990; Slovenko, 1989). Unlike adult survivors who demanded the sanctioning of their unmediated personal memories of childhood victimisation by the criminal justice system, multiples of child alters represented an incontestable mimetic link with the secret world of violation by creating a phenomenological arena in which the suffering and shame of incestuous rape was actually played out. Alter personalities were tangible markers – whose moral authority was guaranteed by an emergent sector of the mental health profession – that confirmed both the reality and the devastating consequences of the hidden evil that society was determined to uncover and eradicate.

During the 15 years that followed the publication of the DSM III, the idea that people can have distinct, autonomous and rapidly alternating personalities captured the imagination of the American public, of some therapists and of thousands of patients (Francis and First, 1998). Moreover, during this period, more than 400 clinical papers, presentations, books, articles, radio, and television programmes, workshops, and seminars devoted to MPD were published and/or presented, including three major international conferences (Greaves, 1986). Significantly, following the example of the DSM III, subsequent theoretical treaties on the disorder focused essentially on the individuality of alter personalities. The physical and neurological anomalies that were exhibited by some multiples were presented as proof of the autonomy and objective reality of these entities (Braun, 1983a, 1983b), whereas the social and psychological implications of the fact that the disorder had been defined as an embodied practice was completely discounted. However, once they emerged and took possession of the bodies of their hosts, alter personalities entered into interactive social space, transforming multiples both physically and symbolically. Like the spirits in non-western societies that sanction ritual possession, for all intents and purposes, late twentieth-century embodied alter personalities constituted a secular form of possession.

Initially, as the numbers of diagnosed multiples in North America rose from approximately one hundred to several thousand, experts pronounced the new diagnosis a resounding success. However, the honeymoon was short lived. As was noted above, the idiom of ritual spirit possession derives its social and political power from the fact that it is a parallel system of communicative behaviours that is circumscribed by ritual space and time. At the end of the ritual, the spirits must leave – and rejoin the supernatural realm – and their hosts must return to their everyday lives. In other words, successful possession in the ritual sphere does not compromise or eliminate the mundane social identity of an accomplished spirit host, it simply enhances it.

In contrast, although theoreticians of MPD acknowledged that prior to diagnosis most multiples appear to have only one identity – because they either ignore the existence of or hide their alter personalities – they maintained that actually from the time that they are created during a multiple's childhood, alter personalities continuously function surreptitiously as members of the cohort of alternating, albeit unrecognised, everyday social identities that are domiciled within their host's unconscious mind. Paradoxically, they also observed that once these elusive other 'selves' have been ferreted out by skilled professionals and identified themselves in the privacy of the clinical milieu, their hosts are constantly at their mercy (Braun, 1984, 1986, 1989a; Kluft, 1985, 1991a, 1991b, 1991c). In other words, unlike spirit hosts, multiples are in a state of permanent possession. When diagnosed multiples go home, their alter personalities go with them. Moreover, since all of a multiple's alter personalities are presumed to have the same ontological status, theoretically, there is no way of distinguishing which one of them is the 'real' personality. Consequently, friends and families of multiples – who were treated as outpatients – were advised that, because alters might emerge at any time, they should always be prepared to adjust their usual behaviours to accommodate the needs and sensibilities of these vulnerable entities (Braun, 1984, 1986, 1989a).

Sanctioned by the authority of medical science, multiples and their alter personalities soon became recognisable participants in everyday American society. Child alters played with multiples' children, adult alters co-authored best-selling biographies, and gave interviews on radio and television talk shows. However, in the clinical milieu, therapists soon discovered that alter personalities' popularity with the mass media appeared to be inversely correlated with therapeutic success. Multiples were proving harder to treat than had been anticipated (Coons, 1986). Since by definition, alter personalities were fundamentally expressions of psychopathology, experts had assumed that once they emerged and revealed their terrible secrets, with the help of their therapists, these entities would fuse together into one person and their host would be cured (Wilbur, 1984b; Kluft, 1985). However, in practice, as often as not, once they had been embodied, alter personalities expressed fear and/or vigorously resisted this type of integration. For example, following diagnosis, instead of improving, some patients began to develop primary social identities as multiples and to insist that society should recognise that being multiple was a legitimate lifestyle and that they should be allowed to refuse further treatment and to remain overtly multiple if they chose to do so (Chu, 1997; Chase, 1987).

Of course, the burgeoning specialised MPD literature contained numerous reports of cases in which intensive therapy, over a relatively short period of time, was apparently effective. Notwithstanding this, a significant perrcentage of these successes were achieved by one well-known MPD expert. In fact, most clinicians reported that their initial successes with multiples were often ephemeral. Once their ostensibly integrated patients left treatment, instead of stabilising, many soon shattered and returned to therapy inhabited by yet another cohort of alter personalities (Coons, 1986). However, whereas at this point, an outside observer, familiar with the sociology of ritual spirit possession, might have suggested that the most plausible reason that many multiples were unable to reintegrate into a single person was due to the secondary psycho/social gains that are associated with the practice of personality embodiment, MPD specialists advised their less experienced colleagues to stay the course, noting that the principal cause of relapse was that when multiples first enter treatment, inevitably some of their personalities may either pretend to be gone or refuse to emerge. They observed that, as a rule, when these secretive entities finally reveal their presence, they either confess that they have evaded detection to avoid being confronted with painful memories and issues or make this clear by subsequent verbalisations and behaviours. Specialists hypothesised that in all probability there was a relationship between the frequency and the severity of abuse that multiples endured during childhood on the one hand and the number of personalities that they harboured and the complexity of their personality systems on the other.

However, although in a few cases, multiples were able to produce independent evidence that corroborated some of their alters' memories of severe abuse, in most cases, this hypothesis appears to have functioned like a self-fulfilling prophecy. As Janet had observed more than a century before, the more therapists concentrated their efforts on uncovering alter personalities, the more their patients produced them. The number of personalities exhibited by individual multiples rose from around a dozen to over 100 in some cases. And with each new generation of alter personalities, to the horror of their therapists, the terrifying memories that these entities produced became increasingly florid and less plausible. In 1986, an informal survey of clinicians revealed that nearly 25 per cent of MPD clients were recovering memories that their childhood care-givers were not only child abusers but Satanists who had subjected them to blood rituals, orgies, rapes, abortions and cannibalism (Braun and Gray, 1987).

Historically, individuals who entered psychotherapy had been expected to gradually assume responsibility for their symptoms. Consequently, reminiscences about their early childhood experiences – that were produced in the clinical milieu – only needed to reflect subjective, psychological truth. However, the traumatic theory of psychopathology and psychological multiplicity transformed psychotherapy into a process of assigning responsibility for mental disorders to people outside of the clinical milieu. Moreover, from 1980 until 1994, essentially all of the significant clinical literature on MPD intimated that memories recovered by multiples' alter personalities were historically accurate. This said, before people can be held accountable for criminal behaviour, the accuracy of their accusers' allegations must necessarily be measured against the objective criteria of the criminal justice system.

Initially, when alter personalities began revealing memories of ritual torture they were taken seriously by both clinicians and law enforcement because, although with the passage of time, even unusually violent child abuse may become difficult to corroborate, criminal activity on the scale that was being described by multiples invariably generates enduring material evidence (Braun, 1989b; Braun, et al., 1989; Braun and Sachs, 1988; Beere, 1989; Greaves, 1989; Hammond, 1992; Lanning, 1992; Young, et al., 1991). Inevitably, when police investigators failed to confirm any of the extraordinary allegations that had been made in any of the cases that were brought to their attention, they became increasingly sceptical (Mulhern, 1991b). Therapists and their patients, on the other hand, were outraged. Almost immediately, the stories of child abusing devil worshippers that had begun raging in the clinical milieu exploded into the spotlight of the secular mass media (Raphael, 1989; Rivera, 1988; Winfrey, 1988). And although television audiences were spellbound when 'cult programmed multiples' regaled them with stories of vagrants being tortured and skinned alive and babies being stabbed to death with inverted crosses (Raphael, 1989), the uncanny resemblance between multiples' uncorroborated stories and the confessions that had sent thousands of women to their deaths during the inquisitions was hard to ignore. Satanic survivors and their defenders proposed a host of bizarre theories to explain why so much murder and mayhem had been going on unnoticed. However, they soon found themselves facing a chorus of social researchers, police investigator, lawyers, and feminists who vigorously objected that the uncritical acceptance of multiples' uncorroborated recovered memories was threatening the integrity of both the practice of psychotherapy and the entire child protection movement (Richardson, Best and Bromley, 1991; Armstrong, 1994).

In June 1994, in response to the growing crisis, the American Medical Association adopted a resolution that created a new policy on memory enhancement methods used with adult patients in cases where childhood sexual abuse was suspected. The policy stated: The AMA considers the technique of 'memory enhancement' in the area of childhood sexual abuse to be fraught with problems of potential misapplication (AMA, 1994). A year later, in the Fourth Edition of its Diagnostic and Statistical Manual of Mental Disorders, the American Psychiatric Association began the sensitive process of revising the diagnosis of Multiple Personality Disorder. To begin with, in an attempt to correct the impression that had been given by the language of the DSM III – that clearly suggested that personalities are separate people inhabiting a single body – the disorder was officially renamed Dissociative Identity Disorder (DID). In addition, unlike personalities that had been described as existing, dissociated identities and/or personality states were described as presences that are experienced by patients that qualify for the diagnosis. Moreover, the attendant clinical description of DID was substantially revised to formally acknowledge that these individuals are highly hypnotisable and vulnerable to suggestion and that consequently, the traumatic memories that they recover in therapy are subject to caution (APA, 1995).

Inevitably, given that like other idioms of psycho/social distress, MPD was so deeply embedded in the historical process that most individual participants – including those who embodied alter personalities, as well as representatives of the cultural elite that sanctioned them and members of the larger society that countenanced them – were unable to step back and examine it objectively. As a result, the deconstruction of the disorder proved to be extremely controversial. Proponents of MPD decried the name change and accused their critics of pandering to incestuous child abusers. Frustrated criminal investigators, who failed to uncover evidence that might corroborate multiples' recovered memories of grotesque Satanic rituals were vilified as being either incompetent or surreptitious members of an international cult of devil worshippers. Some multiples, along with their parents and/or their therapists battled out the meaning of their recovered memories in the media or the courts, whereas others found themselves alone, trying to sort out their shattered memories and lives. And the story goes on, with no conclusive dénouement in sight. Since MPD is still living history it may take many years before objective psychological researchers are able to determine what the sanctioned public embodiment of alter personalities actually contributed to the

understanding of the psycho/physiology of childhood trauma. This said , it remains
true that when this process is examined from the perspective of the sociology of
possession, there is already much to be learned.

References

AMA (1994). *AMA Policy Compendium, 1994*. Policy 515.978. Chicago, IL:
    American Medical Association.
APA (1995). *Diagnostic and Statistical Manual (DSM IV)*. Washington, DC:
    American Psychiatric Association.
APA (1980). *Diagnostic and Statistical Manual (DSM III)*. Washington, DC:
    American Psychiatric Association.
Armstrong, L. (1994). *Rocking the Cradle of Sexual Politics: What happened
    when women said incest*. New York: Addison-Wesley Publishing Company.
Balch, R.W. and M. Gilliam (1991). 'Devil Worship in Western Montana: A Case
    Study in Rumor Construction', in J.T. Richardson, J. Best and D.G. Bromley
    (eds), *The Satanism Scare*. New York: Aldine de Gruyter.
Barach, P. (1992). 'An Integrative Model for Understanding the Clinical
    Presentation of Multiple Personality Disorder', *Ninth International Conference
    on Multiple Personality/Dissociative States*. Chicago, IL. Alexandria, VA:
    Audio Transcripts IIa.
Beere, R. (1989). 'Satanic Programming Designed to Undercut Therapy',
    Sixth International Conference on Multiple Personality Dissociative States.
    Alexandria, VA: Autio Transcripts VIIIa.
Boureau, A. (1993). 'Le Sabbat et la question de la personne dans le monde
    scolastique', in N. Jacques-Chaquin and M. Préaud (eds), *Le Sabbat des
    Sorciers XVe-XVIIIe Siècles*. Paris: Editions Jérôme Millon, pp. 33-47.
—— (1991). 'Satan et le dormeur: Une construction de l'inconscient au Moyen
    Age', *Chimère*, 14: 41-61.
Bourguignon, E. (1967). 'World Distribution and Patterns of Possession States',
    in R. Prince (ed.), *Trance and Possession States*. Montreal: J.M. Bucke
    Foundation.
Braun, B. (1989a). 'Psychotherapy of the Patient with Dissociative Disorder',
    Psychiatric Clinics of North America. Washington, DC: American Psychiatric
    Press, Inc., 12: 307-25.
—— (1989b). 'Psychology and Brain Chemistry in the Programming of Human
    beings', *Sixth International Conference on Multiple Personality/Dissociative
    States*. Alexandria, VA: Audio Transcripts, II-512.
—— (1986). 'Issues in the Psychotherapy of Multiple Personality Disorder', in
    B. Braun (ed.), *Treatment of Multiple Personality Disorder*. Washington, DC:
    American Psychiatric Press, pp. 1-28.

—— (1984). *Dissociative Disorders – 1984: Proceedings of the First International Conference on Multiple Personality/Dissociative States*. Chicago, IL: Department of Psychiatry, Rush University.

—— (1983a). 'Neurophysiological Changes in Multiple Personality Due to Integration: A Preliminary Report', *American Journal of Clinical Hypnosis*, 26: 84-92.

—— (1983b). 'Psychophysiologic Phenomena in Multiple Personality and Hypnosis', *American Journal of Clinical Hypnosis*, 26: 124-37.

Braun, B., J. Goodwin, K. Gould, D. Hammond, R. Kluft, R. Sachs, R. Summit and W. Young (1989). *Ritual Child Abuse: A Professional Overview*. Ukiah, CA: Cavalcade Productions.

—— and R. Sachs (1988). 'Recognition of Possible Cult Involvement in MPD Patients', *Fifth International Conference on Multiple Personality/Dissociative States*. Alexandria, VA: Audio Transcripts Ivd.

—— and G. Gray (1987). 'Report on the 1986 MPD Questionnaire – MPD and Cult Involvement', *Fourth International Conference on Multiple Personality/ Dissociative States*. Alexandria, VA: Audio Transcripts Va-383-7.

Chase, T. (1987). *When Rabbit Howls*. New York: E.P. Dutton.

Chu, J. (1997). 'President's Message', in C. Courtois (ed.), *The International Society for the Study of Dissociation News*, 15/2: 2.

Connerton, P. (1989). *How Societies Remember*. Cambridge: Cambridge University Press.

Coons, P. (1986). 'Treatment Progress in 20 patients with Multiple Personality Disorder', *The Journal of Nervous and Mental Disease*, 174/12: 715-21.

Crapanzano, V. (1977). 'Introduction', in V. Crapanzano and V. Garrison (eds), *Case Studies in Spirit Possession*. New York: John Wiley and Sons, Inc.

Cuneo, M.W. (2001). *American Exorcism: Expelling Demons in the Land of Plenty*. New York: Doubleday.

Delpech, F. (1993). 'Les marques des sorcières', in N. Jacques-Chaquin and M. Préaud (eds), *Le Sabbat des sorciers XVe-XVIIIe siècles*. Paris: Editions Jérôme Millon, pp. 347-69.

Douglas, M. (1995). 'The Cloud God and the Shadow Self', *Social Anthropology*, European Association of Social Anthropologists. 3/2: 83-94.

Ellenberger, H.F. (1970). *The Discovery of the Unconscious*. New York: Basic Books.

Elliot, D. (1982). 'State Intervention and Childhood Multiple Personality Disorder', *The Journal of Psychiatry and Law*, 10: 441-56.

Ellis, B. (2000). *Raising the Devil: Satanism, New Religions, and the Media*. Lexington: University of Kentucky Press.

—— (1995). 'Kurt E Koch and the Civitas Diaboli: Germanic Folk Healing as Satanic Ritual Abuse of Children', *Western Folklore*, 54/2: 77-94.

Esquirol, J.E.D. (1838). *Des maladies mentales considérées sous le rapport medical, hygiénique et médico-légal*. Paris: Baillère.

Ferber, S. (1993). 'Le sabbat et son double', in N. Jacques-Chaquin and M. Préaud (eds), *Le sabbat des sorciers XVe-XVIIIe siècles*. Paris: Editions Jérôme Millon, pp. 101-11.

Frances, A. and M. First (1998). *Your Mental Health: A Layman's Guide to the Psychiatrist's Bible*. New York: Scribner.

Gil, E. (1990). *United We Stand: A Book for People with Multiple Personalities*. Walnut Creek, CA: Launch Press.

Ginzburg, C. (1991). *Ecstasies: Deciphering the Witches Sabbath*. New York: Pantheon.

Greaves, G. (1989). 'A Cognitive-Behavioral Approach to the Treatment of MPD Ritually Abused Satanic Cult Survivors', *Sixth International Conference on Multiple Personality/Dissociative States*. Alexandria, VA: Audio Transcripts: Iva-512.

——(1986). 'Editorial'. *International Society for the Study of Multiple Personality Newsletter*, 2/2: 4.

Hammond, D. (1992). 'Clinical Hypnosis in the Treatment of Multiple Personality Disorder', *Fourth Annual Eastern Regional Conference on Abuse and Multiple Personality*. Alexandria, VA: Audio Transcripts 37-742-92abcd.

Hansen, C. (1970). *Witchcraft at Salem*. London: Hutchinson.

Henningsen, G. (1980). *The Witches' Advocate: Basque Witchcraft and the Spanish Inquisition*. Nevada: University of Nevada Press.

Howard, A. and J.M. Mageo (1996). 'Introduction', in J.M. Mageo and A. Howard (eds), *Spirits in Culture, History and Mind*. New York: Routledge.

Jacques-Chaquin, N. (1987). 'Demonic Conspiracy', in S. Moscovici and C.F. Graumann (eds), *Changing Conceptions of Conspiracy*. New York: Springer-Verlag, pp. 61-87.

—— and M. Préaud (1993). *Le sabbat des sorciers XVe-XVIIIe siècles*. Paris: Editions Jérôme Millon.

Janet, P. (1929/1984). *L'évolution psychologique de la personnalité*. Paris: Edition Chaine.

——(1889/1989). *L'Automatisme psychologique*. Paris: Société Pierre Janet avec le concours du Centre National de la Recherche Scientifique.

Kluft, R. (2005). 'Diagnosing Dissociative Identity Disorder'. *Psychiatric Annals*, 4/8: 633-48.

——(1991a). 'Multiple Personality Disorder', in A. Tasman and S.M. Goldfinger (eds), *Annual Review of Psychiatry*, 10: 161-88.

—— (1991b). 'Clinical Presentations of Multiple Personality Disorder', *The Psychiatric Clinics of North America*. Washington, DC: American Psychiatric Press, Inc, 14/3: 605-29.

—— (1991c). 'Hospital Treatment of Multiple Personality Disorder', *The Psychiatric Clinics of North America*. Washington, DC: American Psychiatric Press, Inc, 14/13: 695-719.

—— (1985). 'The Natural History of Multiple Personality Disorder', in Richard Kluft (ed.), *Childhood Antecedents of Multiple Personality*. Washington, DC: American Psychiatric Press, pp. 197-238.

Koch, K.E. (1973). *Demonology Past and Present*. Grand Rapids: Kregel Publications.

—— (1972). *Christian Counselling and Occultism: The Counselling of the Psychically Disturbed and Those Oppressed Through Involvement in Occultism*. Grand Rapids: Kregel Publications.

Kramer, H. and J. Sprenger (1971). *The Malleus Maleficarum*. M. Summers (ed.), New York: Dover. (Original work published 1486).

Lambek, M. (1996). 'Afterword', in J.M. Mageo and A. Howard (eds), *Spirits in Culture, History and Mind*. New York: Routledge, pp. 237-51.

—— (1989). 'From Disease to Discourse: Remarks on the Conceptualization of Trance and Spirit Possession', in C. Ward (ed.), *Altered States of Consciousness and Mental Health: A Cross-Cultural Perspective*. Newbury Park: Sage Publications.

Lanning, K. (1992). *Investigator's Guide to Allegations of 'Ritual' Child Abuse*. Quantico, VA: National Center for the Analysis of Violent Crime.

Levy, R.I., J.M. Mageo and A. Howard (1996). 'Gods, Spirits and History: A Theoretical Perspective', in J.M. Mageo and A. Howard (eds), *Spirits in Culture, History and Mind*. London: Routledge, pp. 11-29.

Lipsedge M. and R. Littlewood (1997). 'Psychopathology and its Public Sources: from a Provisional Typology to a Dramaturgy of Domestic Sieges', *Anthropology and Medicine*, 4/1: 25-43.

Littlewood, R. and M. Lipsedge (1985). 'Culture Bound Syndromes', in K. Granville-Grossman (ed.), *Recent Advances in Clinical Psychiatry*. Edinburgh: Churchill-Livingstone, pp. 105-42.

Mageo, J.M. and A. Howard (1996). *Spirits in Culture, History and Mind*. New York: Routledge.

Miller, M. (2000). *Zohar*. Michigan: Fiftieth Gate Publications and Seminars.

Mulhern, S. (1991a). 'Embodied Alternative Identities: Bearing Witness to a World That Might Have Been', *The Psychiatric Clinics of North America*, 14: 769-85.

—— (1991b). 'Satanism and Psychotherapy: A Rumor in Search of an Inquisition', in J.T. Richardson, J. Best and D.G. Bromley (eds), *The Satanism Scare*. New York: Aldine de Gruyter, pp.145-72

Peck, M.S. (2005). *Glimpses of the Devil: A Psychiatrist's Personal Accounts of Possession, Exorcism, and Redemption*. New York: Simon and Schuster.

Raphael, S. (1989). *Baby Breeders*. New York: Multimedia Entertainment Inc.

Richardson, J., J. Best and D. Bromley (1991). *The Satanism Scare*. New York: Aldine de Gruyter.

Rivera, G. (1988). *Devil Worship: Exposing Satan's Underground*. The Investigative News Group. New York: Journal Graphics Inc.

Rush, F. (1980). *The Best Kept Secret: The Sexual Abuse of Children*. New York: McGraw-Hill Book Company.

—— (1971). 'The Sexual Abuse of Children: A Feminist Point of View'. Paper presented at the *New York Radical Feminist Conference*. New York.

Russell, J.B. (1980). *A History of Witchcraft*. London: Thames and Hudson.

Sanders, C.J. (1996). *Saints In Exile: The Holiness-Pentecostal Experience in African American Religion and Culture*. New York: Oxford University Press.

Slovenko, R. (1989). 'The Multiple Personality: A Challenge to Legal Concepts', *The Journal of Psychiatry and Law*, 17: 681-91.

Smith, J.Z. (1982). *Imagining Religion*. Chicago: The University of Chicago Press.

Soman, A. (1993). 'Le sabbat des sorciers: Preuve judiciare', in N. Jacques-Chaquin and M. Préaud (eds), *Le sabbat des sorciers XVe-XVIIIe siècles*. Paris: Editions Jérôme Millon, pp. 85-101.

Spiegel, H. (1974). 'The Grade 5 Syndrome: The Highly Hypnotizable Person', *The International Journal of Clinical and Experimental Hypnosis*, 22.

Stoler, P. (1995). *Embodying Colonial Memories*. London: Routledge.

Strathern, A. (1996). *Body Thoughts*. Ann Arbor: The University of Michigan Press.

Weyer, J. (1991) *De Praestigiis Daemonum. Witches, Devils, and Doctors in the Renaissance*. G. Mora (ed.), New York: Medieval and Renaissance Texts and Studies. (Original work published 1583).

Wilbur, C. (1984a). 'Multiple Personality and Child Abuse: An Etiologic Overview'. *First International Conference on Multiple Personality/Dissociative States*. Alexandria, VA: Audio Transcripts Va-1A-127-84.

Wilbur, C.B. (1984b). 'Treatment of Multiple Personality', *Psychiatric Annals*, 14: 27-31.

Winfrey, O., (1988). *Satanic Worship*. New York: American Broadcasting Companies, Inc.

Young, W., R. Sachs, B. Braun and R. Wakins (1991). 'Patients Reporting Ritual Abuse in Childhood: A Clinical Syndrome', *International Journal of Child Abuse and Neglect*, 15: 181-9.

Zane, W. (1995). 'Ritual States of Consciousness: A Way of Accounting for Anomalies in the Observation and Explanation of Spirit Possession', *Anthropology of Consciousness*, 6/4: 18-30.

Chapter 5

Possession and Deliverance in a British Pentecostal Church

Malcolm Gold

The aim of this chapter is to give an account of events which took place during the early to mid-1980s within a conservative Pentecostal Fellowship in the north east of England. Specifically, the focus will be an examination of the doctrines, practices, and outcomes of the ministry of deliverance[1] which was introduced into the church upon the arrival of a new pastor. A concluding section will offer an analysis of the events described here with a view to better understanding the many aspects of the church, at that time, which gave rise to the emphasis on demonic attacks and the strategies employed to counter them.

The Context of the Study

The research entailed an ethnographic framework incorporating participant observation, in-depth interviews, and literature review. For a ten-month period in 1998 I relocated to my home town in the north east of England, Kingston, in Yorkshire, and reacquainted myself with my former church, the City Christian Centre – the prime location for my research. Official interviews in which a specific time and location were set beforehand were used but much data was collected from the hundreds of conversations and encounters with the members of the church and indeed with family members of those who had left the church.[2] Although the ethnographic portion of the study took place in the late 1990s, the description of deliverance sessions in this paper are based upon my own direct observation; during my time as a member of the City Christian Centre (in the 1980s) I attended numerous such occasions.

---

[1]   Exorcism was generally known as deliverance within the churches that practised it.

[2]   Selection of potential interviewees utilised *purposive* sampling, as opposed to non-random, strategies (Dixon, Bouma and Atkinson, 1987). I attempted to interview members and ex-members of the City Christian Centre who were representative of a cross section of ages, gender and race, education and occupation. Educational qualifications and occupations in both groups reflected a broad spectrum: from those with no qualifications to postgraduates and from the unemployed, the manual worker, the clerical assistant, the self-employed to the television producer and headteacher.

The city of Kingston has a long history – some 700 years. Although a relatively large city in Yorkshire (population well over 200,000) its geographical location is somewhat isolated and its more prosperous days as a thriving fishing port and then an industrial centre are now over. Kingston is predominantly working class with the professional class population occupying the small towns and villages in the outlying areas. Within the city boundary, there are a number of large, quite poor, council estates. It is in one such estate, close to the city centre, that the City Christian Centre is located.

At the start of the 1980s the demographics of the City Christian Centre reflected those of the city. There were fewer church members from the middle classes at the City Christian Centre; most working members could be described as occupying skilled and semi-skilled occupational positions. Middle-class representation increased steadily however, throughout the 1980s. This increase was not a reflection of a rise in the status or wealth of the immediate neighbourhood but more a result of the church attracting those in the professional classes from the surrounding suburban areas. The City Christian Centre during the mid- to late-1980s was not a racially or ethnically diverse church. The overwhelming majority of the congregation was white.

The initial research suggested that a synthesis had occurred, over a 20-year period, between classic Pentecostals in the UK and the Charismatic movement and that this fusion had created distinct forms of religious expression that could be viewed as a hybrid of the two traditions.[3] Specifically, in the area of corporate worship, the theology of the Holy Spirit, church leadership, evangelism, and understandings of holiness; each of these reflected the dynamics of this transformation. This chapter will draw on that part of the City Christian Centre's history which was the most volatile with regard to the accommodation of established Pentecostal traditions with the rise of a more experientially based expression of belief. Throughout the episode in the early to mid-1980s, such structural changes explain much of the conflicting practices present in the church. These alone however, do not account for all events which transpired at that time; on a micro level of analysis, it is evident that the interpersonal dynamics of new leadership and the congregational responses to it contributed much to the turbulence described below.

It is necessary, before embarking on an account of what took place in the 1980s at the City Christian Centre, to establish a baseline with regard to the established doctrinal stance of the church. The City Christian Centre had been a member of the Assemblies of God for nearly as long as the AOG had been a recognised denomination (1924) in the UK. The church, up until the 1970s, had only seen three pastors,[4] the fourth, John Hedges (1976-1982/1983), had followed traditionalism

---

[3]   For the complete history and ethnography of the City Christian Centre see M. Gold, 2003.

[4]   The first leaders of the church were its founders in 1909. Two women, Jane Craig and Elizabeth Alan ran a Sunday school from their home which was situated less than a quarter of a mile from where the present day building stands. As their children's work thrived, a congregation

similar to his predecessors, all could be described as classic Pentecostals of the old school.

For the purpose of the study, the Assemblies of God's doctrinal statement provides the traditional theological outlook of the City Christian Centre before the early 1980s and as such becomes a useful baseline for comparison. The AOG's *Statement of Fundamental Truths* has remained constant over time. It sets forth the following tenets:

1. That the Bible is the inspired word of God.
2. God is One Being in three Persons (the trinity).
3. Jesus was born of a virgin, led a sinless life, had a miraculous ministry, died as an atonement for our sin, was resurrected, ascended into heaven to make intercession on our behalf, and will return to claim his own (premillennial second advent).
4. Human beings were created pure (Adam and Eve) but become sinful voluntarily.
5. Only through Christ can a person be saved, know God and be assured of eternity with Him.
6. All who truly believe should be baptised (total immersion).
7. Speaking in tongues is the initial evidence of a believer's baptism in the Holy Spirit and that the gifts of the Holy Spirit are still in operation today.
8. Holiness of life and conduct should be aspired to.
9. God has provided for healing from sickness.

---

of both children and parents grew and a small independent Pentecostal church resulted. Craig and Alan led the congregation until 1948 when Jeffrey Fuller (who had attended the church's Sunday school from an early age and who had been mentored by Craig and Alan throughout his life) became the pastor. Elizabeth Alan died a year later in 1949. Jane Craig continued to attend the church until her death in 1959. In 1976, John Hedges, a former missionary, became the pastor of the City Christian Centre. Sometime in 1982, Hedges felt that his work in Kingston was complete and that God was calling him to other areas of service. His departure was not instant and for more than a year he effectively shared the roles of pastor and leader with Roy Dale. Dale had come from a very strong Pentecostal background. Before he was 25, he had become an assistant pastor, working alongside a prominent Assembly of God figure. Shortly after that, he worked with the Assembly of God Home Missions and pioneered a church in the West Midlands. In the late 1970s Roy and his wife Sandra spent some time with an international outreach ministry which organised large tent rallies, drawing big crowds. This work took them to the United States and many European countries as well as tours around Britain. One such location for a week-long rally in 1979 was Kingston. After internal conflicts within the tent crusade organisation had caused the team to split up, Dale settled in Kingston and became active in the City Christian Centre. When Pastor Hedges decided that his ministry at the church was coming to an end, Dale seemed like the ideal candidate for the job of pastor. After a year of sharing the ministerial duties of the church, Dale officially became the pastor in 1983.

10. Believers should share in communion (Breaking of Bread).
11. Those who are in Christ will spend eternity in Heaven, those who have rejected him shall spend eternity in Hell.

This doctrinal stance formed the standard with regard to theology amongst the believers of the City Christian Centre and had done so since its early days. During the early part of the 1980s and the transition of leadership from Hedges to Pastor Roy Dale, significant changes emerged in the understanding and practice of certain doctrines. It was the perception of most within the congregation that each change was understood as an addition to the existing Statement of Fundamental Truths and not the case that the basic tenets had changed; the tenets were considered foundational to each member's faith and therefore could not be removed or altered. Throughout the episode described in this chapter however, Dale would take considerable liberties in the interpretation of how some of these tenets were expressed. Some of the sources of influence affecting these changes were found to be (1) the direct result of recent (often sensational) 'moves of the Holy Spirit' and their introduction to the fellowship – either though leadership or lay persons; (2) the proliferation of diverse ideas and expressions of religiosity developing organically and permeating the hearts and minds of the congregation through contact with new members and different ministries and (3) A more direct instigator of changes in doctrinal thought lay in the teachings of the new pastor and other senior figures of the church.[5] Each new theological permutation was appropriated via these sources: through global moves of God, the grassroots belief of the congregation and, in particular, the influence of teaching by the leadership.

Between 1981 and 1984 the City Christian Centre tripled in size from approximately 50 members to 150. The growth at this time was spurred on considerably by Dale's teaching and the influx of new members quite overwhelmed the older ones. That is not to say that the existing members did not welcome the newcomers, far from it, to them this was the next step for the church. The numerical growth was simply regarded as what happens to a fellowship when its members 'get serious with God and start preaching the Gospel'. The increase however, had a significant impact on the traditional instruction of the new members. The time and energy spent, prior to the numerical growth, on each new convert instilled

---

[5]   The leadership structure of the City Christian Centre placed authority in the hands of a small group of men who were known by a number of different names – the Elders, the leadership team, the Oversight. The constitution of the church (which saw a number of amendments during the 1980s) stated that the Oversight was required to consist of the resident or senior pastor and a minimum of two other men. Generally, the Oversight during the early to mid-1980s consisted of the senior pastor and between five to seven men. Positions within the Oversight were not by election on the part of the church members but by a decision amongst the existing Oversight members. While the concept of the leadership operating as a 'team' was given considerable lip-service, the senior pastor held jurisdiction over the activities and programme of the church.

traditional church teaching and convention. The fellowship had nurtured each new member and the delicate bonding of relationships had plenty of time to cement. When it came, the increase of membership happened so quickly that interpersonal resources were stretched. Had this particular dilemma been articulated at that time, the response would be one of joyful optimism, 'what a wonderful dilemma to be in'. With new people, however, came new ideas, new forms of doctrinal understanding and a new pastor. Between 1983 and 1987, with the induction of Roy Dale as the new leader, the City Christian Centre entered its most tumultuous phase to date – spiritually, politically and interpersonally.

The Supernatural Realm

A significant component of the teaching Pastor Dale introduced to the City Christian Centre was the issue of deliverance. Deliverance ministry, although not mentioned in the Statement of Fundamental Truths, does exist in Pentecostal circles. Its Scriptural point of reference is found, in a general sense, in Paul's letter to the Ephesians 6:12, 'For our struggle is not against flesh and blood, but against the rulers, against the authorities, against the powers of this dark world and against the spiritual forces of evil in the heavenly realms' (New International Version). More specifically, accounts of possession by evil spirits or demons are documented in the Gospels. The following is taken from Luke, the same story is also told in Matthew 17:14-23 and Mark 9:14-32.

> The next day, when they came down from the mountain, a large crowd met Him. A man in the crowd called out 'Teacher, I beg you to look at my son, for he is my only child. A spirit seizes him and he suddenly screams, it throws him into convulsions so that he foams at the mouth. It scarcely ever leaves him and is destroying him. I begged your disciples to drive it out, but they could not.' 'O unbelieving and perverse generation', Jesus replied, 'how long shall I stay with you and put up with you? Bring your son here.' Even while the boy was coming, the demon threw him to the ground in a convulsion. But Jesus rebuked the evil spirit (Greek unclean), healed the boy and gave him back to his father. And they were all amazed at the greatness of God (Luke 9:37-43, New International Version).

Prior to his induction, Dale's former pastoral and ministry roles, before coming to Kingston and the City Christian Centre, had involved a great deal of deliverance ministry. The theology of this particular issue was not new to the fellowship he now led. There had been a handful of isolated instances in which certain individuals had received ministry for deliverance. Those involved, however, were always careful to conduct the sessions either outside of the regular church schedule or, should the need arise during a meeting, in an office or the vestry away from the congregation. The whole realm of deliverance and possession, even to long-standing Pentecostals, was and is today, quite an uncomfortable area of doctrine to negotiate. There are many different understandings and interpretations of this phenomenon and this has created a confused perception of what deliverance may entail. For most Assemblies, demon possession is an area best left alone if at all possible.

Another problem, besides the potential for theological error in the teaching on deliverance, was how the wider society perceived the notion of possession. It is reasonable to assume that William Peter Blatty's best-selling novel *The Exorcist* (1971) and the subsequent film, less than a decade earlier than Dale's arrival, had created a specific image of this nightmare experience in the minds of a large audience.[6] Any mention of exorcism or demon possession brought to mind the sensational depictions in that film. This was not only true of non-churchgoers but of Christians too. It would be reasonable to suggest that similar perceptions of the diabolical were shared by both camps.

Although no member of the City Christian Centre would have, at that time, even considered going to the cinema to see such a film, the great publicity triggered by its controversial subject matter created an awareness within the evangelical community and many Christians acquainted themselves with its portrayal in order to mount an attack against it. Outraged over some of the film's more graphic (sacrilegious) content, demonstrations were staged outside the cinemas screening *The Exorcist*. Tracts and leaflets would be handed out to those going to see it and long discussions would take place outside the cinema doors. For a city the modest size of Kingston these demonstrations were quite newsworthy, particularly within the churches.

Within the City Christian Centre then, it was the case that leaders and many of the congregation (especially those who were active in ministry) were cognisant of the perceived image of possession. Even so, it was not an image that most Assembly of God fellowships wanted to dwell on. It conjured up darkness and evil and sinister notions of gothic church traditions; it was eerie and foreboding. Most Assemblies wanted to project the exact opposite: they wanted to depict Christianity in positive terms, as 'light' and 'salt' to the world, as joyous and fulfilling; they didn't want to get caught up in the mire of satanic activity. As Walker observes,

> Pentecostalism has not been overcome by demonic infestations … denominations such as Elim and the Assemblies of God have believed in demons but have kept them firmly under the bed and firmly under control. There has been little interest or fascination in the habits, habitat or *haute couture* of evil spirits (Walker, 1994: 57).

Given the integrity of Pentecostals, however, the issue could not be totally pushed aside. The fact remained that there were numerous accounts of possession in the Bible and as the Scriptures were considered to be the infallible word of God,

---

[6]   See Cuneo, 2001 for a useful discussion of the impact of media depictions of possession and exorcism.

a space had to be maintained for it within the experience and beliefs of any given fellowship. It was within the context of a growing congregation that Pastor Dale introduced his own brand of theology concerning deliverance into the City Christian Centre. The fellowship was no longer confined to just 30 or so people who could slowly nurture new members as they arrived in their dribs and drabs. The building was quickly filling to capacity and plans for a new building were already on the agenda. New ministry programmes were being established and the past experiences of many of the 'switchers' who joined the City Christian Centre at that time, presented the 'oversight' (leadership team) with a plethora of new ideas to assimilate.

With hindsight, it is hard to imagine how a church could, over a period of a year or so, become so deeply obsessed with deliverance, unclean spirits and all the manifestations that accompany such phenomena. The deliverance aspect, however, was not thrust on to the people in isolation from other concepts. In the first few months of his appointment, Pastor Dale initiated a series of in-depth Bible studies which covered both the basics of the Christian faith and a number of more specialised subjects. There was a great emphasis placed on these studies and the weekly turnout was usually very high. Dale would often voice his disappointment to the congregation during the Sunday services should the numbers attending the weekday meetings begin to fall. The illustration was sometimes given of a meal that was lovingly and painstakingly prepared; having been invited to dinner, the guests did not arrive.

Juxtaposed with the teaching on deliverance was a new vibrancy in worship services. Under Dale's teaching, both deliverance and corporate worship intersected. Dale was particularly adept at leading worship. In his book *God's People*, Calley suggests that, 'A successful leader is one who can stimulate his congregation to respond as a group, who can make members lose their own individuality in an impassioned, sometimes hysterical identification with the church' (Calley, 1965: 74).

This was certainly evidenced during the corporate worship praise sessions led by Dale. As the worship in the church became more extreme in emotion, losing a former simplicity and stress on adoration based upon the redeeming work of Christ, the fellowship entered into a new era of the experiential over the previous tenets of what some older members regarded as the unquestionable 'Word of God'. Dale was breaking from the traditional expectations of the Pentecostal congregation. As a product of the Assembly of God 'system', he had grown up with an understanding of those church activities which were both accepted *and* expected; even within those denominations (like the Assemblies of God) which are often thought to be extreme in their spiritual exuberance, there is tradition. Perhaps Dale's former church pioneering ministry juxtaposed with the more showman-like Christian tent crusades contributed to the charisma of his leadership. Certainly for a great number of the congregation at the City Christian Centre, Dale's history and flair was regarded as commensurate with Weber's description of the charismatic trait. 'The term "charisma" will be applied to a certain quality of an individual personality by virtue of which he is set apart from ordinary [men] and treated as endowed with supernatural, superhuman, or at least specifically exceptional powers or qualities' (Parsons, 1947: 358).

This shift from the traditional to the experiential was subtle and the congregation largely shared in the excitement of the moment. Exhortations to enter 'within the veil'[7] were given and prophetic messages assumed a more aggressive and direct tone. Times of corporate worship became times of 'proclamation' and 'prophecy'. The 'strongholds of Satan' were torn down and rebuked. For the first time in the history of the fellowship emphasis was placed upon the reaching out to the city and not just to the local housing estate in which the church was situated. Before such outreach could commence, however, it was imperative that the church was ready for the task and this instigated an intense period of introspection. The concept of the need for a kind of spiritual house cleaning was introduced and the former emphasis of outward looking evangelism was replaced by an inward looking purge.

The scene was set for the introduction of deliverance ministry. The teaching on this subject was steadily increased, so too was the emphasis on worship and 'doing battle with the enemy' within the services and in a corporate sense. Each time of congregational worship was highly charged with emotion. Dancing was instituted; marches around the building and around the building site of the soon to be completed new church were frequent, to the bewilderment of the onlookers from the council estate. Wild displays of spiritual perturbation were exhibited during the meetings: individuals would swoon or shake, cry out strange utterances during the sermons and have to be escorted out by the ushers for counselling and quite possibly deliverance. As the various outbursts and displays within the meetings became more frequent, Pastor Dale simply put such manifestations forward as confirmation of his teaching. The Devil was 'hitting out' in fear because of the power generated within the body of believers at the City Christian Centre which was 'breaking down demonic strongholds around the church and in the city'.

In that milieu of highly charged emotionalism and supernatural life, some of the former understandings of holiness and self-discipline fell away. The Assemblies of God official statement reads, 'We believe in holiness of life and conduct in obedience to the command of God "Be ye holy for I am holy". 1 Pet. 1:14-16; Heb. 12:14; 1 Thess. 5:23; 1 John 2:6; also 1 Cor. 13.' Holiness was considered an essential goal to strive towards. Unlike adherents of the Holiness Movement (Bebbington, 1989; Blumhoffer, 1993; Synan, 1997), Pentecostals believed that complete holiness could never be achieved in this life, but that Christians were

---

[7] The concept or image of entering 'within the veil' became an often used metaphor at the City Christian Centre during the time period being discussed. It denoted the aspiration of drawing closer to God and is a reference to the Old Testament Judaic temple structure in Jerusalem (Exodus chapters 25, 26, and 27) in which only the high priest could enter the inner chamber of the tabernacle. The chamber – divided from the rest of the temple by a veil was considered the 'holy of holies' and contained the Ark of the Covenant.

required to continually work towards it, eliminating those actions that were thought to be sinful and offensive to God.

With the former emphasis traditionally placed upon self-discipline at the City Christian Centre, the concept or state of holiness had always been integrally linked with self-control. To be holy was to exhibit the 'fruit of the Spirit' as read in Galatians, 'But the fruit of the Spirit is love, joy, peace, patience, kindness, goodness, faithfulness, gentleness and self-control' (Galatians 5:22, 23). It was believed that problems, within an individual's personal life, could be overcome with prayer, trust in God and a very physical commitment to do something about them. Certain places, through the exercise of the will, would be avoided: cinemas, public houses, and nightclubs were all considered far too 'worldly' for a Christian to frequent and would only lead to temptation and personal 'sin'. Drinking alcohol, smoking, and pornography were considered to be very wrong, so too, of course, was the taking of illicit drugs. Bad language and the use of profanity and blasphemy were also heavily proscribed.

Pastor Dale offered a short cut to holiness. With the emphasis now firmly on spiritual warfare the ministry offered through deliverance was applied to those murky areas of life that had formerly been the focus of much self-discipline. No longer was such ministry restricted to an isolated problem case, quickly hushed up and dealt with in as private a manner as possible. Under Dale's leadership, it became conceivable that every member of the congregation could be in need of that particular kind of help. Nor were the demons restricted to the former (usual) manifestations. In the few isolated cases of the past, a person would most commonly have a 'demon of epilepsy' or 'a demon of depression' and the demon would reveal itself in some obvious physical way, '… causing recognisable symptoms of illness' (Jules-Rosette, 1975: 194). The teaching of the new pastor, however, claimed that demonic activity was thought to be responsible for a whole host of problems. There were now demons of anger, lust, masturbation, nicotine, lack of forgiveness, bitterness, unbelief, alcohol, pornography, defeat, the common cold (and any number of illness-related demons), and many more.

Deliverance sessions varied in time and could be as short as 30 minutes or as long as two hours with subsequent sessions scheduled over a number of weeks. Instruction would be given prior to the actual ministry: Pastor Dale would explain his theological understanding of how to perceive the problem under counsel. Although 'saved', demons could inhabit the believer and be the cause of some particular vice, wrong attitude or mental irregularity; it was possible to rebuke the demon in Jesus' name, to take authority, and to dispel the evil spirit. The problem would then be gone and the individual would be free of it. Dale would look into the spiritual realm and claim to actually see the demon located within the subject; perhaps in the stomach or attached to an arm. He would then explain, specifically, what could take place during deliverance and how the demon would try to fight against the command to go. The demon could well manifest itself in a violent way but would not be able to resist the rebuke; the spirit would, usually, leave the body through the mouth.

Dale would proceed by placing his hand on that part of the body in which the demon had been seen (usually the stomach). A series of loud rebukes would follow, 'In the name of Jesus I rebuke you spirit of _____'. The subject receiving ministry would often react in an agitated and sometimes quite frenzied way. Arms would flail, faces would contort and screams would be emitted. Such manifestations would only fuel the rebuke and eventually, after a series of chokes, the demon would depart. A prayer of thanks would be said by the Pastor and when the subject had collected him- or herself, they would leave, believing in all sincerity that their problem was now gone and that subsequently their relationship with the Lord would be closer. Having bypassed the processes of self-discipline and perseverance, they were a little further on in their journey to holiness. In this mid-1980s period, the basic understanding of what it was to be holy continued in its traditional sense: display the fruit of the Spirit and surrender those things regarded as offensive to God. It was the understanding of how to achieve those ends that had changed: from 'striving towards the goal' to instantaneous deliverance.

The City Christian Centre began to make a name for itself. Although many people were leaving the church on theological grounds, many people were joining the church for the same reason. The church gained quite a reputation: to some, within the evangelical community in the city of Kingston, it was regarded as extreme and fanatical and singularly unappealing, to others it was just what they had been waiting for. With all of its excesses and radical teaching, the City Christian Centre attracted a particular kind of 'seeker-switcher', those who were seeking a Christian experience on the front line of spiritual warfare.

Discussion

Reference has been made to the various influences affecting the City Christian Centre during the early to mid-1980s. This formerly traditional Assembly of God fellowship encountered a new form of charismatic expression as new ideas and spiritual trends surged through the evangelical community at large. On an interpersonal level, the rapid growth of the congregation had a significant impact on the socialisation of new members which resulted in a less stringent grounding in long established, traditional Pentecostal doctrine. The events described in this paper can be seen as part of a transitional phase in the history of this church. There was a move away from the primacy of strict adherence to the bible towards the experiential. This led to a decline in traditional standards of Scripture-based religious practice (as formerly interpreted by Pentecostal believers) and to a greater receptivity for revelation and improvised religious practice. This shift in emphasis was by no means apparent to the vast majority of the congregation who, by and large, considered the often euphoric expression of 'life in the Spirit' to be an indication of God's hand upon their lives. While this shift is extremely significant for an explanation of why religious practice changed so dramatically over a relatively short period of time, it is by no means the only explanation.

In addition, we should consider the role of the leadership of the church and the congregational responses to it.

We find in the person of Roy Dale, a young and energetic rising star within the Assemblies of God. A minister whose earlier pastoral experiences had seen him involved in the realm of demonic activity, to what extent; it is not clear, although he had read, and so was familiar with, the book *Deliver Us From Evil* by Don Basham (1972). This book is one American pastor's account of involvement in the deliverance ministry. Dale was greatly influenced by Basham's story and seems to have followed quite closely (although not totally) the doctrinal interpretation of demonic possession or affliction espoused by the author.

Certainly, Dale's agenda, expressed through the emphasis of his teaching programme and Bible studies, presented a dramatic shift away from the material and subjects of the former minister. Worship, under his leadership, was revolutionised; times of devotion, hymn and chorus singing became proclamations of 'victory over Satan' and exhortations to the congregation to reach for new heights of ecstatic spiritual experience. He was a charismatic leader in every sense of the word; the congregation swelled.

An observer's interpretation of the purge which took place at the City Christian Centre suggests that the social and spiritual context of the church was significantly disordered, with both global and local doctrinal and expressive influences throwing the formerly well regulated community of the fellowship into potential disarray. As a product of the charismatic/experiential surge himself, the newly appointed leader (and his appointees) actually fuelled the instability and yet sought ways to establish equilibrium at the same time. The strategies adopted had to be consistent with the developing spiritual cosmology of the church and so the doctrinal imperatives of spiritual warfare took precedence over the usual spiritual (and practical) injunctions of Christian living.

Within this highly charged emotional-spiritual context, the notion of spiritual 'triumph over evil' was stressed; confirmation of both demonic attack and 'victory over Satan' were considered evident with the concept of possession/affliction by a demon and the subsequent expelling of the demon and the freeing of the subject to live a holy life. Deliverance became a tangible proof that supernatural activity was taking place within the church and that God's work was being done. Members believed that if this was the case, then surely the church was where it should be before God; surely the Body was being cleansed.

A second function of the purge is tied to the maintaining of leadership authority over the congregation. Given the context of the church in flux – a new leader introducing new ideas and modes of operation, the numerical growth, and the collective striving towards the ecstatic and experiential, it is understandable that the perceived need for authority intensified. In many ways, the ritual of possession and deliverance reinforced the power of the leadership team and most notably Roy Dale. He was, after all, the one with the most experience in this area while his 'team' played the part of assistants and apprentices.

Power and position were negotiated through the process of deliverance in a number of ways. Power and authority are always firmly in the person of the exorcist/pastor: they profess to have the doctrinal/biblical knowledge of the subject's condition, they have past experience, they are God's minister, they have supernatural power to look into the spiritual realm, and they have complete faith for a successful outcome. Such were the pastor's prerequisite credentials. The ritual itself is a corporeal experience; a demonstration of physical and verbal exertion, fulminating and ugly; the minister issuing rebukes and commands as the subject contorts, screams, drools, and disgorges. In a very physical sense, it is the image of domination.

A more subtle reinforcement of authority and status was tacitly understood between the parties involved. Although many deliverance sessions took place in which the subject was possessed by some illness or other (a cold, a sore throat and so on), the greater number of demonic cases were linked to some behaviour or attitude considered to be a vice. Deliverance ministry would necessarily follow the confession of the vice. Such confessions were often quite embarrassing for the subject; additionally, possession by a demon of this kind indicated a potentially more serious flaw in the subject's character. Because of the teaching Roy Dale had adopted from the likes of Don Basham, one of the ways demons were able to enter an individual was by that person, '… Indulging carnal appetites …'. Basham writes:

> A … means of inviting demonic torment is to deliberately indulge lustful appetites … a Christian may have a sexual weakness by nature. It is a weakness of the flesh … By repeated indulgence of that appetite, he attracts a demon of sexual lust or adultery which will invade that part of his carnal nature. Then he has double trouble. His lustful nature now is in bondage to a demon of lust which will increase the torment and compel him to commit immorality (Basham and Prince 1977: 55).

The subject is burdened with, not only the guilt of indulging in the vice in the first place, but the responsibility of allowing a demon to take up residence within them. This 'double trouble' can create a serious sense of inferiority within the subject amongst his or her peers and certainly in their relationship to authority.

A final observation draws on various doctrinal inconsistencies regarding the teaching on possession and deliverance in the fellowship at that time. Although Dale gleaned much of his understanding of the demonic from the earlier work of Don Basham, Derek Prince, and the New Testament, he was quite selective in how certain areas of that teaching were applied. As the deliverance ministry developed, there was some initial confusion over the definition of possession itself, and whether or not a Christian could actually be possessed by an evil force or demon given that – if 'saved' – God's spirit now inhabited the individual's spirit thus preventing any such intrusion of evil. Working through this issue, Dale eventually adopted the view that the concept of possession was something of a misnomer and that a more accurate term to describe the experience was 'demonic affliction' or 'oppression'. The demon could not technically possess a Christian, but it could oppress and afflict. The perceived remedy however, was the same regardless of the theoretical change in condition – deliverance. While the above understanding is consistent with Basham and Prince, there seems to be no Scriptural basis for it.

A significant shift away from Basham and Prince (and Scripture again) regarded the issue of children and whether or not children could be possessed, oppressed, or afflicted by an evil spirit in the same way as adults. Basham clearly believed that they could and recounts in his writing (Basham, 1972) one case in which his infant daughter is delivered from a spirit of fear, and another in which a boy is delivered from a demon of epilepsy. Basham also insists that in certain circumstances demons can pass from mother to child. Here he suggests that another way that demons can enter into a subject is through,

> … some weakened area of the personality … traumatic experience which 'fractures' the natural defenses of the personality can allow a demon to enter. A pregnant mother experiencing great fear may not only become tormented by a spirit of fear herself, but her child will be born with a spirit of fear as well. (Basham and Prince 1977: 56)

For Basham, child possession was a very real occurrence. This was not the case with Dale and the situation at the City Christian Centre. At no point during the purge of the 1980s were children ever suspected of being in need of deliverance ministry. Why was this? Certainly there was not an adequate doctrinal/theological answer worked out by the pastor to explain why children were not prone to attacks by evil spirits. This is inconsistent with the literalist reading of the Bible that most conservative Pentecostals hold to; there are numerous accounts of child possession in the New Testament. A generally accepted principle within the fellowship, that effectively countered the notion of child possession, was the connection between demonic affliction and an individual's lifestyle. We have discussed how the reason for a demonic attack was often thought to be, ultimately, the fault of the individual. Repeated 'sin' could pave the way for entry. This was an act of the will, and rational acts of the will with a propensity towards those things considered 'sinful' were not thought to be particularly possible in children of a young age.

Post Script

By 1987 Pastor Dale had, it seemed, exhausted his potential to add anything further to the church. After some years of 'preparing the church' for outreach in what some would later describe as 'a campaign similar to McCarthyism', although numerically speaking, the attendance figures were higher than they had ever been previously, a kind of stasis set in. Membership was high but the church had stopped growing. So emotionally charged were the times of praise and worship that one wondered what could possibly come next. What new exuberance or experience could possibly top the service from the week before?

The 'purging of the Body', also, eventually met with increasing criticism. Pastor Dale's interpretation and implementation of deliverance ministry seemed not to work in all cases: many people who had been delivered of a spirit of nicotine, for example, found themselves slipping back into the habit of smoking. Others, who had struggled with pornography and who had gone to the pastor for deliverance ministry, eventually found themselves going back to it. People still got sick. Even after Pastor Dale wrote and distributed a leaflet entitled *How To Maintain Your Deliverance*, in a rather hasty defence of his ministry, his efforts, though persuasive still to some, simply placed a bigger question mark over his abilities in the minds of others. This leaflet attempted to place the onus for maintaining one's deliverance firmly upon the subject in question. The leaflet appeared to retract Dale's earlier claims which had suggested an instant and complete cleansing of the problem, whatever that may be. The modified notion of deliverance now required a particular application of discipline on the part of the person now delivered. A possible consequence of not maintaining one's own deliverance could be the return of the once evicted demon and the potential for several more demons to re-enter all at once. The Scriptural basis given to support this addendum to Pastor Dale's initial teaching can be found in the Gospel of Luke,

> When an evil spirit comes out of a man, it goes through arid places seeking rest and does not find it. Then it says, 'I will return to the house I left.' When it arrives, it finds the house swept clean and put in order. Then it goes and takes seven other spirits more wicked than itself, and they go in and live there. And the final condition of that man is worse than the first. (Luke 11:24-6, New International Version)

Pastor Dale left the City Christian Centre to take up a high profile post within the Assemblies of God organisation in 1987. Following his rather abrupt departure, the existing leadership team assumed the responsibilities of the pastor and for a period of approximately 18 months the church actually saw a numerical increase in attendance. A majority of new members were, in fact, not 'new' in the proper sense of the word. Most had been former members of the City Christian Centre who had left because of some disagreement they had had with Dale during his tenure. Even so, the church seemed to regain a former innocence as the practice of deliverance seemed to end as abruptly as Dale had left.

Towards the end of the 1980s the church appointed George Young as the new full-time pastor. Young had been a minister within an Assemblies of God church for many years and, after some initial conflicts between himself and the leadership of the City Christian Centre, settled in to the role of church leader. As of this writing, Young remains the pastor of the City Christian Centre. Although less traditionally Pentecostal in his theological outlook than Dale's predecessors, Young has not emphasised deliverance ministry. Although acts of corporate worship (as they were with Dale) approach and encourage the ecstatic, the spectre of demonic possession is absent within the fellowship.

References

Basham, D. (1972). *Deliver Us From Evil*. Washington Depot, CT: Chosen Books.

Basham, D. and D. Prince (1977). *The Unseen War: Basic Training in Spiritual Warfare*. Mobile, AL: New Wine Magazine.

Bebbington, D.W. (1989). *Evangelicalism in Modern Britain: A History from the 1730s to the 1980s*. London: Routledge.

Blatty, W.P. (1971). *The Exorcist*. New York: Harper and Row.

Blumhofer, E.L. (1993). *Restoring the Faith: The Assemblies of God, Pentecostalism, and American Culture*. Urbana: University of Illinois Press.

Calley, M.J.C. (1965). *God's People*. London: Oxford University Press.

Cuneo, M.W. (2001). *American Exorcism: Expelling Demons in the Land of Plenty*. New York: Doubleday.

Dixon, B.R., G.D. Bouma and G.B.J. Atkinson (1987). *A Handbook of Social Science Research*. Oxford: Oxford University Press.

Gold, M. (2003). *The Hybridization of an Assembly of God Church: Proselytism, Retention, and Re-Affiliation*. Lewiston, NY: Edwin Mellen Press.

Jules-Rosette, B. (1975). *African Apostles: Ritual and Conversion in the Church of John Maranke*, Ithaca, NY: Cornell University Press.

Parsons, T. (ed.) (1947). 'Economy and Society', in M. Weber, first pub. 1925, *The Theory of Social and Economic Organization*. New York: Oxford University Press.

Smail, T., A. Walker and N. Wright (eds) (1994). *The Love of Power or the Power of Love: A Careful Assessment of the Problems within the Charismatic and Word-of-faith Movements*. Minneapolis: Bethany House Publishers.

Synan, V. (1997). *The Holiness-Pentecostal Tradition: Charismatic Movements in the Twentieth Century*. Grand Rapids: William B. Eerdmans Publishing Co.

Walker, A. (1994). 'Demonology and the Charismatic Movement', in T. Smail, A. Walker and N. Wright (eds), *The Love of Power or the Power of Love: A Careful Assessment of the Problems within the Charismatic and Word-of-faith Movements*. Minneapolis: Bethany House.

Chapter 6

The *Jinn*, Black Magic and Evil Eye Among East London Bangladeshis[1]

Simon Dein

The east end of London has undergone major cultural changes in the past 30 years. Known in the 1970s for its Jewish inhabitants, their clothing businesses and jewellery shops, the area has changed following an influx of South Asian migrants, mainly from Bangladesh. There has been a growth of mosques and a walk along Whitechapel High Street reveals that most of the shops now are owned by Bangladeshis selling cheap clothing, *halal* food and Muslim books. The influence of Bangladeshi culture can clearly be seen across the capital in Tower Hamlets, Camden, Westminster and Newham. Brick Lane known colloquially as 'Banglatown' is the heart of the community and has become a favourite food haunt for Londoners with many Balti and curry houses and a vibrant market.

From 2004 to 2005 I conducted ethnographic fieldwork among the east London Bangladeshi community specifically focusing upon the role of *jinn* spirits, black magic, sorcery[2] and evil eye in their beliefs in the causes of misfortune. In this chapter I will first describe the east London Bangladeshi community and then move on to discuss the role of these 'invisible forces' in their lives.

The East London Bangladeshi Community

The state of Bangladesh was set up in 1972 after East Bengal split from Pakistan. Throughout the 1960s and 1970s a large number of Bangladeshis migrated to Britain, as economic migrants, particularly from Sylhet – a major city in north eastern Bangladesh; men generally emigrating several years before their wives. Those arriving in the UK often had little command of spoken and written English.

This community is characterised by regular travel to and from Bangladesh and it is common for young people to travel to Bangladesh for an arranged marriage.

---

[1] Some of this material appears in S. Dein, M. Alexander and D. Napier, 2008.

[2] The term sorcery is deployed here in preference to witchcraft. The former refers to the use of black magic or potions. By contrast, the witch has an innate ability to inflict harm and does not require black magic or potions to activate it, just their evil inclinations.

These close links with Bangladesh foster continuity of beliefs and practices between Sylhet and the London communities. As Gardner (2002: 15) points out, 'many so called settlers actually participate in the economic, political and social life of both "sending" and "receiving" societies'. They are 'transnational' communities (Phillipson, Ahmed and Latimer, 2003) and I would contend that traditional ideas, including those relating to misfortune, are maintained through this process. Gardner (1995) has documented how beliefs in magic and *jinn* are prevalent in rural Sylhet. These ideas are also widespread in the east London community who have emigrated from there and pervade every aspect of life from marriage, to health to wealth. Callan (2007) writes: 'Yet in Sylhet there is a tendency to attribute misfortune to other humans' moral shortcomings – in the context of sorcery, spells and spirits are simply regarded as go-betweens enacting other humans' malevolence.' As I shall discuss below, these 'invisible forces' provide an explanatory framework for many types of misfortune and much time and effort is expended in attempting to allay their effects. Bangladeshis have the lowest employment rates of all ethnic groups in the UK (Office for National Statistics, 2002) and in Tower Hamlets only 30.5 per cent of the Bangladeshi population are in employment. Muslim men of Pakistani and Bangladeshi background are disproportionately unemployed relative to other Asians, according to a Cabinet Office report commissioned by Tony Blair. One third of Bangladeshi men work as cooks or waiters (Walker, 2002). A study presented to the Royal Economic Society's 2007 annual conference at the University of Warwick finds relatively stable rates of self-employment among Pakistani and Bangladeshi men. It is possible that discrimination in paid employment against these groups is keeping them in self-employment, working long hours in relatively poorly rewarded sectors such as catering and taxi-driving.

This community experiences a unique set of circumstances – industrial decline leading to unemployment (Cabinet Office, 2003), ongoing immigration from Bangladesh, and the redevelopment and gentrification of the neighbourhoods in which they live. The British Bangladeshi population also has a number of characteristics marking them out from other South Asian groups (Eade, Peach and Vamplew, 1996); they are more segregated residentially than other UK minority groups; their population growth is high; they tend to have large families with a high proportion of young people and they are concentrated within Greater London and especially Tower Hamlets.

These communities have low socio-economic status, high rates of overcrowding: 23 per cent living in overcrowded conditions according to the Commission for Racial Equality (2003), dependence on local authority housing, and the high levels of limiting long term illness: 24 per cent of the Bangladeshi population in England and Wales in 2001 (Office for National Statistics, 2004). Kempson (1999) describes how one in five Bangladeshi homes are overcrowded (with more than four people sleeping in one room) compared to one in 200 overall, and many lack basic amenities. Thus deprivation is prevalent, although there may be significant variation by region, social class, age and gender and younger cohorts may have a more positive outlook. Bangladeshis experiencing the highest levels of social and economic deprivation are those born outside the UK, who are unable to speak fluent English. Racism, especially following 9/11 and Islamaphobia (in which Islam is presented as backward and inferior) are prominent features of the lives of many people in this community. During my interviews several informants stated that they had been victims of racism – from being called a 'Paki' to discrimination in terms of jobs and housing. A minority reported having been victims of racial assault.

Most Bangladeshis living in London's East End are Sunni Muslims who worship at the East London Mosque on Commercial Road. Established in 1941, it was rebuilt in 1985 and can now accommodate 2,000 people. Another important place of worship is the Jamme Masjid mosque on Brick Lane, opened in 1976 in a building built as a Huguenot chapel, which later became a synagogue – a reflection of the changing cultural scene in this area. However it is important to point out that Bangladeshi Islam is strongly influenced by Hinduism and this fact in turn determines their understandings of misfortune, especially the central role of *jinn* possession.

Eade and Garbin (2002: 12) have pointed out that the east London Bangladeshi community is subject to a process of Islamic revivalism, a reflection of a similar movement in Bangladesh: 'As Bangladesh becomes more formally Islamicised, so Bangladeshis in London and elsewhere in the West come under pressure to conform to everyday practices, which reflect this Islamicising development.' The religious leadership of the prominent East London Mosque is highly influential in this process. It provides literature and organises activities including study groups, conferences and social support to the local Bangladeshi (and Somali Muslim) population, aimed at bringing young Bangladeshis back to Islam, as an alternative to the increasingly prevalent 'gang culture' (Alexander, 2000). The mosque holds regular introductory classes in the teachings of Islam and these are generally very well attended.

The *Jinn*

Islam describes various classes of beings, which populate the universe: *jinn* (spirits), *shaitan* (satanic beings), *marrid* (demons), *bhut* (ghosts – applied to someone who has died an unnatural death such as from an accident or suicide) and *farista* (angels). In the framework of Islamic religion there are two types of spirits. The first are good; they have been converted to Islam by Muhammad. The second are bad; they follow Iblis, the fallen angel who was expelled from the Garden of Eden (Qur'an, Surah Al-Hijr). The *jinns* possess free will like human beings; as such they may be divided into two main groups according to their faith, Muslims (believers) and *kuffar* (unbelievers). The *kuffar jinn* are referred to as *shaitan*. The Qur'an also refers to human beings who become enemies of righteousness as *shaitan*. *Jinns* are described both in the Qur'an and Hadith (the sayings of the Prophet Mohammed) as a race of intelligent beings that are normally imperceptible to the senses. In fact *Sura* 72 of the Qur'an named *Al-Jinn* is entirely about them. 'Indeed we created man from dried clay of black smooth mud. And We created the *jinn* before that from the smokeless flame of fire' (Surah Al-Hijr 15:26-7).

Like human beings *jinn* are rational and possess intellect and have freedom of choice. This is reflected in their ability to choose between right and wrong and thus they are accountable for their actions. They are held to marry, procreate, eat, drink and die. However, unlike humans, they have extraordinary powers to take on different shapes such as the ability to take on the form of birds, animals and even humans, can move rapidly from one place to another, and have the ability to move heavy objects instantly from place to place. The word *jinn* derives from the Arabic root *Jann* which conveys the idea of protecting, shielding, concealing or veiling. They are said to occupy dark places or graveyards and are most likely to be found at dusk. They are attracted to people of the opposite sex whom they might marry and young women in 'transitional states', for example pregnancy, menstruation or post-partum. *Jinn* can have sexual relations with women if their husbands do not mention the name of Allah before engaging in sex. (Ibnal Jawsee vol. 27:119). Unlike angels, who are created from light, *jinn* are said to be created from smokeless fire.

Jinn Possession

Most Islamic scholars accept that *jinn* can possess people. Some scholars disagree and assert that *jinn* can only influence mankind and cannot literally take up physical space within a human's body. Both, however, would agree that there are clear criteria which need to be applied before concluding that a *jinn* has had a role in an individual's situation, whether through possession or influence. Various passages in the Qur'an and Hadith affirm the belief that *jinn* can cause erratic behaviour in one's words, deeds and movements. This one is commonly cited as evidence for the possibility of *jinn* possession: 'Those who eat *Ribaa* will not stand (on the day of resurrection) except like the standing of a person beaten by *shaytaan* (*shaitan*/Satan) leading him to insanity' (Qur'an Al-Baqarah 2:275). It refers to the Islamic prohibition of charging interest (*Ribaa*) on a loan. Those who do this will be driven mad by Satan.

In the UK, *jinn* possession is most likely to be seen among people from Pakistan, Bangladesh, the Middle East, Somalia and North Africa. Although many western educated Muslims might deny the possibility of *jinn* possession, it appears that this possibility is still accepted by most members of these communities. Specifically in the Bangladeshi community possession by a *jinn* spirit is commonly cited as an explanation for a wide range of misfortune among members of this community. Problems believed to be caused by *jinn* possession range from low mood, withdrawal, speaking 'rubbish', a failure to observe Islamic practices, and deviant behaviour including stealing and unfaithfulness in marriage. It is the suddenness in the change of behaviour, rather than the behaviour itself, which suggests *jinn* possession. Children are held to be especially vulnerable to *jinn* possession on account of their inherent weakness. As will be described below, occasionally violent means are deployed to drive the *jinn* out and this can result in serious injury or even death.

In one case, Abdul visited a local *imam* (the leader of a mosque's congregation) with his 20-year-old son Rashid. Both had been devout Muslims regularly attending mosque and praying five times a day. For about one month, his son had been angry, shouting and threatening and refusing to attend prayer. This was very much out of character for him. There were no major stresses in his life to account for his sudden change in behaviour. The *imam* agreed with his father's view that a *jinn* had attacked Rashid. His behaviour improved somewhat after the *imam* recited several passages from the Qur'an. Abdul speculated that this attack by a *jinn* had occurred during a visit to Sylhet several weeks previously.

On the other hand it is commonly posited that it is possible to protect oneself against *jinn* possession by being good and obeying Allah's words. In my interviews with members of the community there was much variation in the frequency with which *jinn* were cited as a cause of misfortune. The older (and less educated) members of the community were more likely to invoke *jinn* than the younger community members. All were however in agreement that *jinn* exist and can influence the human world. The following case is typical of what several younger informants stated about *jinn*.

Syed, a 20-year-old restaurant worker who had immigrated from Sylhet at the age of five stated that all Muslims believe in *jinn*. However *jinn* only hurt people who upset them by entering prohibited spaces where they live. He went on to point out that those who are 'modern' – being young and brought up and educated in the UK – do not believe that *jinn* can cause harm. For him these 'modern people' could not accept anything for which they did not have an adequate explanation. Because *jinn* are invisible, they believe they cannot hurt people. However his belief in the malevolent influence of *jinn* derived not from the Qur'an but from his parents who told him stories 'from long ago' involving people harmed by *jinn*. This is what caused him to believe that *jinn* could hurt people.

Black Magic

Another frequent explanation of misfortune is *Sihr* – black magic – performed for a fee by 'specialists', known in the community as *jhadu kor*. It is typically held that *Sihr* is practised by members of their community, as a way of forcing someone else to be compliant to their wishes, for example engaging in a relationship contrary to their will. (It was commonly held that hair from the victim was needed to perform *Sihr*.) Women particularly fear *Sihr* because of its use in inducing them to go to Bangladesh to marry someone against their will. *Sihr* is cited as a means of inducing illness, but is not implicated as often as *jinn* possession.

Sabira, a 50-year-old woman who had lived in the UK for many years, explained that the Qur'an talks about *Sihr*, which is black magic, but felt that people took this idea too far. For instance her aunt suffered from a form of arthritis and over time became very withdrawn and spent long periods lying in a darkened room. Her family were obviously concerned about her and wondered about the best course of action. Her son, born and educated in the UK thought she might be mentally ill, but two nieces recently arrived in the UK, held that her condition was caused by black magic and advised visiting a local *mullah*.[3] Her son consulted a religious teacher who advised that she be taken to her GP first, who prescribed a course of antidepressant treatment. This case study vividly illustrates the contested interpretations of psychological disturbance in this community, with different family members variously holding to either psychological or spiritual explanations.

Sorcery is sometimes deployed to prevent another person attaining success. In these instances this act is usually driven by envy. For example several informants implicated black magic when a relative had failed an important exam.

Shahad, a 25-year-old student, recounted how he had failed his exams in Sylhet despite the fact that he had been studying very hard. For several weeks prior to the examination he had experienced severe migraines which had distracted him from his studies. He believed that his neighbours would be envious of his success, therefore they had employed black magic to cause him to become ill and therefore fail.

The term *Sihr* literally refers to anything the cause of which is hidden, and everything that may be imagined as being other than what it is and happens by way of concealment of deceit. Typically a person who wants black magic performed approaches a sorcerer and asks him to harm someone. The sorcerer asks for the name of the potential victim and the name of his or her mother and for something which belongs to him or her such as hair, nails, clothing or his picture. Following this a charm or amulet is manufactured and incense is burnt as an offering to the *jinn*. It is held that the best way to protect a person against black magic is to strengthen faith in Allah by reading the Qur'an and by reciting the *Adhkaar* (the remembrances of Allah) regularly. For instance *Ya Sin sura* (chapter 36 of the Qur'an) is said to be effective in the treatment of sorcery, while chapters 109 and 112-14 are used for its prevention. Black magic and *jinn* possession are not two mutually exclusive explanations of misfortune. As one *imam* explained, magic might be deployed to bring about *jinn* possession in another person. Conversely, those who deploy black magic may be persuaded to do it in the first place through the agency of a *jinn*. A popular custom for women is to wear a *kabaj*, a metal case, which contains a *tabij* (amulet*)*, which is a passage from the Qur'an or the name of one of the angels. This is deployed to protect a person from the evil eye, or from witchcraft. Although the Qur'an prohibits the use of these amulets, they are widely available from shops in Muslim areas, for example in Brick Lane, East London.

---

[3]   In large parts of the Muslim world, particularly Iran, Turkey, central Asia and the Indian subcontinent, it is the name commonly given to local Islamic clerics or mosque leaders.

At times those deploying magic make use of Qur'anic verses written in the wrong order, perhaps buried under the bed pillows or carpet. One *imam* recounted the story of a couple in London who began arguing after receiving a *taviz* (the same as *tabij* – an amulet) from a family member in Bangladesh and explained that in other cases a poorly written amulet could result in someone becoming sleepy and losing their appetite. He emphasised that this belief in magic and the evil eye is based in the Qur'an.

> There is a story about the prophet who 1,424 years ago had fallen ill. This is because of a curse by a 'black magician', who I think was Jewish. One of the prophet's hairs had fallen into the hands of the magician. The magician tied eleven knots in the hair and the prophet became ill because of this. Allah sent eleven verses of the Qur'an to undo the eleven knots in the prophet's hair. The verses are in the last two chapters of the Qur'an. When one is ill one should recite these eleven verses.

Nazoor – Evil Eye

Many informants spoke of the evil eye. This refers to the malevolent influence of one person's envious glance on another. Those who give the evil eye are often unaware that they are doing it. Although certain individuals may acquire a reputation for *nazoor*, personal blame is rare: their destructive power is not thought to be under conscious control. Envy and the evil eye are potentially harmful to the thing that is liked or envied. Sometimes a person comments on how pretty fruit looks, only to find the following day that the fruit is rotten. A compliment might turn out to be destructive. Everyone in the community is vulnerable to *nazoor*, but some are held to be more vulnerable on account of their weakness, for example babies. To avert the effects of the evil eye, a black mark is often painted on the head of a baby, or the baby might be covered. An amulet (*tabij*) similarly is held to deflect and counter the effects of the evil eye. Another popular method is *foo* – blowing over someone after having memorised Qur'anic verses. Those who give compliments and their recipients often mutter under their breath *Ma Ha Shallah*, 'thanks be to Allah' to prevent the compliment having evil effect.

Nazoor is often implicated in cases of weakness, especially in children who fail to thrive or lose their appetite. Only one female informant spoke of the possibility of the evil eye directly causing illness. A young child in Sylhet threw temper tantrums whenever she was given food. She went on to lose considerable weight, but two doctors could find no obvious physical cause. The child's parents attributed the problem to the envy of a neighbouring family who had lost a child.

Spiritual Healing

Not surprisingly, given such beliefs, appeal is often first made to *imam*s to find religious solutions for problems. This is not to deny that members of this community make regular use of western medical services for sickness. However levels of complaints about both hospital services and primary care run high in this community. During my fieldwork several informants mentioned that General Practitioners had little respect for them and provided overall poor services for their families.

Imams point out that these *jinn* explanations are 'overused' and emphasise that most people who consult them are not possessed by *jinn* but rather, are suffering from psychological disturbances. They deploy Islamic prayer, often reciting *suras* (verses) from the Qur'an for healing purposes. In cases which are thought to be 'genuinely possessed', they may call in a local expert in *jinn* possession who will attempt to eliminate the *jinn* by similar means. They themselves do not generally claim to have the expertise to exorcise such malevolent spirits.

It is common for members of this community to consult several types of healer simultaneously.[4] The healers most often consulted are *hakims*, *kabiraj* (traditional healer who generally employs herbs) and *mullahs* (religious leaders). *Hakims* are defined variously by informants as medicine men or herbalists and are consulted more often by women, often on account of marital disharmony or because a woman is afraid that her husband may be seeing another woman. *Hakims* visit from India or Pakistan and can cost up to £500 a consultation. Alternatively, people may travel long distances to find a reputable *hakim*.

Resort to folk healers is commonplace especially when Western medicine is not perceived to be effective. Healers often advertise in local Bangladeshi newspapers and claim to be devout Muslims with a thorough knowledge of the Qur'an. They often claim a long lineage with their fathers and grandfathers being healers and may trace their ancestry back to well known *mullahs* or *pirs* (the title of honour given a holy man or religious leader). They deploy various techniques in their healing practices: blowing over the patient (*foo*), the recitation of Qur'anic verses (*mantra*) and the prescription of amulets (*tabiz*). Healers appeared to specialise in particular treatments or illnesses, some for example claiming the ability to find lost objects or people, for instance a wife who has left the household following domestic violence. Yet others were consulted for purely malevolent purposes, such as inflicting harm on someone they did not like, or with a view to changing someone's mind, for example to facilitate amorous feelings. Below is an example of one such advertisement from *The Asian Times*.

---

4   See also S. Dein and S. Sembhi (2001).

Mr Khalil
International healer and spiritualist The first African man to combine the power of voodoo, black and white magic, juju and many other spiritual methods including the use of the Holy Quran. Born from a strong family of Shiekh and Mulana – with over 100 years experience of helping people. Such as; relationship, curses, unknown and unexplained illnesses and diseases. A stop or break of an unwanted marriage, union or separation, immigration, or any court matter, protection, exam, rebirth of luck or affection, business to be more successful etc. Please put an end to all your worries in 7 days by phoning: Mr Khalil: 020 XXXX XXXX Guaranteed to be 100% successful. Payment after result.

I now present two cases which exemplify *jinn* possession. The first derives from a newspaper report, the second from my own fieldwork.

Sureha

A newspaper article in *The Asian Times* (24 September 2005) reported on the case of Sureha Begum, who for some months had been quiet, crying and self-harming. She spent much of her time crying. Her parents believed she was possessed by a *jinn* and took her to a healer, who took £3,000 from her parents in an exorcism. Sureha was in a relationship with her Bangladeshi boyfriend. Her parents found out about the relationship and disapproved strongly, panicked and arranged a marriage with a cousin in Bangladesh. In the two months prior to the marriage she became quiet, not eating and didn't go out. According to her, 'life didn't seem worth living'.

She was aware that her cousin was not right for her and she would be unhappy with him. She cut off all ties with her boyfriend and became distant from her friends. She spent many hours in her room just staring out of the window. Her parents did take her to Bangladesh and she was married. Following this she stopped talking to people. People thought generally she would get back to her normal self. However, nothing changed and her in-laws noticed her behaviour and became worried. One night she was in her room talking to herself asking God 'Why me?'.

Her husband walked into the room and thought she had gone mad. He called his parents who started saying their son had married 'a loony'.

Following her return to England her mental state deteriorated further. Rumours started to circulate that she had become a *phagal* – a possessed person. Her parents felt there had been a *jinn* overtaking her in Bangladesh. They suggested she should go to a *mullah* in London, who claimed to be an expert in possession. The *mullah* lived in Stepney Green. Her parents explained to him that their daughter had become withdrawn, did not eat and cried all the time. She also did not want to bring her husband over. She didn't speak to anybody. The *mullah* readily agreed that it was a *jinn* who had possessed her. He asked them to bring her back in one week so that he could read special prayers over her and get rid of the *jinn*. When they arrived home in Manchester neighbours clamoured to see her because they wanted to see what 'a *phagal*' looked like.

Sureha began to have nightmares. It was a *jinn* causing her bad dreams. They didn't go back to London as the parents decided to go to a local faith healer. He examined Sureha and prodded her body with a stick before agreeing that she was indeed possessed. According to Sureha,

> he poked me so hard it hurt. I tried to move away from him but my parents held me down. I hated him being there. This faith healer claimed he worked with the special spirits who visited him at midnight and told him how to help people. He promised my parents I would be okay again and they must give him at least £500 to start the healing process.

He prayed over Sureha and she was taken back the following week. On this occasion he sat in front of her and wrote prayers on a sheet. He then burned pieces of paper and put the ashes in water and said that she must drink it. When she refused, he told her parents that the *jinn* was causing her to refuse the drink.

The healer restrained her and she was forced to drink the water. She screamed to be let out of the *mullah*'s house. Everything she did, however, was blamed on the *jinn*. She went home that night scared and shaken. She thought of suicide and had a small knife. She cut her arms just to see how the pain felt, but she was afraid to do anything. However, when she did cut herself she felt relieved, as though the physical pain would take away the mental pain. This pattern continued and she started to do it regularly. Within the next year her parents spent over £3,000 visiting faith healers all promising to bring back the old Sureha. However, all of them failed.

Eventually Sureha's ex-boyfriend and his sister heard that she was ill and went to visit her. The ex-boyfriend was shocked to see her. Sureha opened up to his sister. The following day her ex-boyfriend and sister returned with an older member of the community and insisted that Sureha should be taken to a doctor as soon as possible. According to Sureha, 'my ex and his sister are very educated and don't believe in *jinn* possessions. I think they could see straight away that I was ill and not possessed. Nobody realised I was suffering from depression as these faith healers were so convincing.' Finally in desperation her parents took her to a doctor and she was diagnosed with chronic depression and was helped immediately. She was given antidepressants and saw a counsellor.

Sureha finally stated that her parents were wrong but she did forgive them for what they had done. She emphasised that 'faith healers only prey on your weaknesses'.

Muzassar

Muzassar, a shop owner, recounted the following story to me. Two years previously his sister, then aged in her thirties, began to behave quite strangely. She became withdrawn and she had problems sleeping and was up most of the night. She reported having bad nightmares. This went on for some time. Her husband was quite concerned and took her to a local healer in East London. Having spent a short period of time with her the healer felt that she was possessed by a *jinn* spirit. He told her husband that his sister needed to have the spirit removed. He did this by blowing water over her and also reciting various passages of the Qur'an. This, however, was not successful. Her husband then took her to a second healer. This time he was even more expensive. The healer listened to the story and again felt, not only was she a victim of *jinn* but that a friend had caused this spirit to possess her. He told them he could perform a ceremony to get rid of the spirit and also to stop her friend harming her. This would cost a couple of hundred pounds. The sister tried this but to no avail.

After several months her state was getting worse. She became quite low and withdrawn. The husband then asked her brother, Muzassar what he should do. Muzassar felt the healers were charlatans and were not successful in helping her. He advised she go along to a local doctor. The doctor diagnosed depression and she was started on medication. After a month or so he reported that she did feel considerably better.

Jinn and Violence

Sometimes families take matters into their own hands and attempt to eliminate the *jinn* through violent means such as beating the victim until the *jinn* has gone. In a few instances this has resulted in tragic consequences with the victim dying. There have been several high profile cases of members of the community who have been convicted of assault or even manslaughter on account of such activities.

Samira Ullah

The BBC website (21 December 2005) reported upon the case of Samira Ullah who was murdered by her father. She was born at St Mary's Hospital in Paddington, West London, on 19 July 2004, two months premature, and was discharged home four weeks later. When a health visitor came to see her at home a month later she described her as 'thriving, gaining weight and reaching all her development milestones'. However she died three months later from horrendous injuries.

Her father, Sitab Ullah, had worked as an educational development officer at a school in Westminster and was described as a 'positive influence' on the children, a third of whom were, like him, of Bangladeshi origin. When his own father died in

November 2003 he broke down and became addicted to heroin and crack cocaine. His personality changed and he became violent and expressed delusions. He came to believe that his wife Begum was unfaithful and that his daughter Samira was possessed by a *jinn*.

After Samira was born Ullah became more violent towards Begum and started hallucinating – seeing writing on her body and on the walls. On one occasion he chopped up the marital bed with a samurai sword, claiming that Begum's lover was hiding inside. When Samira was brought home from hospital he became convinced she was possessed by spirits.

Ullah later claimed in court that he had employed an *imam* to drive out the spirits. But the *imam*, Abu Ahmed, told the trial he had never been to the house, had never performed such a purification ceremony and did not know the family.

Begum told the court how Ullah's delusions about Samira became worse and said:

> He did not want me to feed her too much. He complained she was becoming greedy because he thought the thing inside her wanted to be fed all the time. She once chastised him for flicking the soles of Samira's feet. He replied: 'I'm not hurting her. I'm hurting the thing inside her.' Throughout September and October Ullah's physical assaults on Samira became worse, culminating on 16 October 2004 when Ullah shook her so violently she incurred a fatal brain injury.

The post-mortem revealed a 'catalogue of injuries', including cigarette burns to the face and lips, nipples had been 'destroyed' by pinching, badly damaged feet and several fractured ribs. Damage to her ears suggested she had been picked up by them and the piece of skin connecting her gums to her top lip was torn away.

Ullah was found guilty of murder. Interestingly, his mental condition was not raised as a defence in his trial. This is quite unusual since generally a detailed psychiatric opinion is sought in cases of murder. Why this was not done in this specific case remains uncertain.

Conclusion

Beliefs in *jinn*, evil eye and black magic are still prevalent among the east London Bangladeshi community. Such beliefs influence health related behaviours and may detract from sick people obtaining the help they require. There is frequent resort to various types of folk healers and magicians. Apart from their expense, there is little evidence that they are effective. However it remains to be seen whether these beliefs will persist when this community becomes more acculturated. Although these beliefs are less prevalent among second and third generation east London Bangladeshis than among the older less educated community members, many of the younger generation still hold to them.

There is some reason to believe that sorcery accusations may in fact increase following migration to the UK. Inequality may provide fertile fuel for the growth of these mystical explanations. Callan (2007: 341) has pointed out how in Bangladesh

> Sorcery persists in Bangladesh despite the impact of global forces. Global capitalism has given rise to new inequalities locally. Inequalities have always been present between families, but overseas migration leads to new inequalities within the joint household, giving rise to tensions which constitute the perceived increase in sorcery accusations.

It is possible that a similar process of intensification will occur in the UK.

References

Al Baqarah, Commentary on the Qur'an cited in Ameen (2005).

Alexander, C. (2000). *The Asian Gang: Ethnicity, Identity and Masculinity.* Oxford: Berg.

Ameen, K. ibn I. (2005). *The Jinn and Human Sickness - Remedies in the Light of the Qur'an and Sunnah*, N. Al-Khattab (trans) and A. Ahad (ed.). Riyadh Darussalam.

Aslam, M. (1970). *The Practice of Asian Medicine in the United Kingdom*, Ph.D. thesis, University of Nottingham, UK.

Cabinet Office (2003). *Ethnic Minorities and the Labour Market*, London: Cabinet Office. Chapter 7.

Callan A. (2007). '"What Else do we Bengalis do?" Sorcery, Overseas Migration, and the New Inequalities in Sylhet, Bangladesh', *The Journal of the Royal Anthropological Institute*, 13/2: 331-43.

Commission for Racial Equality (2003). *Survey of English Housing, Provisional Results: 2002-2003, based on 1999-2000 data.* London: CRE. Table 2.

Dein, S. and S. Sembhi (2001). 'The Use of Traditional Healers in South Asian Psychiatric Patients in the UK; Interactions between Professional and Folk Remedies', *Transcultural Psychiatry*, 38/2: 243-57.

Dein, S., M. Alexander and D. Napier (2008). '*Jinn*, Psychiatry and Contested Notions of Misfortune among East London Bangladeshis', *Transcultural Psychiatry*, 45/1.

Eade, J., C. Peach and T. Vamplew (1996). 'Bangladeshis in Britain: The Encapsulated Community', in C. Peach (ed.) *Ethnicity in the 1991 Census*, (vol. 2). London: HMSO for Office for National Statistics.

Eade, J. and D. Garbin (2002). 'Changing Narratives of Violence, Struggle and Resistance: Bangladeshis and the Competition for Resources in the Global City', *Oxford Development Studies*, 30/2: 137-49.

Gardner, K. (2002). *Narrative, Age and Migration: Life History and the Life Course Amongst Bengali Elders in London*. Oxford: Berg.

—— (1995) [reprinted 2001]. *Global Migrants, Local Lives: Migration and Transformation in Rural Bangladesh*. Oxford, Oxford University Press.

Kempson, E. (1999). *Overcrowding in Bangladeshi Households*. Policy Studies Institute.

Office for National Statistics (ONS) (2002). *Annual Labour Workforce Survey, Working-Age Employment Rate by Ethnic Group, 2002/03*. London: HMSO. Table 3.1.

Office for National Statistics (ONS) (2004). *Focus on Social Inequalities*. London: HMSO. Chapter 6, 'Health', Table 6.14.

Phillipson, C., N. Ahmed and J. Latimer (2003). *Women in Transition: A Study of the Experiences of Bangladeshi Women Living in Tower Hamlets*. Bristol: Polity Press. Chapter 5.

Walker, D. (2002). 'Study Reveals the Plight of Muslims: Cabinet Office Highlights Wide Ethnic Gaps in Jobs', *The Guardian*, 20 February.

Chapter 7

The Practice of Spirit Possession in Haitian *Vodou*

Bettina E. Schmidt

In 1998 I participated at a *Vodou* ceremony for the first time. I have investigated Caribbean religions since 1990 but mainly in Puerto Rico. But, though I observed possession of mediums in Puerto Rican Spiritism (*Santería*) several times I was never allowed to join the members of an Afro-Caribbean temple at a spirit possession ritual. I was told that it would be too dangerous for me to participate at such a ceremony. Because I was not trained in handling an *orisha* (the name for the divine entities in *Santería*) it would be difficult for me to get rid of one if he/she would possess me. I had to limit my research therefore to conducting interviews and observing other ritual activities (such as oracle readings) during my time in the Caribbean. Though I noticed an ambivalent attitude towards possession among different priests, I lacked any personal experience.[1]

In 1998 I decided to follow the migrants and to conduct a research project about religion and diaspora in New York City. There I noticed a more open attitude towards non-believers. And in November 1998 a colleague invited me to my first *Vodou* ceremony in a *Vodou* temple of a Haitian woman living in Long Island. I was very curious (and a bit nervous) about what awaited me. When we arrived at the house of the *mambo* (the *Vodou* priestess) – a small terraced house in a quiet neighbourhood – the ceremony had just started. The temple was in the basement of the house. A group of people sat in front of the altar, mostly women dressed in white, and sang the first prayers.

At the beginning only a few people sat on chairs but after some time the basement was full of people, mainly Haitians and Haitian Americans, descendents of Haitian migrants. More chairs were brought into the room, and I was glad to find somewhere to sit. No one seemed to take notice of my presence; I was accepted as a friend of a friend.

---

[1] There are several spellings of Afro-Caribbean religious terms, in particular '*Vodou*' is written in various ways (for example Voodoo, Vodu, Wodu). In order to distinguish the religion from its negative image that is portrayed in many Hollywood movies most scholars today use the Creole spelling, for example *Vodou*. *Vodun* is used as a term for the African spirits, the equivalent of *lwa* (see below) in Haiti.

During the night the *mambo* was possessed by several *lwa*[2] (the name for divine spirits in Haitian *Vodou*, pronounced: *loa*). Not only was her paraphernalia changed every time – the dresses, the objects, their colours and so on – but also her movements, her attitude, her body language. It was no longer the *mambo* but the *lwa* speaking to the participants. At the end, when we left at dawn, I asked whether I may approach the *mambo* and thank her for allowing me to come; my friend said 'Well, you can do it but be careful, she is still not here, it is still a *Gédé* speaking.' I must admit, I was scared though I approached her and thanked her. I was emotionally overwhelmed by this unfamiliar situation. But why?

During my time in Puerto Rico I participated in several spiritistic[3] séances and meetings, all in a friendly homely atmosphere; I felt protected surrounded by people I knew and their friends. Though I was startled when one medium addressed me personally (Spiritism deals with the spirits of the dead and I was still recovering from the early death of my mother), I never felt reluctant to approach the mediums. What was different in the *Vodou* Temple? Coming from a working-class background and a family of refugees I thought that I had more in common with the Haitian migrants than with most of the Puerto Rican spiritists. Another difference between Puerto Rico and New York was race. I was an outsider in both situations, a blond stranger speaking their languages (Spanish, French and English) with a German accent. But while the Puerto Rican communities were very mixed with regard to race, I was one of few white people at the *Vodou* temple in New York City. However, it was not the first situation where I was surrounded by people of a different colour, and I never felt so strange before.

I realised later, after having participated at several rituals and getting used to it, that my feelings at the end of this first night were influenced by my experience with spirit possessions. Though I was not afraid, I was touched by this experience when I left the temple physically exhausted from the long night. I still can remember the smells, the music and the intensity of this night ceremony.

In this chapter I want to explain the religious practice of spirit possession in Haitian *Vodou* so that people are less afraid of it. *Vodou* is one of the most fascinating religions, open towards foreign influences and ideas and foreign people. But it is also one of the most frightening belief systems for outsiders. When people hear that I work on Caribbean religions, they always ask about *Vodou*. Everyone seems to have an opinion, but no one really knows about it. I

---

[2]   *Loa* is the Creole spelling. It is used to be consistent with the Creole spelling for *Vodou*. *Lwas* are very similar to *orishas* in the Afro-Cuban and Brazilian religions. However, *orishas* derive mainly from the Yoruba deities in Nigeria and Benin while *lwas* include, in addition to the Yoruba spirits, other categories of spirits, derived from other African ethnic groups, indigenous spirits and even human beings. There are also some differences in the religious practices directed to *lwas* and *orishas*.

[3]   Spiritistic meetings are the central gatherings in Latin American spiritism, a system of beliefs and practices that derives from French kardecism but includes African and indigenous influences as well as elements from Spanish popular Catholicism.

will therefore write about the historical background of *Vodou* and the differences between the African religion and the Haitian religion and then present the system of beliefs and practices before showing its development in the diaspora. My focus will be on the practice of incorporating a divine being in a human body, so-called spirit possession.

What is *Vodou*?

Originally, the term '*Vodou*' (or '*Vodun*') was used in Benin, the former kingdom of Dahomey in West Africa, for ancestor spirits or other divine entities. Each group (each family, village, or association) worshipped its own spirit, its own '*Vodou*', in specific rituals. There was no common belief system but a collection of various practices and beliefs. But when people started to move, they carried their beliefs with them. Hence, through migration to other areas, information about a '*Vodou*' arrived in an area where people used to worship other spirits. After some time the local beliefs in single '*Vodou*-s' were combined into a common system with various immigrant spirits. *Vodou* in Benin today is still a predominately urban religion though its practices are popular throughout the region, even beyond Benin's borders. Its strong position was recognised when *Vodou* became the official religion in Benin in 1996.

However, despite its African origin, *Vodou* as it is known today originated in Hispaniola, the Caribbean island, as a consequence of the transatlantic slave trade. The slave trade forced people of various religious and ethnic backgrounds together. In the slave barracks enslaved people had to develop the means for survival, not only physical but also spiritual. One way was to create a common system of beliefs and practices that combined various practices from different origins. Though the practice of African religions was strictly prohibited by the *Code Noir* (1685), enslaved people were given some freedom under the protection of the Roman Catholic Church. Enslaved people were baptised and encouraged to join the Church for some ceremonies. As a consequence, enslaved Africans started to adapt some Catholic elements (such as prayers and Catholic iconography) but reinterpreted them according to their own traditions. *Vodou* as a complex religious system became enriched by elements from French Catholicism, freemasonry, indigenous traditions and the worship of African deities, in particular the Dahomey spirits but also some from other ethnic religions (for example Yoruba). The moment when we really can speak about *Vodou* as a homogenous belief system is still a debated issue. Some scholars doubt its existence in this early stage because enslaved people were not allowed to meet outside a limited number of places such as a working space and church buildings. How could they agree, for instance, on the ceremonial order of important rituals or the categorisation of the spirits? On the other hand it would be a mistake to overlook the creative potential of oppressed people who searched for escape and revenge from the moment of their capture. Religious activities represent an important part of this escape. Nonetheless, lack of information makes it impossible for us to date the origin of *Vodou* religion. All we know is that *Vodou* became part of the oral history of Haiti. Today people believe that the religion played an important part in the uprising against France and the declaration of independence of Haiti in 1804. One of the leaders against France, the 'maroon'[4] Boukman Dutty, was apparently a *Vodou* priest who started his acts of revolt against slavery with a *Vodou* ceremony. Though some historians doubt whether it really happened, Boukman's ceremony in 1791 is celebrated today in Haiti as the initial event of the fight for independence. Unfortunately, the connection to this victory, the declaration of independence, led also to a negative evaluation of *Vodou*. People outside Haiti, in particular white owners of sugar, tobacco and cotton plantations that were economically dependent on slavery, became so afraid of Haiti and the events on this island that they tried to isolate it from its beginning. The aim was to prevent the spread of knowledge about the victory of enslaved people over their oppressors. In addition to prohibiting ships with cargo from Haiti from entering a harbour in North America or chaining black sailors to the ships' masts while in port to prevent them escaping, one common strategy was to associate Haiti with evil, black magic and even cannibalism. The ceremony in 1791, for instance, became increasingly embellished with bloody elements. Nearly one hundred years after the ceremony Spenser St John wrote (in 1884) that during the ceremony a young white woman was sacrificed in a cannibalistic ritual – but only in the second edition of his book, while the first edition mentioned only the sacrifice of a pig.

Several leaders of the young republic tried to separate Haiti from its negative reputation and in 1835 *Vodou* practices were prohibited as superstition. Nonetheless, the lack of dedication of the Catholic Church in Haiti until the concordat in 1860 allowed *Vodou* to stabilise as a popular religion, in particular in rural areas of the island. Despite its negative reputation among non-Haitians *Vodou* is part of Haitian history and presence. In 1987, a new constitution finally deleted the prohibition of *Vodou* practices, and in 1991 the 200th anniversary of the *Vodou*-ceremony at the beginning of the struggle for independence was commemorated in a state ceremony. In 2003, *Vodou* was finally acknowledged as Haiti's second national religion. However, most practitioners of *Vodou* in Haiti do not locate their religion outside Catholicism but as part of it. If someone would ask them what religion they practise, they would answer 'I am Catholic', and add probably in a second sentence 'but I serve the spirits'.

Serving the Spirits – How Does One Practise *Vodou*?

Vodou practitioners believe that God (*Bondye*) created the world. More important for daily life are, however, the spirits (*lwa*) who can influence human destiny

---

    [4] 'Maroon' is the name for a formerly enslaved person who ran away and lived with other maroons in isolated independent settlements in the mountains or the hinterland of the islands.

according to the belief. People must honour them (for example with offerings or prayers) in order to avoid punishment and misfortune. Most of the *lwa* represent African deities though some spirits derive from Native American origins or from *maroons*, hence are human beings. Most of them are also connected to Catholic saints, though the *Vodou* believers distinguish between the two divine entities. *Lwa* are thought to be present in nature, for instance in trees, rivers or mountains. They are associated with human activities such as healing, fighting, farming, or love, as well as aspects of nature (for example thunder, rain and storm). *Lwa* are divided in categories (*nanchons*), each with a specific ritual and its own song, prayer, movement, rhythm and offerings.

Communication between *lwa* and human beings is the centre of the religious practices. In case of a problem, people consult a priest (*houngan*) or priestess (*mambo*) who will search for the causes of the problem using specific divination techniques (oracles) and then suggest possible treatments. Apart from the oracles there is another direct way of communication. *Vodou* practitioners believe that *lwa* can materialise in a human body by 'possessing' or 'mounting' a person (*monte chwal*). This should always happen during a ceremony, hence within the protected area of a *Vodou* temple and a community of *Vodou* believers. However, *lwa* can approach a human being at any time, sometimes even during the Holy Communion in a church, though this is then interpreted as a call of the *lwa* and will often lead to the initiation of this person.

Every *Vodou* ceremony is divided into sections which address specific categories of *lwa*. Even if the ceremony is to honour one particular *lwa*, the ceremony must include rituals for the other *lwa* categories. The ceremony I mentioned at the beginning, for instance, was celebrated in honour of the *lwa Erzulie*, who belongs to *Rada* category. The *Rada* part of the ceremony was therefore longer and more elaborate than the other parts; nonetheless, no ceremony can be successful without honouring some of the other *lwa*. As an example I will continue describing my first *Vodou* ceremony.

The ceremony started with Christian prayers in front of the altar. The *mambo* and her assistants were all dressed in white. The voice of the *mambo* led us through the whole ceremony though she was supported by some members of her temple. After the prayers *Legba* was honoured with his songs. *Legba* is a trickster spirit who guards and opens doors. He has to be addressed at the beginning of every ceremony; otherwise the door between the world of Human beings and the world of *lwa* would stay closed. Every *Vodou* temple has a *Poteau-mitan* (a kind of world tree, a 'pole' that connects the levels of the cosmos). Attracted by rhythm and prayers a *lwa* can descend from the level of the *lwa* to the level of human beings via this pole and materialise in the body of a person. It is not only the *mambo* who is possessed.

After the songs for *Legba*, the small chairs in front of the altar were taken away, and the drummers changed to the *Rada* rhythm. The *mambo* urged everyone to join her singing and the music got louder and louder. After a while a *Rada-lwa* approached the first person to be possessed. The approach of a *lwa* is visible in convulsive body movements. I was told that the reason for these movements is that the human soul struggles against the powerful force of the *lwa*, against the domination of the body until it finally has to surrender. In order to protect the body, members of the temple look after a person as soon as he or she starts behaving in such a way. Sometimes they take away glasses or other sharp objects so that the human body as well as other people are not harmed by these convulsive movements.

After a while *Erzulie*, the main spirit at this evening, announced her arrival. The room was already prepared for her. On the altar, members of the temple had put a statue of Our Lady of Lourdes, her Catholic equivalent, and her favourite offerings such as perfume, sweets, a large cake and biscuits. Finally *Erzulie* materialised in the body of the *mambo*, who fell on the floor. Some men carried her body carefully to a small chamber where she was dressed in the favourite colours of *Erzulie*. Wearing new dresses *Erzulie* made her grand entrance. Flirting with the men (and ignoring most women) she held court. People came forward to ask *Erzulie*'s blessing and an answer for their problems. *Erzulie* deals, for instance, with problematic relationships and with the failure to conceive a child.

More than two hours passed. The air became sticky, full of incense, perfume and the alcohol that was spat in all four directions. Because of the neighbours who had already called the police on more than one occasion, the windows had to remain closed. The sounds of the drums and the singing became louder and louder. The *mambo* urged the participants to sing louder, in order to support her effort to call the *lwa*.

The next part was in honour of *Nago lwa*. People changed from white dresses into red. Again the body of the *mambo* was 'possessed', this time by *Ogou* who was immediately handed a red bandana, a machete and a cigar. *Ogou* presents himself as being very aggressive, very 'male' though he is an ambivalent character, a warrior but also someone who causes disorder and other problems. After supper the celebration continued with *Petro lwa*, a very colourful experience. These *lwa* are not considered as individual spirits but as a collective entity. The last part of the night was then dedicated to the *Gédé*, the spirits of death and of new beginnings. This part was the funniest; people made jokes, they laughed and drank. But *Gédé* are very demanding and need careful attention. At dawn the ceremony came to an end.

Though I focused in my description only on some aspects in order to introduce spirit possession, it is obvious how important the *mambo* was. While she was possessed, it was possible to consult her, or more precisely, the *lwa* who materialised in her body at that moment. Though other members of her temple also became possessed, the *mambo* was the main character who led the whole ceremony with her voice, even when her body was 'mounted' by a spirit. She paid attention to every detail, gave orders to her assistants and demanded the support of all participants. While in Haiti a temple normally has more senior members who support the priest or priestess in their effort, only few diaspora communities can even afford to hire musicians and hardly can have someone to hold *Vodou* flags or for other special functions. Consequently the range of work of the priest or priestess who founded the temple increased, as I could observe at this ceremony and at later ones. By the end, after nearly eight hours, the *mambo* was physically exhausted, not only because of the series of spiritual manifestations in her body.

In other Afro-Caribbean religions such as the Cuban *Santería* a person has such a strong relationship to one divine entity that only this one will manifest itself in the body of the practitioner, who is often called the child of this *orisha* (*Santería* spirit). In *Vodou* everyone is also connected to one *lwa*; nonetheless, gifted people such as the *mambo* in this ceremony can incorporate more than one. This relationship between a *lwa* and a human being is regarded as ambivalent. On the one side it is a special gift, but on the other it can become a burden. The manifestation is physically exhausting for a person, and if it happens too often, perhaps even outside the temple, it can interfere with ordinary life. People are afraid to lose their job or to be rejected by friends and family when someone happens to see the manifestation. Sometimes the spirit can become too demanding, even jealous, for instance, when the individual is married and directs their attention away from the spirit. People therefore often resist the call of the *lwa*. While in former times the duties of a priest and a priestess were inherited within a family (hence a grandchild carried the burden of a priest or priestess after the death of the grandparent who trained it), migration from the countryside to urban areas and then abroad changed *Vodou* and individualised the decision of becoming a priest.

Experiences with the Spirits Outside Haiti

I visited a temple of a young Haitian *mambo* in Brooklyn, a single mother with two daughters, several times. She told me once how she became a *mambo*. She had her first experiences with the *lwa* manifestations as a child in Haiti but struggled against it. At the age of 14 she received messages from the *lwa* about other people whom she was able to help. Nonetheless, she still fought against it. Then she moved to New York City for her education, but again she was called by the spirits. Only after she had suffered more and more problems (at work and at home) did she decide to return to Haiti and to accept the call of the spirits. In Haiti she became initiated as a priestess and after her return to New York she founded her own temple. In her description of her call she made a clear distinction between her first experiences with the *lwa* as a child and the first manifestation of her guiding spirit as an adult. Only the second one she described as 'possession', not the first ones. In the literature one can find similar differences. Elizabeth McAlister, for instance, quotes a *mambo* who received her call as a child during her first Holy Communion in the Church (McAlister, 2002). While the priest saw an epileptic attack, the relatives and friends of the child recognised at once the significance of the body movements. Nonetheless, it is not described as possession but as the call of the *lwa*. One speaks only of spirit possession when the *lwa* takes control over the human body. Though my description of the ceremony already demonstrated that the *mambo* was still able to ask for more chairs or louder singing, it is debatable whether it was the *mambo* or *Erzulie* (or one of the other *lwa* who materialised in the body of the priestess) who demanded the support. Scholars developed typologies of spirit possession based on the differences between the presence and lack of a conscious mind in the 'mounted body'. For the believers the question is irrelevant. As I mentioned at the beginning, I was warned to be careful approaching the *mambo* at the end of the ceremony because her body still incorporated a *Gédé*, one of a category of playful tricksters who like to play nasty jokes on people. Whether it was the *lwa* or the *mambo* asking for something, the orders had to be obeyed, though the participants knew to whom they were speaking in every moment of the ceremony. Nonetheless, I observed different kinds of spirit possession during my research in New York City. Sometimes it became very obvious that the body of a person was possessed by a different entity, not only because of the different dresses and decorations but also because of different characters. A man possessed by *Oshún* (an *orisha* in *Santería* similar to *Erzulie* in *Vodou*) became a graciously behaving goddess; his whole body movement and attitude changed. A woman possessed by *Ogun* (a warrior *orisha*) became aggressive and tossed a sword around the hall at amazing speed. I was fascinated but not terrified; these were trained people, initiated into their religion. They knew what they were doing (and when *Ogun* came a bit too near to me and someone in the crowd hit my glasses, members of the congregation protected me and recovered my glasses). An important part of the initiation process is teaching; every new initiate has to learn how to recognise and to handle the spirit. I was told once that an untrained person would not know how to get rid of the spirit, hence to end the manifestation. The consequence would be that this person would remain controlled by the spirit and lose its personality. During the initiation process a new initiate learns therefore how to control the spirit during the manifestation. When a pregnant woman becomes initiated, the unborn baby is often also considered to be initiated without being trained; nonetheless, at a later stage in its life this person, too, has to learn what is involved, otherwise it would be too dangerous when an uncontrolled spirit dominates a person.

While initiated people embody the spirit in such an impressive way, untrained people normally should not do so. Nonetheless, they too can experience the power of the spirits but in a different way. I already mentioned the convulsive movements in a human body when a spirit approaches it. It is described as a painful experience when this happens and the untrained person resists. The person can become sick and the training during initiation is considered to be the only cure.

The problem in the diaspora is the lack of understanding in outsiders. Caribbean people know how to react and where to send someone who experiences such spiritual contacts. Even people who are not members of *Vodou* temples know where to find one in Haiti because most ceremonies such as the one described are celebrated in public. It is even considered to be very important to involve the whole community, the village or the neighbourhood in a ceremony in Haiti. But in the diaspora these ceremonies are hidden in basements. Instead of inviting everybody in, no one is supposed to know when a ceremony is prepared. Even the existence of a temple is a secret, in New York as well as in London. While this secrecy is connected to the negative image of *Vodou* and is done to protect the members, it increases at the same time the stereotypes about the religion. Outsiders think that in *Vodou* communities, secrecy exists because they have something to hide, instead of realising that *Vodou* has to be practised in secret because otherwise the practitioners would put themselves at risk.

The lack of communal involvement has another side effect that can cause serious problems. In the Caribbean, *Vodou* priests and priestesses act in public. People know who a priest is and what his or her reputation is. Religions such as *Vodou* depend on trust. While certain rituals are conducted behind closed doors, their outcome needs a public arena. The public acts as a kind of safety net; if a priest misbehaves, his or her reputation will decline, fewer clients will come and their income will decline. Hence, few priests will do anything to endanger their reputations.[5] But lack of public acceptance and control in the diaspora creates a vacuum and opens the door for the improper behaviour of some individuals who only want to earn money. They ignore the damage done to the reputation of an entire religion, if even one out of hundreds of priests and priestesses acts improperly.

Vodou serves an important function in the diaspora. It can signify home for first-generation migrants and its practitioners offer support in a hostile environment, but it can also mark cultural or ethnic identity for succeeding generations whose home is the diaspora. Many of the second and third generations of migrants have parents with mixed ethnic background. The question 'Who am I?' becomes impossible to answer. What ethnic identity has a girl whose father is Haitian and her mother is African American or Latina or European? How does she identify herself? She will probably declare in one moment that she is American, and in another moment that she is Caribbean or Haitian. However, when she joins a *Vodou* temple, she will begin to emphasise her Haitian heritage. Hence, the decision to join a religious community goes often hand-in-hand with a new self-identification with Caribbean descent. I noticed in New York City how passionately young Caribbeans search for an understanding of the Caribbean home of their parents. They go to drum classes or dance workshops to learn more about their cultural background. And some join religious communities such as *Vodou* temples. The religious tradition presents a different link to the Caribbean, and some religious festivals become touchstones for the strength and cohesion of an ethnic group within a white mainstream society. But not only Caribbeans join the communities. A steadily increasing group of followers consists of people of different ethnic backgrounds who discover the openness of *Vodou* communities and the creativity of its traditions.

---

[5]   During the time of François Duvalier and his son Jean-Claude (presidents between 1957 and 1986) some *Vodou* priests were involved in the activities of the government's secret army, which harmed the reputation of *Vodou* priests in Haiti and led to the murder of priests in 1986. Nonetheless, this was an exceptional event, caused by a brutal political regime.

Vodou ceremonies are performed nowadays not only in New York and Haiti but in Quebec, Paris, London and many other places. However, in every city, at every location the religion has a slightly different meaning for the practitioners. Though the belief system is of course identical, the meaning for the individual can be slightly different. In London, contact with other traditions and religions may have altered it from the form of *Vodou* I studied in New York, but there will certainly be common features that indicate its origins.

References

McAlister, E. (2002). *Rara! Vodou, Rave, and Performance in Haiti and its Diaspora*. Berkeley: University of California Press.

Schmidt, B.E. (2007). 'Misuse of a Religion: Vodou as Political Power Rooted in "Magic" and "Sorcery"'. *Diskus, The Journal of the British Association for the Study of Religions*, 8. Available online at: http://www.basr.ac.uk/diskus/diskus8/schmidt.htm

St John, Spenser (1971/1884). *Hayti of the Black Republic*. London: Frank Cass & Co. Ltd.

PART II
Possession as Contact with the Divine

These two chapters offer further examples of possession as a positive religious technique but they are written from the point of view of practitioners, rather than observers. They are examples of what Professor Littlewood designates 'voluntary possession'. Dr Harrington is a leading member of a new religion that its practitioners call Wicca. Her Chapter 8, 'Possession as a sacrament: The perspective of Wicca'[1] begins Part II. Although new, Wicca is modelled on ideas of pre-Christian pagan religions and early in its history was known as Witchcraft, although it does not resemble what people usually mean by that term at all. Wicca's priestesses become possessed as part of their most sacred rite and this article describes what its meaning is for the central figure, whose body receives the goddess who is worshipped in it. Like *Vodou*, Wicca places possession at the centre of its rituals, although unlike *Vodun* spirits, the Wiccan Goddess is not manipulated for mundane purposes.

Chapter 9, 'Possession in The Celestial Church of Christ' by Mercy Magbagbeola,[2] describes how holy figures in an African Christian church, known there as prophets, may serve as the channel through which the Holy Spirit can communicate with members of the Church. Dreams and visions experienced by the prophet in trance are conveyed as messages and warnings to the members of the congregation for whom they are intended. Members of the Celestial Church of Christ believe that Satan or his subordinate devils may enter the bodies of human beings, including children. She describes, very vividly, what people believe about the witchcraft initiated by the evil spirits and its harmful effects. Those suspected of the possession of evil spirits will be the object of concerted prayers and are expected to help by praying at the same time. Children are less able to do this, Mercy Magbagbeola says, and therefore are harder to exorcise. But nothing other than prayer should be used; she is firm that only prayer is effective. Her paper illustrates the fact that African churches have different perspectives on possession and cannot be assumed to fit a particular pattern.

---

[1]   First given as a paper at the Inform conference of May 2006.

[2]   First given as a paper at the Inform conference of May 2006.

Chapter 8

Possession as a Sacrament: The Perspective of Wicca

Christina Harrington

My title, 'Possession as a sacrament', is deliberately provocative – not to cause offence, but rather to get people's attention. Although I have a doctorate in history, specialising in religious history, I attended Inform's conference in May 2006 not as an academic but as a representative of a religious tradition that deliberately invites a deity into the body of its priests for them to be possessed. It is, for me, uncomfortable territory, for I am more at home speaking of the beliefs of others than of my own: of the practices of others, not my own. I am acutely aware how much easier it is to speak about ideas than about inner experiences, for which only poetry really has the true words.

For those unfamiliar with the pagan religions of today, Wicca is a nature-based, initiatory religion with a theology centred around two cosmic deities, known as the Goddess and the God. I should say that Wicca has a mystical tradition and requires a vocation (or calling) to join. Only adults can be members and membership requires application, probation and a year's wait before initiation. It shares many characteristics with the mystery religions of the ancient world, such as the cults of Isis (best known from Apuleius' account, 1998), Dionysus and Mithras; all of which have been written about extensively by scholars such as Walter Burkert (1988). We also hold that only a minority of people will ever be drawn to our tradition. We are a path for the few rather than for the many, and it is a matter of being chosen by the gods and of having a personal vocation. We in Wicca believe in a largely benevolent spirit-world, and we believe that the body of the dedicated can be taken over, and shared with, the gods. Therefore, Wicca employs the practice of deliberate possession – not of demons, I stress, but of our gods. We share this with Afro-Caribbean religions such as *Vodou* and *Santería*. We, like they, call our patron deities to be present in our rituals by possessing the bodies of some of the practitioners. There are other tribal, ecstatic mystical religions which share this feature, mostly I believe in Africa. With these I am unfamiliar, so I will not try to make broader or comparative remarks; but I mention these because I feel it is worth remembering, particularly among religionists concerned with demonic possession, that the world contains religions – albeit small ones – which contain sacramental, deliberate deity possession. I am conscious that people are most familiar with the Christian belief in demonic possession, and are concerned also with the ways in which exorcists (priests) drive devils out. Therefore, a certain discomfort arises because demonic attributes have been applied to deities of pagan religions: Wicca, *Vodou* and other tribal religions. If people in a pagan religion invite their deities to inhabit their body in ritual, then we should be aware that past monotheists have labelled this as deliberate demonic possession. This causes me no small sadness.

My experiences, which are the subject of this chapter, commenced with my initiation into Wicca. You must imagine the year is 1990, and I am a rather serious young woman of 27, somewhat bookish and fond of poetry, medieval mystical writing and late Latin poetry. I have grown my hair long, and am immured in the nature mysticism of the romantics; my favourite work is Walt Whitman's *Leaves of Grass* (originally 1855). I have recently moved to London to study for an MA in medieval Celtic studies, having previously been living on a remote Orkney island where I had been surrounded by the wilder elements of nature, taking an extended spiritual retreat. For roughly four years, I have been looking for a group of Wiccan initiates, hoping to find traditional teachers who could take me in, apprentice me in the tradition and help me grow spiritually. My solitary devotions and rites have served me so far, but I have always hoped for more. (I should interject to say that this is typical: initiatory Wiccan groups are few in number, have relatively few members per group – ten is a rough average – and accept relatively few applicants for initiation.) Now in London, I have finally met a solid group who are considering me – having felt ready to take on a new person. I would be their first in several years.

After spending almost a year at the outskirts of the group, getting to know its members (my conduct during which time being quietly assessed); and having passed the subtle tests, I was accepted for, and eventually passed through, the rite of initiation. My initiation was the most important day of my life so far. Anyone who has a religious calling will understand the feeling of being admitted to the body of one's religion.

Once an initiate, I could attend the private, secret rituals. As I recall, it was at the first ritual after my initiation that I first saw what we call 'the Drawing Down of the Moon'. The high priestess of the group had the Goddess of Wicca called into her, and the Goddess was made present in her body. In that possessed state, she spoke a beautiful inspired speech, that I recall as being poetic and deeply emotionally moving.

A little about the context: we met in a temple room, and there were about ten people present in a chalk-marked circle. The Wiccan circle – the sacred space that keeps out undesirable forces whilst containing the power of the ceremony – had previously been blessed with consecrated salt water, and protective guardian spirits called forth to guard the rite. These protective spirits act as the sentinels of protection against any unwelcome supernatural forces that might be about; and whilst for us the unseen realms are not believed to be filled with evil forces, we do not want undesirable or incompatible presences in our place of working, particularly when we are working the possession rites. In Christianity, these guardians are the four archangels; the guardians of our tradition are ancestral forces, also associated with the four elements of earth, air, fire and water.

There was drumming, and dancing to raise energy; which is considered very important for what happens next: the drawing down. We believe that the energy of the practitioner's body has to be enlivened, because the power emanating from bodies is what connects us to a divine force-field. Everyone in the ritual is to be in a heightened state to be most effectively receptive to the God. All that being done, the priest as partner of the priestess 'drew down the moon' into her. A poetic invocation was, and is, used to accomplish this in conjunction with a spiritual petition and act of will. He called for the Goddess to come down, to be drawn down through the force of the moon into the priestess's body, so that she might be present among us.

I experienced a great and peaceful stillness. The poetry was extraordinarily beautiful – quite a contrast to the ecstatic, free dancing and drumming. A serenity came upon me, and I was somehow at one with the whole cosmos. I saw a woman I knew, a gracious and serene woman in her sixties; yet she was transformed: she looked like herself, but was also infinite. And then she spoke these words, hers but yet *not* hers. I was moved by a sense of being beyond the world. Those of you who have studied a little bit about Wicca will probably be familiar with the words she delivered, which are called 'The Charge of the Goddess': the most famous text we have. These words came through her, yet it was some part of her, an eternal part, that was speaking them. They were for everyone, and yet they were for the most intimate inner part of me individually. I confess I felt touched by the most tender force imaginable, and I felt that in whatever happened to me – for the rest of my life – all would be well, for she was with me always. She was standing still whilst this was happening, and she was speaking. After that, we each came and saluted her, and as a woman I made my offering of devotion to her by bowing. When it was over, the priestess then became herself again. Some other things were done in the ritual, then we had a marvellous feast. At the end of the night I went home a very happy young initiate.

Interestingly, I perceived and sensed in the ritual a few apparent inconsistencies. Every religious practice has a world-view underpinning it, and Wicca is no different. I had long known that, in Wicca, nature is sacred – every person is sacred, the body is sacred. It teaches that the world is sacred and that it is a blessing to be here on earth having life: a very pantheist, benevolent kind of theology. However, one thing that struck me this time – now actually participating – was that the priestess had started the rite by marking out the sacred space, making the circle in which we were met, implying that the world outside sacred space was 'profane'. I was reminded of the anthropological work on the distinction between the sacred and the profane in religion. Moreover, as if to further enforce this seeming distinction, the initiates called up guardians for protection and sprinkled the space and the bodies of the initiates with blessed salt water. Yet the general theology of Wicca is that every place is sacred. Hmm. 'Odd', I thought to myself. And if one contradiction concerned the space of ritual, the other concerned the act of possession itself;

for Wicca teaches that every person is sacred, and that the world goes wrong when and where people begin to hate their bodies; for the physical world is divine, and a person's divinity is intrinsic to them – including their physicality.

When we, as humans, begin to hate other people; and when we see ourselves as not connected to others – when we do this, we forget their sacredness. I was curious. If every woman is already sacred, why then does Wicca have a tradition in which a discarnate[1] deity is called into a woman's body? If Wicca is pantheist, then surely the priestess, as all physical beings, ought to be considered innately divine? How could there be an incorporeal deity, if the religion is pantheist? Yet my experience did not give me the feeling of mutual inconsistency. I felt fine, indeed wonderful, when I was in the presence of the Goddess in my priestess. I did not feel that it made any less of the woman she was, or of me, or of the physical world. The resolution of my confusions came much later, and through my feelings of the experience itself.

After my initiation, I did what every new initiate does: I participated in the group for some time, attending rites and helping in minor ways; I learnt about moving energy, doing the ritual chants and dances, making herbal preparations, meditating, praying. This went on for months and months. An initiate is trained in having the deity drawn down on them after they have been in the tradition for some time, usually when they have grasped both their own practical abilities and some certain spiritual principles. Male initiates will eventually learn to have the male God of Wicca drawn down on them; women the Goddess. I knew that, some day, it would be my time to be trained and prepared to have the Goddess drawn down upon me.

Of the spiritual lessons a person needs to have in place, the first is that our job is to help people. Our main 'magical' work is healing work, and we cultivate certain spiritual or energy techniques that can be for people's assistance. We are warned against feeling superior, and encouraged to do our healings and other work in a spirit of friendship. I learnt that I must remember that I and my fellow initiates are simply *people amongst people*, and that everybody is sacred. It was recommended for me to keep a diary for self-reflection, and to keep my self-awareness acute.

Having reached a sufficient level of spiritual maturity, as well as proficiency, I was put through another initiation in which I became a priestess of the tradition at the level where I could undergo the possession. After the initiation – quite traumatic and emotional, but utterly exhilarating – there was a gap of about a week, and then my priestess (a remarkable woman in her sixties), suggested to me that I visit her so that she could start teaching me the drawing down. I was desperately excited, honoured and nervous as I travelled across London on the tube, my bag of ritual tools in hand, on a weekday afternoon. And this is how it would happen: I would go to her house, we would have a cup of tea, and we would dedicate the afternoon to it. Firstly, I had to make the magic circle. She took me through the techniques. Ah, the old 'sacred v. profane' dichotomy, I thought! However, as I was learning and

---

[1]   Discarnate meaning not normally present in a body.

practising this, I found that the making of the sacred space didn't feel as though I were making the rest of the world profane: I was making the circle sacred.

What I mean is this: it felt that I was making a space in which certain things could happen, and that it was purified *not* against dirtiness, but purified so that it was *for one thing only*. Most of the time, the world is full of a variety of thoughts – reminders and events from all walks of life – and it is not single in purpose. For example, I am thinking about my job, I am thinking about my bank balance, I am thinking about my mother's birthday, and the space is mixed just so. To make a circle, our religious space, is to make a space that is dedicated to one intention only. Everything else is put outside, aside temporarily. I realised then, and fully realised in my very body, that the world is not profane. We do, however, need to make a space that is dedicated and set apart – the circle is a world condensed, microcosmic, and devoted to our relations with spiritual powers. Certain things are shut out, so that other things can happen.

Then we moved on. I began to be trained in the 'drawing down'. I had all sorts of inner experiences that are impossible to put into words – I am sure that many of you know what it is to experience things for which there are no words – but a few things stand out. One is the way in which the energy moved (in the room and inside of me) during the process of possession. In our tradition, the Goddess is seen as the moon in the night sky, almost as though the moon is her soul and the night sky her body. The priest kneels in front of the priestess and calls to the Goddess through her eyes and through her body to the universe beyond her, and she is called into the body of the priestess. I recall standing still with my arms out to embrace the moon, and before me was a man kneeling, speaking to the Goddess to 'descend into the body' of the priestess that was me. He was gazing into my eyes, but at the same time he was behind and beyond me. There seemed to emanate some rays of power from him, travelling in the vibration of his words. This vibration entered my chest somehow, filled up my being, and carried on into the space behind me – which I felt to be infinite.

Through it all, I never felt I was losing myself, but rather that the part of me that is caught up in daily life linked to (and embraced into) a more still and eternal Me, which in turn is a part of a divine universe. My consciousness pulled back into a night sky, so eventually I was looking down at a young woman's body, and seeing her look at a man kneeling before her. I saw all this through the eyes of a Goddess, not through personal eyes. When I spoke the words of the Charge, the poetry came through me from a far greater place than I had ever been able to imagine. The poetry of the Charge (the poetic oracle) was integral. Sometimes a priestess does speak spontaneously, as the oracles of the ancient Greek and Roman world; but the words of the charges that we know by heart, and which generally are delivered through us in our altered state, are not a literary recourse; rather, the Goddess comes through the words – and the words came out like a stream, and pure love was in them, and the deity travelled in the vibration created by my human voice, travelling on the air, like a blessing to all the initiates in the ceremony. It was ineffable; but perhaps I could summarise it as an experience of being myself, but also of being something much larger than myself: of being connected to all women and being connected to all nature. I was both myself and more than myself, both myself and another. My puzzlements of dogma were finally resolved, to my satisfaction at least.

To experience oneself as both woman and Goddess is exhilarating. I was warned that there is a danger that women, once they begin to have the 'drawing down' done upon them, go through a period wherein they are prone to grandiosity. To prevent this, I was reminded of the sacredness of everybody, mainly by the quiet dignified example of my initiating priestess and mentor. In my 17 years within the tradition, I have seen a few succumb to grandiosity, with massively inflated egos for two or three years after starting this practice. This passes – generally – as life teaches them some hard lessons. The grandiosity is knocked out of them by nature (or the gods of Wicca) sending them some events that bring them down to size. The gods are wise with us.

To draw some threads together towards a conclusion, I would say that in Wicca our version of possession, or 'possession as a sacrament', acts as a microcosm of some of our most important tenets, including some of the seemingly contradictory ones. Firstly, in Wicca we are fluidly mystical and experience-oriented, and this practice is a perfect example. Religious scholars often talk of religions as defining divinity to be either immanent or transcendent, and I think that here is a tradition which blurs the distinction; and that our 'drawing down' practice brings the group (and the person being possessed) to experience something that flickers between the two states of divinity. Secondly, and finally, in drawing down the gods upon ourselves, we have a ritualised way to move the small, daily self. If we get it right, the individual is at once themselves and something far, far beyond themselves.

As pantheists, we believe that this is really true about each person, whether or not they are experiencing it consciously. My initiating priestess is a lovely individual: she is now 79 years old, lives in Crouch End and belongs to Friends of the Earth; I do not worship her personally, but I reverence the divine in her, just as I reverence the divine in the lady who sells me my newspaper every morning. Being part of a tradition where one witnesses, and then participates in deity trance possession, gives us a ceremonial, regular reminder of the fact that we believe in the sacredness of each individual. Surely, this is something that I could only describe as a sacrament.

References

Apuleius (1998). (new edition). *The Golden Ass*. Penguin Classics, Penguin: Harmondsworth.

Burkert, W. (1988). *Ancient Mystery Cults*. Cambridge, MA: Harvard University Press.

Whitman, W. (2005). (new edition). *Leaves of Grass*. Penguin Classics, Penguin: Harmondsworth.

Chapter 9

Possession in The Celestial Church of Christ

Mercy Magbagbeola

The Celestial Church of Christ originated in the Republic of Benin, West Africa nearly 60 years ago. It spread to Nigeria and I joined it there. I have been a member of the Church for about 37 years and it has had a presence in Britain for about 32 years of them. Although I am Nigerian by birth I have lived in Britain for 34 years. I am a nurse, a general nurse trained in Nigeria but also trained as a psychiatric nurse in Britain. I am currently practising as a psychiatric social worker, taking part in mental health assessments of clients with or without admissions to hospital, in the community and in the hospital as well.

In our Church we believe in the power of the Holy Spirit and its manifestation in people. This can happen anywhere – in the tube, in a bus, at home or in church and at any time. I am a prophetess, which means I receive the Holy Spirit when called upon. My special gift is the Gift of Revelations which includes dreams, visions, prophecies, hearing messages from God, either as a clear vision or as God speaking directly into my heart.

As Christians we are all filled with the Holy Spirit but possession, according to our faith, is attributed to the Powers of Darkness or to affliction by a demonic power. We link possession with something like an illness that controls people, takes them over and is manifest in shaking and hearing voices that tell you to do evil things, like 'go and kill', 'go and kill'. The Holy Spirit comes and goes; it comes peacefully and calmly with instruction, but demonic possession seizes a person and does not let go.

In the society that is my background, that we Nigerians have come from, it is generally acceptable to believe that another person is responsible for your misfortunes or problems, because of the experience we have of demonic power being active in our society. This is not just talk, this is what goes on. People are afraid of what the powers of darkness could do with them and to them. We are not wrestling with flesh and blood wickedness but as the Bible says: 'with principalities, powers, [fighting] against the rulers of darkness of this world and against spiritual wickedness in heavenly places'. Those who experience the activities and powers of darkness have wickedness in their lives. When they hear about witches or wizards (male witches) they are petrified and the only place of refuge to come is the church. So they come with the belief that the Power of Darkness is not something you can take as a joke, like Hallowe'en. People fear witches as much as they fear God.

A witch has demonic power as the human agent of Satan; some know about it, others do not. But they cannot control it; they are controlled by it. Witchcraft may be handed on from a senior generation; mothers may even give the power to practise witchcraft to a child before they die if they have no one else to give it to. Children can be as powerful as witches as adults, but sometimes if they are given the powers of witchcraft it lies dormant until puberty. Witches use the power of darkness. Sickness that cannot be healed, barrenness, working hard (like an elephant as we say) but getting nowhere – all this can be caused by witchcraft. They plan evil by night but their actions are carried out by day. Witches can use their power to affect specified places such as Islington or more widely to affect London or even cause a natural catastrophe like a tsunami.

When they come to church with their problems people do not say: 'I'm possessed', no, people will give you the symptoms of their experience that worry them. For example they will say 'I had a dream last night that I was bitten by a snake' or 'I saw a big bird attacking me in my dreams.' If you have these dreams for some time and they coincide with inexplicable misfortune in your life, you know definitely there is witchcraft involved. It might be that you get a Ph.D. but then find that there isn't a worthwhile job for you. Or you have a sore that, unlike normal sores, will not heal. There are also dreams with definite meanings: for example, dreams of whippings herald bad events to come. People tell you the symptoms of what is happening to them or what is happening to someone back home, or something that has happened in the past but the effects of it are still continuing. If such people show signs of thought disorders, that is, their words do not make sense, even in terms of their own culture, or what they say is quite impossible, like the claim that they have jumped off a high building and survived, then they are ill not possessed, and need psychiatric treatment.

Then what is the solution for those who are not mentally ill? The solution concerns God. How does it reach God? It will need the combined gifts of the pastor and a prophet or prophetess, sometimes several. The pastor will pray over the prophets or prophetesses, the number of whom will depend on how many people there are to be healed; then the spirit of the Lord will descend upon them and then they will dream whatever is happening and what should be done about it. The whole process is for the resolution, restoration, and solution of the problem this person brings to the church. And when a solution has been prescribed, then you act accordingly. It could be in terms of several members of the Church praying for this person or three members to pray for this person, for several days, or it could be for one day, or it could even be for the whole church to pray for that person. The solution could be in the form of water for a bath to wash away the mark of the enemy, the mark of Satan, to get rid of poverty or barrenness, or affliction or sickness – whatever is the area in which people are suffering from the power of witchcraft or the power of darkness.

So the solution depends on what the Holy Spirit has revealed must be carried out. It comes in different forms which are all written down and are carried out accordingly. Sometimes it is acted out. It may be acted out in movements with palm fronds. Palm fronds are like sacred swords that cut away every activity of the enemy around us. We chant: 'I cut them off, I cut them here, I cut them off there, off my floor, off my ceiling' – all acted out to match the words. The Word of God in Genesis says that He will put an enemy between us, to stop him bruising your heel, bruise his head. So we may start praying that we will bruise the head of Satan, saying, 'It is my hope that I bruise the head. I bruise his head at home, at work, by day, by night, in my family, in my marriage – I will bruise his head.' And we believe that if we bruise the head of the enemy enough he will not come back again. Putting it in actions, stamping to match the words, that is our faith. The solution comes in different forms depending on what the Holy Spirit has asked us to do. It is all written down and will be carried out accordingly. We pray again and again until the behaviour changes or the problem goes away. Children are too ignorant to participate in these prayers so they are sometimes more difficult to treat than adults because they are not joining in, which helps the healing.

My experience of prophecy is that God speaks to me. It might be for a short time or a long time depending upon the person. Sometimes I hear the voice say 'Tell my daughter so-and-so to go and do something' or for somebody not to travel, as a precaution. For protection and directions, that is the purpose of prophecy and that is what we use it for. I'll give you an example: you are watching a television programme, suddenly it's changed. It is no longer the television programme; it is just like a dream going on. Somebody is shown in it, the problem is shown and the solution is put there. This is something different from the television you were watching. In less than two minutes it shows itself like that and you're not even given a name for what you see. But when you get the shock of a vision then you look for someone who it is likely to be, someone who you have seen in that small vision and then you go to them and say: 'This is what God did to me yesterday and this is what you should do about it.' Most of the time they confirm that the vision is true and then they go and do whatever it is that God asked them to do. For example if now, at this minute God wants me to see something, I will stop seeing you and will see whatever it is God wants me to see. Within that space of time, those two minutes, I will not know what is happening around me, because I will be cut off from it. When the vision is over, I will come round and I will be able to write down what God has revealed to me regarding the individual, or the church or the family or the whole congregation; it may be for protection like advising someone not to travel or telling somebody to pray against a mishap, or to pray for your children. The way they carry it out depends on what the Holy Spirit has asked us to do. If there is a spiritual message for someone and he is not present in the church at that time, the name can be written on a piece of paper and put in the Bible for another time, or you could pray for them straight away. These visions could suggest you pray at a particular time or a particular day. The message could be for the whole church, or to a family or an individual. Whatever the problem is, it is always revealed. I believe this practice solves problems.

As a social worker I have been involved in mental health assessment in quite a few cases. One example was on an African woman who was praying loudly in her room in the middle of the night. You know we have loud voices, it is quite typical of Africans to have a loud voice and this woman was praying in her own room in rented accommodation. With everything that was happening to her she was desperate to pray and she was praying loudly: 'Jesus help me, Jesus help me, Jesus help me.' Unfortunately this was misinterpreted by the neighbours who heard her and called the police. Anyway this woman was admitted to hospital and it was recommended that she be sectioned, that is, that she should be compulsorily detained in a mental hospital. I was involved in the assessment to decide on the recommendation and I interviewed the lady. What happened was that she had told the psychiatrist who was brought to see her that she was hearing voices from God and seeing visions, which was misinterpreted as hallucination and delusions. After all this, the woman was crying: 'How have we come to be like this? What am I doing here? This is not my house.' So I interviewed her and she could explain what she was doing so I realised she was not mad. I said: 'No, doctor so-and-so, there is nothing wrong with this woman, she is just acting on her religious beliefs.'

When people say that they hear voices and see visions, what they say can be misunderstood like this; they may be acting on their religious beliefs in their own way, talking very loudly or praying night and day. We believe in night visits to tackle our spiritual problems and that the problems that come in the night (that is, they are evil) have to go in the night. Then we pray aloud in the middle of the night and in the process it sometimes disturbs the neighbours. I am not saying it is right to disturb other people's sleep but sometimes I pray loudly to send away an evil spirit: 'In the name of Jesus you must go, you must go.' You have to express in prayer what is happening, negatively or positively in their dream. The word of God says: 'Whatsoever you bind on earth shall be bound in heaven.' People want to get rid of their problems and so they just act on their belief and hope that it is not misinterpreted.

Let me think if there are other ways that we work: we pray from time to time, sing songs of Praise, we dance and we believe strongly in the power of prayer and all that the Holy Spirit can give us in response to our prayer, setting us free from affliction. We also do deliverance prayers (a form of exorcism) as warfare. We do not target children as witches; even if there is a child who is a witch the public reaction is less. Children are not actually considered in that context, it is adults, because normally they inherit the Power of Darkness from an ancestral God, from their mother or wherever, God knows, and that is a different context entirely. If the children are possessed at all, then we bring them into the Church to pray for them, using the prayer of spiritual warfare to save them; we are using the power in the blood of Jesus, in the name of Jesus, and the power of the Holy Spirit to deliver and destroy every work of Satan in their lives. Only if children's abnormal behaviour coincides with misfortune in their family are children thought of as witches. Beating them will not change anything; only the power of prayer, the power of the Word, the power of the Name and of the blood or of the Cross could rid them of the evil.

Back home in Nigeria there is a lot of prejudice; an adult woman can look like an old witch. They may not be one, but because of their area or if there has been a witch identified in their family background they are thought to be witches. Witches may confess what they do to people, which often sends a chill down your spine to hear it. So when you hear of a witch, you tremble because of what they looked like, like the person I dreamed of last night. Some people might not go near a street they dreamed of because of the fear of it they feel. The identity of a witch can be revealed to a prophet or prophetess in a vision but this is just for their information. They will then take care not to expose the person to the whole church but make sure that she is not included in prayer groups (with those who lead prayers) for fear of retaliation from the witch.

This is our reality. It is not just gossip and it is not just odd ideas, it happens in people's lives.

PART III
Children Accused

In Part III, the book moves into the detail of cases in which children have been accused of practising witchcraft as the result of being possessed by devils or demons. Jean La Fontaine's Chapter 10, 'Child witches in London: Tradition and change in religious practice and belief', concerns the history of the idea of children as witches in Africa and traces its origin to a blend of Pentecostalism and the traditional idea of witchcraft. The accusations that are made indicate an intolerance of children whose bodies and behaviour do not conform to the rather narrow view of normality in children that has become general. Filip De Boeck, in Chapter 11, 'At risk, as risk: Abandonment and care in a world of spiritual insecurity'[1] gives a comprehensive analysis of information on children in Kinshasa, Democratic Republic of Congo, who have been accused of witchcraft and who are living on the street, having been rejected by their families. By contrast, Eleanor Stobart's Chapter 12, is a slightly abridged version of her report entitled: 'Child Abuse linked to Accusations of "Possession" and "Witchcraft"' written for the then Department for Education and Skills about children accused of witchcraft in Britain. This shows that a similar pattern of accusations to that detected in Kinshasa obtains in Britain.

---

[1] Given as a presentation at the Inform conference of December 2005.

Chapter 10

Child Witches in London: Tradition and Change in Religious Practice and Belief

Jean La Fontaine

On 3 June 2005 at the Old Bailey, two women and a man, all from Angola, were convicted of cruelty to an eight-year-old girl.[1] The child was in the care of one of them, a woman who claimed to be her mother, although DNA tests subsequently revealed her to be a more distant relative. The household contained another woman, not apparently related, and her son. The victim (referred to throughout as Child B to maintain her anonymity) had been accused of being a witch, initially by the child of the other woman. She was grossly abused by the adults and only saved from death by drowning by the boyfriend of one of the women who argued that the British Police would doubtless find out who had killed her. The maltreatment: starvation, beatings, cuts made on her chest and chilli pepper[2] rubbed in her eyes, were attempts, it was alleged, to force the devil responsible for her witchcraft to leave her body. This was the first time such beliefs and practices had been made public in the British press, although some five years earlier a girl of a similar age, Victoria Climbié, had had a deliverance ritual[3] performed for her by the pastor of the church she had attended and had subsequently died at the hands of the woman she lived with, also a distant relative. In the case of Victoria Climbié, the allegations of witchcraft or possession by demons were downplayed in the press accounts; in 2005 they were the central focus. By 2006, when Eleanor Stobart's report for the Department for Education and Skills was published, the existence of many more similar cases was revealed. In 2005 there had been some 18 cases in which children had been abused as a result of their having been considered to be possessed by an evil spirit or to be engaging in witchcraft against their accusers. This was nearly half the total number of cases studied by Stobart, who wrote that: 'even at the time of writing other cases are coming to light' (Stobart, 2006: 3).

---

[1]   The case was widely reported in the press. This account has been taken from *The Guardian*, 4 June 2005.

[2]   As Stobart reports (see Chapter 12 in this volume) the use of chilli pepper as punishment need not in itself entail beliefs that the child is a witch. Here it seems to have been ancillary to other physical means of exorcism.

[3]   Exorcism – Pentecostals use the term deliverance rather than the older 'exorcism'.

It seemed to be the general opinion that what was happening was that migrants from other countries had brought their traditional beliefs with them. There is, however, one major objection to this view. Traditional African beliefs in witchcraft did not usually associate children with the practice of witchcraft. They were victims, the vulnerable possessions of adults who might be attacked through them. In Bugisu, Uganda, where I worked in the 1950s, adults would have dismissed the idea of witchcraft by children, for they were not considered strong or knowledgeable enough to exercise such powers. This, as far as I know[4] was the pattern almost everywhere in Africa.

In 1970 the earliest anthropologist to describe child witches, Robert Brain, wrote of the Bangwa of Cameroon that children were accused of witchcraft and might confess to using it, giving the names of their victims (Brain, 1970). However, he also pointed out that 'most misfortunes are explained through the maleficence of *adult* witchcraft' (Brain, 1970: 162 my emphasis) and he cites some evidence that the beliefs in child-witches (Brain, 1970: 178) were new. Accusations against children were linked, by his informants as well as by Brain, with the changes following colonialism, and with the gradual disappearance of beliefs in children being set apart as 'children of the gods'. 'Children of the gods' were affected by the gods of the earth to which they yearned to return in death.[5] They had the power to return to the world of unborn children if they wished it strongly enough and their attachment to the earth was seen as fragile, so ritual treatment was required to keep them in the land of the living.

By contrast, 'children of the sky' were children supernaturally punished for the crime of witchcraft. Both were set apart from other children and were 'subject to mystical dangers that could only be removed through ritual' (Brain, 1970: 162). The witchcraft of the 'children of the sky' was only a part of traditional Bangwa witchcraft. It might be displayed in the child's illness or shown by autopsy after the child's death. Children might also be implicated in the confessions of other witches or their witchcraft might be detected by diviners. Their victims were usually close kin but confession and the appropriate ritual were believed to cure both the sinner and the afflicted.

Child witches might have been a new phenomenon in Bangwa, but they were 'everywhere'. 'Witchcraft accusations and exorcisms were ten a penny' (Brain, 1970: 178). One paramount chief called a meeting of experts to advise him on why this was so. Brain was also concerned to explain the increase and particularly the increase in accusations against children, by association with rapid social change (Brain, 1970: 177). He pointed out that although there had been a great deal of

---

[4]   Luena Pereira (forthcoming) tells me that she has found information that children believed to be witches were sold into slavery in the Kongo region during the nineteenth century. (Luena Pereira personal communication.)

[5]   Similar beliefs, about children with spiritual gifts and those with spirit doubles, sometimes seen as a twin who died, are common in West Africa. They are thought to yearn to return to the spirit world and must be placated or they will die in order to do so.

social and political change, there was no Christian mission in the area until the late 1960s. And, he remarked, missionaries appeared not to discourage the ideas of witch children as they did beliefs in 'children of the gods' (Brain, 1970: 178), which they classed as superstitious. On the other hand, wrote Brain, 'they are fascinated by witchcraft' (Brain, 1970: 179). One priest gave people holy water to protect them against witchcraft and another told of his having killed a witch that he found lurking round his house at night. Christianity might thus be presented as a weapon against evil that was conceptualised by the priest as a demon, but in popular thought personified as a witch. Thus the earliest mention of child witches is accompanied by the implication that they owe their perpetuation, if not their origin, to the syncretism of Christian and African belief.

Little further was published until 1980 when Geschiere recorded a 'new type of child-witchcraft' *mbati*, which appeared among the Maka of South Eastern Cameroon in the 1970s, lasting only two or three years. It was said to have been adopted from the North; according to Geschiere the Maka adopted ideas and beliefs from their neighbours and from Europeans with ease (Geschiere, 1980: 270). *Mbati* attacked only virgin boys and those in the cases described by Geschiere were probably in their early teens. As his title, 'Child Witches against the Authority of their Elders: Anthropology and History in the Analysis of Witchcraft beliefs of the Maka (Southeastern Cameroon)' indicated, Geschiere saw this as a symbolic rebellion against traditional authority. He argued that it should be compared to the witch-cleansing movements of central Africa whose members were also young. (The latter were however old enough to be characterised as men and were identifying, rather than claiming to be, witches.)

The Maka boys had been 'given' their witchcraft by an unnamed other and no mention was made of possessing demons. Like the Bangwa children, the Maka boys confessed to and elaborated on their wicked plans, claiming to be taking revenge on their parents for failure to feed them enough meat. Although the boys were not accused of causing specific harm that had led to their detection and did not confess to having harmed anyone in particular, the subsequent illness of the father of one boy led to the adults taking the matter seriously. Like the witchcraft that would later be linked to possession by the Devil or evil spirits, *mbati* required exorcism carried out by a specialist. This appears to have cured it. Geschiere concluded (1980: 283) that this was a symbolic rebellion made possible by the fact that the elders' authority had already been seriously undermined by the colonial regime and by the introduction of a money economy. Thus he did not consider it to be the effect of Christian missionary activity, but explained it as an epiphenomenon of colonialism.

Subsequent writing on the impact of Christianity on African religions (often referred to, inaccurately, in the singular) is largely agreed on its effects. To begin with, many missionaries, unlike those in Bangwa during Brain's field-work, denounced belief in witchcraft as pagan and as manifesting a lack of faith in the power of God. The majority of Africans found this hard to accept. As is amply demonstrated by a whole plethora of writers, African and non-African, over the course of time ideas about witchcraft were assimilated into ideas of the devil's work and, as Christianity offered no competing explanation of misfortune, beliefs in witchcraft survived. Among African Christians, witchcraft was established as the work of the devil, although Western missionaries might try to eradicate the belief.

A century or more later, with the rise of fundamentalist and particularly Pentecostal Christianity in the West at the end of the twentieth century, new Christian churches began proselytising in Africa (Meyer, 1999; Ellis and ter Haar, 2004). They were preoccupied with fighting evil and both missionaries and their converts believed in the existence of Satan, the prevalence of devils, his servants in promoting evil, and in the use of demonic powers to practise witchcraft. The African churches that sprang up under the influence of this fundamentalist Christianity, particularly the Pentecostal variety, naturally resembled Pentecostal churches in Britain and the US whose missions had inspired them. Many of these independent African churches now have congregations throughout the African diaspora, including London. Speaking in tongues, exorcism for possession by devils and belief in the power of witchcraft are characteristic of these African Independent churches. Moreover, their focus on success, measured in wealth and possessions as the mark of God's favour, included the belief that those who did not succeed were prevented from doing so by witchcraft. De Boeck is definite: 'Beyond any doubt the Pentecostal churches play a "crucial" role in the production of the figure of the witch' (de Boeck and Plissart, 2004: 173). There seems to be no obvious doctrinal origin in any of these forms of Christianity for the belief that *children* are particularly vulnerable to possession by the devil and thereby gaining witchcraft powers. There is no discussion of original sin in the large literature about the new African churches, nor mention of the frailties of children making them more likely to be possessed of demons or to exercise the powers of witches, unlike Bangladeshis who do think children are more vulnerable to possession by demons because of their weakness, as Dein notes in Chapter 6. Thus while the surge of accusations of witchcraft in Kinshasa and even in London can be explained by the rise of the new African Christianity and its preoccupation with the Devil, the problem remains: why children? Why was there this major change of target for witchcraft accusations?

The explanations I have cited imply that the accusations follow after a change in 'religious belief'. Two of them, Brain and de Boeck, refer to the syncretism that followed the introduction of Christianity into Africa, but interestingly there was no immediate increase in witchcraft accusations. The, unintended, preservation of beliefs in witchcraft by the initial missionary endeavour did not provoke a rash of new accusations, nor were children accused. Other factors were clearly needed before children would be accused, and in very large numbers.

In Geschiere's account it was the allegation of a child who claimed to have been frightened to join in that brought his peer's witchcraft to light. The accused children confessed to having accepted the offer to teach them *mbati*, a form of magical knowledge. The allegation was not taken seriously at first by the adults and none of the children were said to have been possessed by evil spirits or demons.

By contrast in Kinshasa, as in the two cases in London with which this account started, it is adults seeking the cause of misfortune in their own households who have identified children as harbouring demons who had inflicted suffering upon them out of malice. It is the link between possession by demons and the power to harm others that is characteristic of the new evil-doing. This must be distinguished from the other phenomenon that has appeared in multi-ethnic London, the belief in children's possession by evil spirits (see Dein, Chapter 6 in this volume).

Filip de Boeck, writing a generation after the first descriptions of child witches in Africa (de Boeck and Plissart, 2004; de Boeck, 2005 and Chapter 11 in this volume) argues that in central Africa there was a change in the whole concept of childhood. He attributed this to the results of violent upheavals in the area causing large numbers of deaths and displacement. In particular he emphasises the part played in this changed view by child soldiers, children who became diamond hunters and others who survived without adults. A report by Molina for the Save the Children Fund (Molina, n.d.) office in Kinshasa supports this view and both refer to thousands of children living on the street after having been rejected for being witches. While similar cases of rejected children do now occur elsewhere in Africa, the Democratic Republic of Congo (DRC) was the earliest recorded site of what might be called an epidemic of such accusations that spread through the Congo basin. The exact numbers of such children is uncertain but all estimates I have seen are in the thousands. It is unlikely to be coincidental that Child B and the people she lived with came from the Cabinda enclave which lies in this area. However, Victoria Climbié came from Ivory Coast and the latest severe epidemic of accusations of witchcraft against children has been reported in the delta region of Nigeria, in Akwa Ibom State. This area, like that of the Congo basin, inhabited by the poor and uneducated, has been devastated by rebellions, kidnappings and the uncertainties of political strife. It is reported, however, (Foxcroft, 2007) that the accusations stem from the influence of one particular pastor, Helen Ukpabio, founder of a Pentecostal church, who also makes religious videos. One of them in particular accuses children of responsibility for the sufferings of people in the region through their witchcraft and has been widely sold. A local charity that is struggling to look after children thrown out of their homes by parents who accuse them of witchcraft, holds her activities responsible for the witch hunt.

As de Boeck points out, the Christian Church involvement in the twenty-first-century phenomenon of child-witches goes beyond the mere provision of ideas which have been incorporated into the belief system of churches of African origin (de Boeck and Plissart, 2004). He and Molina make this clear. The pastors of African churches in Kinshasa can be seen to encourage accusations. They are asked to diagnose the cause of the child's condition, or to confirm suspicions; they also exorcise the devil responsible for the witchcraft. There is a suggestion that prophets obtain not only considerable material rewards, but the prestige of increasingly large congregations, by their successful exorcisms, so that it is clearly in their interest to identify children as witches. Splits in congregations have resulted in more leaders available for consultation. The epidemic could thus be said to be driven by competition among the leaders of the new churches (compare Gold, Chapter 5 in this volume). In sum, we have a background of changed concepts, both of evil and of children, activated by religious entrepreneurs who encourage the diagnosis of witchcraft in the households of those who are searching for an explanation of their misfortunes. Such a clustering of factors can be found elsewhere in Africa and throughout the African diaspora; so too are accusations against children.

Child Witches in the African Diaspora

The activities of African churches in diagnosing and treating child witches continue in the African diaspora. De Boeck recounts (de Boeck and Plissart, 2004: 163) how he first became interested in the phenomenon, not in the DRC, but in Belgium, where he came across a video of the cross-examination of three Congolese children, who were accused of being witches. Recent reports on the phenomenon in the UK (for the DfES published last year and for the Metropolitan Police[6]) make clear that there have been a number of cases over and above those that reach the newspapers. More are being reported all the time (see the abridged version of Stobart's report published as Chapter 12 in this volume).

The particular factors that seem to have been involved in the DRC in creating an evil image of children are obviously absent in London. Yet, while free of the effects of war, of epidemics and of fleeing from genocidal armed forces, migrants to London may still suffer anxiety, poverty and suffering. The need to find causes for failing to succeed even after having reached the promised land of a western city may sustain beliefs in child witches as a threat to the households in which they live. Once formulated, and accepted, the changed view of children was not so easily abandoned.

The main church associated with the detection and exorcism of child witches in Kinshasa, Combat Spirituelle, has branches in London and many adherents among the large Congolese community here. Eleanor Stobart's study, commissioned by the DfES mentions a 'significant cluster' (Stobart, 2006: 12) of cases from the DRC and the importance of the phenomenon in the community has been confirmed by other individuals I have talked to. However, the problem is not confined to recent migrants; a sizeable proportion of the children in the cases studied by Stobart for the DfES were born in the UK.

For reasons both geographical and social, it is not possible (yet) for young children to survive on the street in Britain as they do in Kinshasa, although a few teenagers may do so. Those concerned with the problem point out that the accused children form a very small proportion of all children who are abused in Britain (for example Stobart, 2006: 28; R. Pull, Report on Project Violet given as a paper

---

[6]   Unpublished but referred to by DI Robert Pull in a presentation at a conference organised by Inform in May 2005.

to Inform conference May 2006). There is only anecdotal evidence of one case in which children were kept on church premises until they were exorcised; nor are children forced onto the street, although in some cases the adults responsible for the child have been recorded as asking social services to take him or her into care. One charity formed to help neglected and deprived children admitted that some of them have been virtually driven from home as a consequence of being accused of witchcraft. Some children have been repatriated to be exorcised and some seem to have been abandoned there (see Stobart, Chapter 12, this volume). One pastor was said to have encouraged parents to send their child back to Kinshasa where he would be killed. Another child allegedly abandoned in Kinshasa has been publicised by Richard Hoskins, a free-lance researcher who has presented his findings on child-witches in the media (Hoskins, 2006). In general, however, the British problem is both less visible and much smaller than that in Kinshasa.

Street children in Kinshasa survive outside any domestic organisation and are subject to no parental or other authority, apart from occasional attacks on them by the police. To a large extent they can be said to be out of control and outside normal social life. It could be said that a similar problem exists in London. In recent years much attention has been paid by the media to British children who are beyond parental control and who take drugs, drink alcohol, truant from school, steal and vandalise their environment and indulge in shocking, often random, violence. Remarks about the break-down of society are made while the debate about how to get rid of the problem continues.

These highly visible anti-social children represent in an exaggerated, but all too credible form the fears of many immigrant parents about what will happen to their children in this country. They are said to be shocked at the extent of unbelief among British adults, and view the society into which they have come as immoral and as one in which children are ill-disciplined by their parents, who allow immoral behaviour in their children as well. The police seem unable to exercise any control. To these immigrants, British regulation of immigrant parents prevents their exercising the punishments they expect to use in order to control their children and bring them up 'properly'. The present National Society for the Prevention of Cruelty to Children (NSPCC) campaign to make smacking illegal is seen as depriving parents of their natural rights. If the children who are difficult to control are also not closely linked to the adults by ties of blood, their relationships with the adults are further jeopardised. They fear that their own children, who may go to schools with these evil children, will be contaminated and grow up like them. Even those who do not accuse their children of witchcraft may send them back to their country of origin, where they can be disciplined and avoid the influence of their British contemporaries. Others see their children growing up like their British age-mates and when there is conflict about their behaviour, parents are afraid that the children may even be possessed by demons.

Another finding in Kinshasa is mirrored in contemporary London and that is the existence in some African households (how many, no-one knows) of children who do not belong to its core family. They may be distant relatives, but often they are unrelated children who have been brought into Britain to help in housework or as baby-sitters, to attract child benefits or in some cases to be forced to work as prostitutes or in other illegal enterprises such as the growing of cannabis (*Missing Out*, report by End Child Prostitution, Child Pornography and the Trafficking of Children, ECPAT 2006). Child B, in the case with which this account started, was living with a distant female kinswoman who had brought her to this country. Victoria Climbié was killed by a distant 'aunt' (some say great-aunt) who had brought her from Ivory Coast. Stobart (2006) comments that '… it has become apparent that children including unaccompanied minors can travel internationally and nationally with considerable ease in a way that is very difficult to monitor. This lack of monitoring can increase their vulnerability.' (Stobart 2006: 25 and p. 168 this volume). These children will be the marginal members of the households in which they find themselves and like other survivors of displacement may well show the behavioural effects of their distress.

Possession by demons is not solely a Christian idea. However the beliefs in different religious systems are not identical. Some Pentecostal churches may believe in possession by demons but believe it to be confined to adults (see Gold, Chapter 5 this volume) while other religions believe in possession as a means of communication with the divine and induce it in their religious ceremonies (see C. Harrington, Chapter 8 and B. Schmidt, Chapter 7 in this volume). Some religious groups who do hold the idea of children being possessed by demons do not associate this with their becoming witches and harming others, but as the cause of sickness and failure to thrive. Dein (Chapter 6 this volume) makes clear that this is the case among Bangladeshis in east London. A social worker who has had some experience of such cases informed me that in Asian families generally children might be believed to be possessed by evil spirits, but they were not usually witches. Another case described to me as being a matter of child witches in fact concerned children said to be endangered by the witchcraft of their parents' enemies – a traditional African idea. The idea of children using witchcraft may be being promoted by religious leaders but little is known. There are said to be fewer prophets (who usually diagnose possession) in the diaspora churches but prophets from the country where the church originated may pay visits to Britain from time to time. However, during the writing of this article the Revd Tukala was acquitted of causing harm by accusing children of witchcraft, a conclusion hard to match with the video shown on television that recorded him doing so.

In Britain children who were accused often showed some disability as well as displaying signs of distress and neglect. Fourteen of those in the cases studied by Stobart showed one of a range of disabilities, physical mental and emotional; the children were also described as showing 'difficult behaviour', including being rebellious, disobedient or overly independent. Three however were described as 'exceptionally bright' and this may have been the reason they were difficult to control. Added to that, the households of immigrants, even those who have been here a number of years, are often under severe pressures: they may be waiting for papers and hence find it difficult to get jobs. The promise of migration is not fulfilled: expenses are higher than expected and incomes lower, so money is not being accumulated; the lack of success or the occurrence of illness add to the likelihood of a magical cause being sought.

Anthropological Explanation

The problem of explaining beliefs in witchcraft has been central to the anthropological endeavour for more than half a century. During that time, anthropologists have established that beliefs in witchcraft provide explanations for the uneven distribution of health, prosperity and good fortune and have tied these beliefs to the nature of social relationships, in particular the known and common propensity of human beings to suffer envy and jealousy of those more fortunate. Beliefs are activated within the context of human lives, by those who hope to improve their circumstances and by those with an interest in proving their power to make this happen. Individual circumstances are involved in transforming these general beliefs into specific accusations against named individuals. Moreover beliefs in witchcraft are not a substitute for other, mundane, explanations; witchcraft explains why misfortune happened to a particular person at a particular point in time, not how it happened. Crops must be well planted and tended to produce a good harvest; witchcraft explains why they fail to do so when all the technical requirements have been fulfilled. In the cities of Western Europe immigrants struggle to explain why they have not got their resident permits when others have; why they fail to land the good jobs that are available despite their best efforts; why their children behave badly and show no traditional respect for their elders.

Some anthropologists studied religious movements of witch-finders in Africa that occurred during the 1930s and 1940s (Redmayne, 1970; Richards, 1935; Willis, 1968) although they were rather few. More recently the interest of the present generation of scholars (Comaroff and Comaroff, 1993; Geschiere, 1997) has been attracted by the outbreak of witch-hunting in many parts of Africa (Ralushai, 1996). They have identified a variety of causes for the phenomenon from system change (the effects of colonialism to globalisation), religious change (Pentecostalism and the entrepreneurial activities of pastors of Independent African churches) and the break-down of traditional institutions. Yet most of them, with very few exceptions (de Boeck, 2004; Meyer, 1999) have described the accused as adults or at most adolescents.

That those accused of witchcraft should be children, rather than adults,[7] is a marked change that could not be adequately explained by the classic anthropological theories of African witchcraft. This recent phenomenon was both described and analysed by de Boeck's work in Kinshasa, in which the numbers of those accused and their fate was vividly presented. Subsequently Pereira (forthcoming) has

---

[7]   Filip de Boeck states that adults were also being accused in Kinshasa when he was doing his research (personal communication).

reported on a similar situation in northern Angola, whose peoples are of the same linguistic and cultural group as people in the adjacent DRC. The pattern there seems very similar in both places and indeed resembles the pattern of accusations in the delta region of Nigeria. By studying the situation in the African diaspora where some of the social features that de Boeck includes as explanatory factors also exist but others are missing, we can hope to refine the explanation further.

Equally, if not more important are the social problems involved. Both children and their carers suffer: the children may be abused, neglected and humiliated causing them long-term emotional damage even where they survive abusive exorcism; the adults suffer fear and the frustration that they are not supported by the society in which they live but must try to solve their problems by their own actions. When they take action against what they perceive as deadly evil, their host society defines their acts as illegitimate and punishes them. There are some recent cases in which immigrants attempt to manipulate the authorities' views by claiming that a spouse with whom they are in dispute has accused their children, or some of them, of witchcraft, thus hoping to mobilise the scepticism of the British majority in their favour. The exorcism of demons from children is likely to become more secret and less easily combated. The vicious circle is unlikely to be broken until we understand more and can offer more to both accusers and accused.

References

Brain, R. (1970). 'Child Witches', in M. Douglas (ed.), *Witchcraft Confessions and Accusations*. London: Tavistock Press.

De Boeck F. (2005). 'The Divine Seed: Children, Gift and Witchcraft in the Democratic Republic of Congo', in A. Honwana and F. de Boeck (eds), *Makers and Breakers. Children and Youth in Postcolonial Africa*. Oxford: James Currey.

—— (2004). 'On Being Shege in Kinshasa: Children, the Occult and the Street', in T. Trefon (ed.), *Reinventing Order in the Congo. How People Respond to State Failure in Kinshasa*. London: Zed Books.

—— and M-F. Plissart (2004). *Kinshasa: Tales of the Invisible City*. Ghent/Tervuren: Ludion/Royal Museum of Central Africa.

—— and M-F. Plissart (2003). 'Geographies of Exclusion: Churches and Childwitches in Kinshasa', *Beople: A Magazine About a Certain Belgium*, 6.

Comaroff, J. and J. Comaroff (1993). 'Introduction', in J. Comaroff and J. Comaroff (eds), *Modernity and its Malcontents: Ritual and Power in Postcolonial Africa*. Chicago: University of Chicago Press.

ECPAT (End Child Prostitution, Child Pornography and the Trafficking of Children) (2006). 'Missing Out', A Report on Child Trafficking in the North-East, the North-West and the West Midlands.

Ellis, S. and G. ter Haar (2004). *Worlds of Power: Religious Thought and Political Practice in Africa.* Hurst Series in Contemporary History, London: Hurst and Co.

Foxcroft, G. (2007). 'Supporting Victims of Witchcraft Abuse and Street Children in Nigeria'. Paper to Africans United Against Child Abuse (AFRUCA) Conference. Available online at: www.steppingstonesnigeria.org

Geschiere, P. (1980). 'Child Witches Against the Authority of their Elders: Anthropology and History in the Analysis of Witchcraft Beliefs of the Maka (Southeastern Cameroon)', in R. Schefold, J.W. Schoorl and J. Tennekes (eds), *Man, Meaning and History.* The Hague: Verhandelingen van het koninklijt Instituut voor Taal-Land-en Volkenkunde 89.

—— (1997). *The Modernity of Witchcraft: Politics and the Occult in Postcolonial Africa.* Charlottesville/London: University Press of Virginia.

Hoskins, R. (2006). 'Torment of Africa's "Child Witches"', *The Times*, 7 February.

Meyer, B. (1999). *Translating the Devil: Religion and Modernity Among the Ewe of Ghana.* Edinburgh: Edinburgh University Press.

Molina, J.A. (n.d). 'The Invention of Child Witches in the Democratic Republic of Congo. Social Cleansing, Religious Commerce and the Difficulties of Being a Parent in an Urban Culture'. Summary of the research and experiences of Save the Children's 2003-2005 programme funded by USAID.

Pereira, L.N. (forthcoming). 'Families, Churches, the State and the Child-Witch in Angola', in Luis N. Pares and Roger Sansi (eds), *Sorcery in the Black Atlantic.* Chicago: Chicago University Press.

Pull, R. (2006). Paper on 'Project Violet' to Inform conference, May 2006.

Ralushai, N.V. (1996). *Report of the Commission of Inquiry into Witchcraft, Violence and Ritual Murders in the Northern Province of the Republic of South Africa.* Unpublished ms.

Redmayne, A. (1970). 'Chikanga: An African Diviner with an International Reputation', in M. Douglas (ed.), *Witchcraft Confessions and Accusations.* London: Tavistock.

Richards, A.I. (1935). 'A Modern Movement of Witchfinders', *Africa*, 8: 4.

Stobart, E. (2006). 'Child Abuse Linked to Accusations of "Possession" and "Witchcraft"'. London: Department for Education and Skills Research Report RR 750. Available online at: http://www.dcsf.gov.uk/research/programmeofresearch/projectinformation.cfm?projectid=14953&resultspage=1

Willis, R. (1968). 'Kamcape: An Anti-Sorcery Movement in South-West Tanzania', *Africa*, 38: 1.

Chapter 11

At Risk, as Risk: Abandonment and Care in a World of Spiritual Insecurity

Filip de Boeck

This chapter focuses on the production of child witches in the Democratic Republic of Congo (DRC). After a brief description of the phenomenon as it occurs today in the capital, Kinshasa, I will try to analyse this phenomenon by looking at the intricacies of intergenerational relationships in the DRC's contemporary urban scene. Rather than describing children as mere victims of irresponsible parents, elders and other figures of authority such as preachers (belonging to the so-called 'churches of awakening', often of neo-Pentecostalist persuasion), who relegate them to new zones of seclusion and social abandonment, I will try to outline the specific forms of social and spiritual insecurity to which both children and adults are exposed, and which have thoroughly transformed family life and the shape of networks of care. The emerging picture is one of highly complex intergenerational interactions unfolding within Congolese cities, as well as in their various diasporas, and forcing us to reconsider standard notions of agency and victimhood. I will end this chapter by briefly discussing the responses of local and international Non-Governmental Organisations (NGOs) to the phenomenon of 'child witches'.

Introduction: The Production of Child Witches in Kinshasa[1]

Increasingly, street children are a part of the urban fabric of Kinshasa, the capital of the DRC. Referred to as *moineaux* (swallows), *phaseurs* or *bashege*,[2] their presence used to be restricted to the more important traffic arteries and public spaces of Gombe, also referred to as La Ville, the former white colonial heart of the city where embassy personnel and other expatriates still mostly live today. In recent years, however, street children have become a familiar part of street life everywhere in this vast city. Rather nomadic in their existence, they try to survive in the streets and markets of the city, and periodically retreat to their shacks and cardboard boxes (referred to as *baguesta*, 'guesthouses') around the main football stadium, under bridges, along the railroad tracks, near rivers, and in the numerous cemeteries of the city.

According to various statistics, Congo's capital currently 'houses' between 20,000 and 50,000 street children, many of them so-called 'witch-children' (Lingala: *bana bandoki*). Forced to take to the street after family members and relatives or neighbours accuse them of practising witchcraft, they are blamed for everything that goes wrong within the family, from common misfortunes, the loss of one's job or the break up of one's marriage, to illnesses or deaths. Children, sometimes as young as two or three, are generally believed to be the sources of

---

[1]   Trained as an anthropologist, I have worked in both rural and urban environments in Southwest Congo and Kinshasa since 1987. In 1994, I became interested in the phenomenon of child witchcraft, both in the Congolese diaspora context in Belgium and in Congo itself. I have continued to follow and analyse the growth of that phenomenon ever since. I published extensively on the phenomenon of child witches in a number of books and journals (see de Boeck, 2000, 2004, 2005; de Boeck and Plissart, 2004), and also co-curated an exhibition, *Kinshasa: The Imaginary City*, for the Nineth International Architecture Biennial in Venice, 2004, in which the stories of accused children figured prominently. In my most recent work, an ongoing ethnography of several cemeteries in Kinshasa, I document the ways in which the management of death in Kinshasa increasingly seems to have become the prerogative of children and youngsters (de Boeck, 2006). In 2005, I was also asked to prepare an expert report on behalf of Sita Kisanga, a 35-year-old woman who was tried in the Old Bailey in London for conspiracy to murder and several counts of child cruelty in 2003. The victim was an eight-year-old girl whom Sita and the girl's aunt suspected of being a witch. The court case received a lot of media attention, both in the UK and internationally. See BBC report, 'Girl Tortured "for Being a Witch"'. 9 May 2005. [Online]. Available at: http://news.bbc.co.uk/1/hi/england/london/4530197.stm [accessed: 10 September 2009].

[2]   Originally a derogatory Hausa term, used to denote a bastard child, or someone without roots or established origin, the word *shege* was adopted in Kinshasa in the 1990s. Local popular folk etymologies link it to Shengen, the little town in Luxemburg where a treaty was signed to abolish Europe's internal frontiers. Not without humour, street children call the street their Shengen, a world without borders where one can enjoy the fruits of globalisation. The slang term 'phaseur' can be glossed as a person who is cool, has street cred and is a trendy dresser.

maladies such as madness, cancer, heart attacks and AIDS. In some cases, young girls have been accused of transforming themselves into stunningly beautiful women who lure their fathers and uncles into bed to snatch away their testicles or penis, and cause their impotence or even death.

A thoroughly modern and primarily urban phenomenon which has little in common with longstanding notions of witchcraft as they continue to exist in more rural areas, this new form of witchcraft transcends rank and class, and is not limited to any particular ethnic group. Believers in witch-children distinguish between the embodied form these children take in the 'first world' (or waking world of daily reality), and the more sinister form they assume in the spectral 'second world' where they are capable of giving birth to other children – their offspring also become witch-children and roam the streets of Kinshasa. It is believed that witch-children are able to transform themselves into mystic serpents, crocodiles or Mami Wata sirens.

It is very common for witchcraft accusations involving children to result in violence. As a consequence of emerging suspicions and accusations, children are often severely beaten, and in some extreme, though by no means isolated, cases, even killed. Most often, though, suspected child witches are taken to an *église de réveil*, church of awakening, sometimes also referred to as a miracle church, by the adults who are responsible for them. There the preacher engages in a diagnostic procedure during a private consultation, in order to identify the children as possible witches. A number of churches in Kinshasa have made the exorcism of child witches their speciality. It is important to note, though, that in most circumstances, church leaders themselves are most often not the source of witchcraft allegations against children. Taking on what would formerly have been the role of a diviner, preachers merely confirm (and thereby legitimise) accusations and suspicions which already exist within the child's family environment or neighbourhood. In doing so, they help to relocate and reformulate the (sometimes extreme) physical and psychological violence accused children undergo in their family. Their diagnosis (often referred to as 'prayer control') turns the already existing allegations into an official diagnosis and by that fact offers an alternative solution to the problem, proposing the church as a therapeutic 'healing' space. Removing children from the (often abusive) family environment in which they are accused, they are taken in by the church. Here, children usually face a period of seclusion and quarantine, either individually or collectively with other 'child witches'. During their seclusion, the children are subjected to a period of fasting and ritual purification. The administration of laxatives and emetics aims at cleansing the witch-children's bodies from the meat of the victims that they supposedly ate. During that period, which may last a couple of days but sometimes also weeks or even months, the children are urged to confess the number of victims they have bewitched or 'eaten'. Undigested pieces of meat or bone, but also objects of all kinds which are found in the children's vomit and faeces will be used as corroborants during their public confession before the assembled members of the church. The children are regularly subjected to interrogations. During these interrogations, and in collaboration with the leaders of the church, the children will slowly construct a narrative about how they became witches. This narrative will then be presented to the church community during masses and collective prayer meetings, where children are urged to make a public confession and reveal their true nature as witches. Usually, the structure and content of such a narrative is very standardised and stereotypical. It relates the descent into the second world, usually starting with the child receiving a gift from an adult during the day (very often not a member of the child's family, and very often a woman). At night, however, this person returns to demand a counter-gift in the form of human meat. From then on, the child is drawn into the world of the occult and will start killing people. I will comment upon the meaning of these stories below.

Following the crucial moment of public confession (*témoignage*), the church community will then engage in subsequent prayer meetings, rituals of deliverance (*délivrance*) and 'soul-healing' (*cure d'âme*) to untie the knots that link the child to the forces of evil, the devil and everything that is considered as belonging to Satan's realm (and for these churches that includes the autochthonous moral frameworks that refer to the world of the ancestors and to 'local tradition'). The child will be exposed to collective prayers in order to exorcise or deliver it from the powers of darkness that hold it in their grip. These prayer meetings may last for weeks and take place on set intervals throughout the week. Such forms of ritualised exorcism are often carried out under the guidance of female church members known as *intercesseuses* (intercessors). The child is placed in the middle of a prayer circle while the women participants regularly lapse into glossolalia (speaking in tongues), a sign of the Holy Spirit's presence. Usually, one woman takes the lead in prayer, while the others sustain her by regularly punctuating her preaching and her laying on of hands with religious songs and hymns. Depending on the type of church, these sessions unfold in collaboration with the child's mother or some relatives, in the hope of facilitating a reintegration of the cleansed witch-child within its family. In many cases, though, parents are not very collaborative, and such reintegration often remains problematic: the child's parents and other members of the kin-group often remain too afraid to accept children accused of witchcraft back into their midst. It is usually in those all too frequent cases that young children are forced to take to the street in the end.

The Portrayal of Child Witches in the Media

The creation of new 'zones of social abandonment' (Biehl, 2005) through the production of child witches is not restricted to Kinshasa alone. Over the past two decades the notion of child witchcraft has spread across Congo and indeed Africa and beyond, on a scale that is unprecedented. Most of the time, the occurrence of child witchcraft seems to be linked to Congolese (and increasingly also Angolan)[3] diasporas in Africa and Europe, often connected to the existence of Pentecostalist communities or other types of churches within the new brand of Christian fundamentalism, which currently flourishes in Africa and in its various global diasporic movements. Because of their increasing visibility, child-witches in Kinshasa and elsewhere have received a lot of attention from the media.[4] Similarly, child witches have become the focus of a growing humanitarian market. In recent years, local and international NGOs, the most active of which has no doubt been Save the Children, as well as an increasing number of other relief organisations and international institutions such as the Red Cross, Amnesty International, Human Rights Watch, United Nations Children's Fund (UNICEF), United States Agency for International Development (USAID) or MONUC (the UN mission in the DRC), have placed the plight of child witches in Congo and in diaspora contexts in Europe on their agenda.[5] Similarly, the existence of child witches in Congo has attracted a great deal of attention from photographers and documentary film makers. To my knowledge documentary films of Belgian, Dutch, Canadian, French and American origin have already been made on the subject in the past

---

[3]   There have been some recent reports of similar outbreaks in the Delta area of Nigeria (Foxcroft, 2007). [Ed.]

[4]   See for some examples of recent press releases: Barthélémy Bosongo, 'Les "enfants sorciers", bouc émissaire de la misère à Kinshasa' (*Agence France Presse*, 13 October 1999) During the same period BBC2 *Newsnight* devoted a whole programme to the phenomenon of child-witches in Kinshasa (12 November 1999). In March 2000, APA (*Agence Presse Associée*) also issued a report on mass exorcisms of children in Kinshasa. See also the Dutch *NRC Handelsblad*, 24 March 2000: 'Mothers in Congo Give Birth to "Witches"'; the BBC's Mark Dummet's report from 17 January 2003: 'DR Congo's Unhappy Child "Witches"'; an article by Christophe Boulierac on the MONUC website, 18 November 2003: 'The Bad Fate of So-Called Child Witches in DRC' (*Le mauvais sort des enfants dit sorciers en RDC*); See also *The Scotsman*, 26 January 2003: '"Bewitched" Children are Forced to Bear Curse of Congo'; James Astill, *The Observer*, 11 May 2003: 'DRC Casts Out its "Child Witches"'; Julie-Ann Davies, *The New Humanist*, 1 March 2004: 'Witch-Hunt. Julie-Ann Davies on the Torture of the Congo's Child "Sorcerers"'. Reuters, 4 October 2006: '"Sorcerers" Swell Ranks of Congo Street Children', a report also used by CNN, 4 October 2006: 'Congo Orphans Accused of Sorcery, Cast into Mean Streets'; *The Times*, 21 November 2006: 'DRC: Children's Lives Torn by Accusations of Witchcraft' (an article re-issued by the Child Rights Information Network (CRIN); Afrol News/IRIN, 25 March 2007: '"Witchcraft" an Excuse for Child Abuse in Angola'; Muriel Devey, *Afriqu'Echos*, 11 April 2007: 'Child Witches: When "Awakening" Turns into a Nightmare' (*Enfants sorciers: quand le 'réveil' devient cauchemar*). A longer journalist's account of the plight of child witches in Congo is D'Haeyer, 2004. High profile court cases involving children accused of witchcraft in the UK and Europe have also received a lot of attention from the media (see footnote 1).

[5]   Aguilar Molina, n.d.; Human Rights Watch, 2006; Stobart, 2006. See also an unpublished preliminary report by Ekholm Friedman and Biluka Nsakala Nenga (2002) on the situation regarding child witches in Angola.

few years, while many more are being finalised as I write, amongst others by the Canadian Broadcasting Corporation.[6] Child witches in Congo and elsewhere have also become a theme that captures the fancy of playwrights and novelists.[7]

Some of these news stories, reports, novels and documentary films try to contextualise the phenomenon of child witches in terms of local understandings, practices and discourses concerning the world of the occult. In fact, my own anthropological analyses of child witchcraft in the DRC have been frequently used and referred to.[8] Yet, for most journalists or development workers child witchcraft remains an issue that is extremely hard to place and understand. In itself, witchcraft is already a very complex and tricky topic, difficult to de-exoticise and contextualise correctly, let alone fully comprehend. In combination with the figure of the child, the subject easily turns into an explosive cocktail, often leading to interpretations in which both fascination and moral indignation fight with each other to get the upper hand.

---

[6]   See for example the documentary film by Elisabeth Burdot and Edith van Hove (2004), *La nouvelle stratégie du diable*. See also the texts and photographs on Congolese child witches by Marco Trovato, an Italian photographer and freelance journalist, or an interview with filmmaker Angela Nicoara (from Internews-Rwanda), 'The So-Called Child Witch: The Creation of a Local Human Rights Story in the Democratic Republic of Congo' on the website of the Brandeis University International Center for Ethics, Justice and Public Life (15 September 2005).

[7]   See for example Cameroonian writer Léonora Miano's recent novel *Contours du jour qui vient* (2006), in which the main protagonist is a young girl, Musango, accused of witchcraft. Miano's novel directly draws from the Congolese context, whereas another recent novel by Nigerian novelist Helen Oyeyemi, *The Icarus Girl* (2005) links children to the world of the occult in the Nigerian context, as did Ben Okri's acclaimed novel *The Famished Road*. In 2007, Roland Mahauden, director of the *Théâtre de poche* in Brussels, toured in Congo with a play called *Un enfant n'est pas sorcier*. Similarly, Amsterdam based director and actor Guido Cleene and his theatre group, Compagnie Dakar, went to interview child witches in Kinshasa in 2006. He is currently working on a theatre play dealing with the subject of child witchcraft and organised a number of public debates on the subject in *De Balie*, a well known cultural centre in Amsterdam.

[8]   Anthropologists often complain that their work is not taken into account by decision makers and development organisations or that it does not impact enough on the way in which the media report on local realities. In my experience, however, media and policy makers often try hard to find more information and use anthropological insights. In my opinion, anthropologists, myself included, have often been too timid or reluctant to share their information or frame it in such a way that it can make a difference. Often also, the social and cultural realities under scrutiny are so complex that knowledge about them eludes simple conclusions and cannot readily be turned into strategies for action.

Accusations of Child Witchcraft as a Response to Poverty?

Many of the above-mentioned reports seem to start from the presumption that accusations of witchcraft targeting children are related to *poverty*. Indeed, Kinshasa has lived through difficult years, due to the continuing economic crisis and years of war and political violence which. Even as I write (March 2007), Kinshasa is undergoing another urban war (between militias loyal to former presidential candidate Jean-Pierre Bemba and the government troops of Joseph Kabila) which caused the death of hundreds of people, most of them civilians. Needless to say, the unstable political context has greatly impacted on life in the city. More generally, there is a widespread feeling that the city, and indeed the country as a whole, is being dragged into an unending downward spiral, condemning the urban dwellers to levels of poverty and hardship hitherto unknown.[9] 'We have started to live like animals' (*tokomi kovivre lokola banyama*) is an often heard remark in the streets of Kinshasa. In such a context, in which parents have a hard time to feed their children properly, accusing one's children of being witches indeed seems to offer a possibility to get rid of excess mouths and stomachs. In this interpretation, witchcraft accusations become a form of *a posteriori* birth control.

I have no doubt that poverty enhances the problem of child witchcraft. Yet the emergence of the phenomenon cannot be limited to that factor alone. Many of the children whom I interviewed in churches were from families that were indeed very poor, but others were rather well off, including children of university professors, high-ranking government officials, and even ministers.

Similarly, the occurrence of the same phenomenon in Congolese diaspora contexts in Europe, for example, where for many life is often more relaxed, economically speaking, seems to indicate that poverty alone is not a sufficient explanation. This reminds me of an incident a couple of years ago, while I was interviewing children accused of witchcraft in the compound of a prayer group on Kabambare, a main road in one of Kinshasa's older neighbourhoods. In this compound some 30 children were awaiting exorcism. They all lived together in a tiny little room, filling their time with praying, sleeping and waiting. Amongst the children one girl in particular drew my attention because she did not seem to speak or understand Lingala. Her name was Ginette and she was 12 years old.[10] For three weeks she had been waiting for her father to come and pick her up. She had lived all of her life in Paris, where she grew up in a Congolese household. After the death of her mother, her father remarried. The stepmother had started to spread the rumour that the girl was a witch and made it clear to her husband that she would leave if he did not do something about it. The father decided to buy two Air France

---

[9]   Contradicting these widespread feelings of ever increasing poverty, recent analyses by economists seem to suggest, rather surprisingly, that the economic capacity of most Kinois (residents of Kinshasa) has not significantly altered over the past decade or so – see de Herdt (2004).

[10]   I have changed all names throughout this chapter.

tickets and travel to Kinshasa with his daughter. There he brought her to the church
where I found her. According to the preacher, the father had abandoned his child
there and had already returned to Paris, unknown to the child.

Incidents like these clearly illustrate that material insecurity is often not the
sole driving factor behind witchcraft accusations against children, but that there
are also other elements related to more complex forms of *social* and *spiritual*
insecurity that may explain why children are seen as witches.

Accusations of Child Witchcraft as a Response to New Forms of Social Insecurity: Redefining Networks of Kin and Care

One dominant factor is constituted by the changes that have started to occur within
the landscape of family and lineage. These changes are more pronounced within
the urban environment. It is a fact that many of the children that are singled out
as witches already occupy a structurally weak position within the family in which
they live, either because they are orphans, or because they are growing up with
their grandparents, aunts, uncles, a co-wife of their mother's or other classificatory
or more distant relatives, rather than with their own parents. This in itself makes
the position of these children more vulnerable.

The increasing number of children who are 'displaced' within the physical
and mental maps that constitute the landscapes of kinship in the city indicates
that family structures themselves are undergoing increasing pressure. Labour
migration, war, AIDS and other factors have contributed to the fact that families
are increasingly disrupted entities.

The specific character of new forms of polygamy which exist in the urban
context as well as in the diaspora have added to this. These arrangements have very
little in common with the highly regulated polygamy as it existed and continues
to exist in more rural communities, where co-wives live in the same compound
as their husband, where social control is much greater and where the choice of
and access to marriage partners is much more regulated. In Kinshasa, however,
it frequently happens that co-wives do not even know of each other's existence,
for they may be located and housed in different neighbourhoods of the city. When
one of the co-wives dies, for example, her children will end up in the household
of one of her 'rivals' (*mbanda*). As one can well imagine, this may cause a lot of
conflicts. Indeed, as in the example of Ginette, the 'stepmother' (*marâtre*) often
seems to be a key figure in the production of accusations of child witchcraft. In this
respect, one should also note that women (mothers, grandmothers, aunts) are more
often than men accused by children as being the instigators of children's initiation
into the world of the occult. This in itself is indicative of the changing perception
and status of women in the urban field, a change which is linked to the new social
and economic position of women in the urban context. Here the authority of male
elders and heads of household has gradually been eroded, and women have often

become the main providers of income, a process that is even more pronounced in the setting of the diaspora.

The existence of specific forms of urban polygamy is not the only factor altering networks of care and rendering the position and movement of children more problematic. The changing nature of marriage itself is also partly responsible for the new status and significance attributed to children. Paradoxically, while some Kinois are capable of investing in more or less formalised polygamous relationships, an increasing number of young people are confronted with the impossibility of ever marrying. Indeed, for many youngsters it has become financially impossible to accumulate the bridewealth necessary to conclude an officially recognised marriage.[11] Condemned to the status of eternal youth, many men resort to what is known as a 'short-circuit marriage', and set up a household with their girlfriends without the consent of her family members. More often than not, this short-circuiting of the cycle of gifts and counter-gifts between wife-givers and wife-takers leads to disputes between the two groups concerned, and often the liaison itself proves to be short lived. All of this impacts on the position of the children such a union might produce, as well as on the more general nature of social relations in the urban context. In the end, children often seem to have become a burden, rather than the social and symbolic capital which they tended once to represent in the Central African socio-cultural configuration.

More generally, it is clear that in Kinshasa today there is a widespread tendency to redefine the very notions of kin and family, narrowing them down to the members of the nuclear family. This is a process to which the charismatic churches have contributed to an important extent. Formerly, one belonged to an extended kin group, which functioned as a wide-ranging network of solidarity. Today, in many of the new charismatic churches and prayer movements, the members of the extended family are almost invariably labelled as *bandoki*, witches. In fact, the churches' attacks on extended family relations focus on the gift obligations which underpin these larger kin-based solidarity networks. To underline their argument, church leaders refer to the Bible passage in which it is stated that one should earn a living and work 'by the sweat of your brow', that is, through one's own effort. In the past, those family members who came to ask a relative for food, shelter, money and other forms of support, were fully entitled to do so in the open gift logic of kin-based solidarity and reciprocity that has always been so characteristic of the social architecture throughout Central Africa. Indeed, refusing such a request constituted an insult and could lead to a legitimate witchcraft attack. In these Central African worlds, also, the vocabulary of kinship has always been used in much more encompassing ways as a metaphor for opening up

---

[11]   Marriage means a threefold financial sacrifice, for one ideally should organise a traditional wedding (*coutumièrement*), as well as contract a legal marriage (for the state administration), and a religious marriage (with one's preacher and church community). Each of these marriages involves huge costs, and people often only manage to conclude the three marriages over a period of many years.

kin-based networks. By redefining strangers and outsiders as kin, for example, gift cycles were widened and new levels of trust summoned. In this way a political economy of gift exchange in the form of tributes between real, putative or fictive kin has always formed one of the most important organisational modes to create, enable, maintain and broaden the network of political relations. Tributary relations institutionalised the personal sphere and personalised the institutional level.

The new regimes of knowledge that are currently being installed in the urban context introduce a radical break with these longstanding moralities of transmission and exchange. In these new religious arenas, which to a great extent pervade and shape the public sphere in the urban realm, the open social field of relations, constantly generated and renewed through the flow of gifts and transactions, is increasingly becoming more closed. Basically, all those who fall outside the scope of the nuclear family are now being denied the right to enter into such gift relations. What this means in practice is that they are not only being labelled as evil witches when they attempt to do so, but also that, as witches, they are redefined as non-kin.

In summary, Kinshasa is currently witnessing a total breach with older concepts regarding both the morality of gift exchange and the delineation of the relationships between kin and non-kin, inside and outside, or endogamous and exogamous. The redefining of networks of kin, and therefore of care, greatly impacts on the way in which children are circulated between families and relatives within kin groups, and it drastically transforms the relationships through which child circulation is negotiated. This is even more the case in migratory and diaspora contexts.[12]

Spiritual Insecurity and the Transformations of Notions of Witchcraft and Gift

This reconfiguration also transforms the very notion of witchcraft itself. It is important to underline once more that the realities referred to as 'witchcraft' (*kindoki*) in urban Congo have very little in common with older forms of witchcraft and their mechanisms of attack and accusation. Reflecting the new social and moral grounds around which the urban world constructs itself, the phenomenon of 'child witches' is a thoroughly modern phenomenon that is shaped, amongst other things, by the specific forms of a global capitalism that increasingly impacts on the ways in which lives are lived locally. Unlike more traditional patterns of witchcraft, for example, where the witch always was a family member, or someone from within one's own social world, the new forms of witchcraft in the urban context are no longer seen as restricting themselves to such inner social realm. Not only, as I outlined above, has the circle of kinship become much smaller through the restricting redefinition of lineage and clan relations propagated by the churches, but the outside world is also increasingly, and often in very brutal ways, penetrating the intimate circle of

---

[12]   For a comparative example on transnational networks of care see Oien, 2006. The article focuses on Angolan children in Portugal.

the nuclear family. Contrary to older forms of witchcraft, therefore, the witchcraft 'new style' is experienced as being wild, random and unpredictable. The threat of witchcraft and the dangerous possibility of being harmed are always there, perhaps even more so in the urban context, but the reason why one is attacked is no longer clear. In more traditional forms of witchcraft, the witch will never attack one just for the fun of it. Whether meant to be a punishment or revenge, the attack always has a clear purpose, and there always seemed to be a good reason to justify such an attack. Today, however, it is no longer because one has not respected certain rules or norms, or has not fulfilled certain obligations towards family members, that one may be attacked. Witchcraft in the urban context does no longer need such a specific reason to set itself in motion. It is without specific direction or intention. This unpredictability has also greatly affected local concepts of the causation of disease and has drastically altered older explanatory and diagnostic frameworks. Because the possible sources of witchcraft are oftentimes disconnected from kinship relations, the danger may now come from anywhere. One runs the risk of becoming bewitched for no apparent reason in public places like markets and shops, and through relations with unrelated or anonymous people, as is attested by the narratives which children construct about how they entered the world of the night.

In addition, the nature of the gift itself has dramatically changed in the urban context. It no longer is what it appears to be. Underneath the visible gift lurks another invisible pattern which corrupts regular patterns of exchange. In the urban realm what poses as gift actually creates a debt obligation. More important, the receiver of the gift does not even realise that he is actually contracting a debt and engaging in a relation of a totally different nature: that of a nocturnal capitalism, with all that this entails: debts, unstable prices, interest rates, and laws of supply and demand.

In this sense, children's narratives about how they became a witch may be read as commentaries on how urban dwellers in Congo experience and interpret the switch from a gift-based social world to a market driven, 'modern' capitalist environment, a dangerous passage that puts older social rules and structures under a lot of strain (changing gender relations, the breakdown of masculine structures of authority and of gerontocracy, new labour divisions, the breakdown of marriage and the transformed nature of the circulation of women, the drastic restructuring of kinship models and the transformed nature of the circulation of children within networks of care, the disconnection between kinship and witchcraft).

Not surprisingly all of these factors also produce a great deal of anxiety and, what Ashforth in a recent book on emerging patterns of witchcraft in Soweto has termed, 'spiritual insecurity' (Ashforth, 2005). This insecurity is illustrated in the fact that, for a growing number of people, the realities of city life are increasingly hard to decipher and comprehend. The shifting boundaries between insiders and outsiders, between life and death, between the dimensions of everyday reality and an underlying world of the occult, or between the day and the night, have provoked a profound interpretive crisis. For most people in the city it has become difficult to read and understand the meanings generated by the social life forms currently emerging. A word that is constantly used in current parlance to evoke this sense of the uncanny is *mystique*. Things, people and social transactions are increasingly described as being 'mystical', meaning that it has become increasingly hard to place and understand them. The general feeling is that what you see is not what really counts the most, as if there are constantly other, more hidden and invisible, forces at work which complicate and impact upon the daily life of most citizens within the urban environment.

The Impact of Social and Spiritual Insecurity on Children and Adults as Social Categories

In order to understand how it is possible that the phenomenon of child witchcraft has taken on such an important dimension in the urban locale it is therefore necessary to look more carefully at the new forms of social and spiritual insecurity that city life has engendered. The restructuring of kinship relations and forms of alliance, in combination with the crisis of the gift and the passage to a modernity defined by a monetary logic, has generated new uncertainties, as well as new human geographies of inclusion and exclusion that deeply affect the position of both children and adults.

To begin with, let us consider the role and place of children themselves. In a seminal book on children and the politics of culture, Sharon Stephens outlined the ways in which the Western spaces of childhood seem to be increasingly threatened, invaded and polluted by adult worlds (Stephens, 1995: 8ff). Hand in hand with the notion of children at risk, however, is also the growing fear of and anger at children. Stephens's twofold interpretation of children *at* and *as* risk is very useful to describe what is currently happening in Kinshasa.

Confronted with the daily realities of a city such as Kinshasa it does not take a great deal of imagination to discover why children are at risk. As Non-Governmental Organisations (NGOs) and human rights activists constantly remind us, they are often reduced to the status of victims requiring help due to the political, socio-economic, psychological and sexual violence that pervades Congo today. To deny the realities that correspond to this general victimising discourse with regard to children would be very short-sighted. Yet, children, especially in the often extreme living conditions in which they grow up in the African context, are not only vulnerable and passive victims, *subjected* to, or 'made and broken' by the contexts in which they live, but they are also active *subjects*, 'makers and breakers', of that reality (de Boeck and Honwana, 2005). Children in these societal contexts often have the capacity to act strongly on the worlds in which they live, in both positive and negative ways. In line with more local notions of agency, children and youngsters are often not regarded, nor do they regard themselves, as future or proto adults in need of protection, but as social actors in the present with a marked role and presence in the very heart of the societal context, and fully responsible for their own actions.

On the one hand, then, children in Kinshasa are increasingly relegated to sites of exclusion (chased onto the street, expelled from the kin group, secluded in churches, or rounded up by the government and sent to re-education camps[13]). On the other hand, however, children have never before been so prominently present in the urban public space, where they have increasingly been perceived as constituting a risk for the rest of society. There is, of course, the inescapable demographic fact that over half of Kinshasa's population is under the age of 20. In sheer numbers alone, the young have become very visible and as such, they are increasingly determining not only the city's public space but also its public sphere, in military as well as political, social, cultural and economic terms.

In particular, children have come to represent the very real and violent power 'from the barrel of the gun'. In 1997, when child soldiers made their entry in Kinshasa as Laurent Kabila seized power, this was a totally new and rather shocking fact for most of the capital's inhabitants. Since then, street children have been playing an increasingly prominent role in shaping and (re)defining political events in the capital and throughout the country. That became very clear in the 2006 electoral process during which *bashege* switched their allegiance from Kabila towards his opponent Bemba, and actively participated in the heavy fighting that broke out between the two rivals in downtown Kinshasa in August 2006. In the recent urban war of March 2007 street children were prominently present again.

More generally, street children are increasingly defying the authority of parents, elders, preachers and politicians. Some years ago, after a street child was killed in an incident with local policemen on Kinshasa's Central Market, *bashege* started a riot and gained total control over the city's main market. Only after the city governor agreed to come over to negotiate in person with these children were they willing to leave the market (and only after they were promised a free concert by Werrason, a popular musician). Similarly, in a 2004 documentary film on child witches (by Burdot and van Hove, see footnote 6), the spectator can witness how children accused of witchcraft and placed in seclusion in a church compound, threaten to bewitch and kill the Minister of Social Affairs during a visit he pays to the church after alarming reports on the children's situation. Other changes also indicate to what extent intergenerational relationships have changed over the past few years. A drastic transformation of existing structures of authority and gerontocracy is operated through new cultural forms of managing death. Funerals have not only become a means for political contestation by children and youngsters but, in a much broader sense, death has also become an occasion for these youngsters to criticise and defy the role of parents and elders, whom they accuse of not fulfilling their role properly. It is common to hear children and youngsters say that their

---

[13]   See for example the BBC report by Arnaud Zajtman, 24 September 2006: 'DR Congo Children Held After Riot'. Also see *Congo Indépendant*, 25 September 2006: 'Kinshasa Police Hunts Down Street Children' (*La police kinoise fait la chasse aux 'Shégués'*).

elders have *démissioné*, (retired) have abandoned whatever responsibility they have towards their offspring, or that elders behave selfishly and fail to work for the betterment of all of those placed under their authority. This aspect of contestation of the elders' authority is most poignantly expressed when a young person dies. Inevitably, his parents and elders will be accused of having 'eaten', that is killed, the victim by means of witchcraft. In such a case the funeral and mourning rituals almost invariably turn into 'disorder' and become an intergenerational battlefield. The young 'people of disorder' (*bato ya désordre*) will attack the deceased's parental home (frequently destroying it or burning it down), and they will also chase away or physically harm the parents, aunts, uncles and preachers gathered there to mourn the deceased. Frequently, it is only after completion of the burial that the responsibility for the dead person is handed over again to his family, and only after long negotiations (de Boeck, 2006).

All these elements point to the changing position that children and youth occupy in the contemporary urban context. Economically as well, young adolescents occupy a more central position than ever before. For the past two decades numerous youngsters have been participating in the diamond rush in the Angolan province of Lunda Norte. Upon their return, these youngsters have often acquired a financial power that exceeds that of their parents by far. Together with youth's (instantaneous though often not long-lasting) new financial independence also comes social power, most tangibly demonstrated in the context of family and kin, and allowing these youngsters to speak out of turn. In Kinshasa today, those in possession of dollars inevitably also become the boss (*mokonzi*), regardless of their age. The young have in this way become *bana ya kilo*, 'children with weight' and with a social status exceeding that of their elders.

The discourse of witchcraft often proves to be as empowering an idiom for the young as that of diamonds and dollars. By using the witchcraft idiom of 'eating' (an idiom that used to be the prerogative of elders and always had strong political connotations as well, Fabian, 1990) youngsters appropriate domains of speech and action that they could not possibly have accessed before. It fully illustrates the switch of social and political power from elders to the young. The idiom of 'eating' also forms the translation of the contents of juvenile economies of desire. It is believed that the nocturnal consumption of one's elders gives straight access to, and is quite literally an incorporation and ingestion of, modernity's technology and its spaces of wealth and consumption.[14] In this sense, by using the vocabulary of witchcraft, and by controlling a dream-like, imaginary economy of the occult in the second world, children and youngsters create possibilities of accessing worlds of consumption from which they are very often excluded in the realities of the first world. This also means that the space of the street and the time of the night, the two worlds to which children are relegated, are perceived by many children not as spaces of exclusion and social abandonment but, on the contrary, as spaces of possibility and promise, of empowerment, of play and diversion and, above all, of

---

[14]   For examples see de Boeck and Plissart, 2004: 183.

freedom. As Barry (1998/1999: 143) points out in an interesting article on street children in Ouagadougou, a prominent but scarcely debated motive for children to take to the streets often also is a longing for freedom. Sometimes, children themselves make the decision to wilfully detach themselves from their family context and from the responsibilities, futures, and expectations that lie embedded within a regular family life. The street then becomes a space of opportunity to escape from the poverty or the violence of the family home; a place, also, where adolescents believe they can realise all their consumerist dreams. In Kinshasa, calling yourself a witch is certainly a way to attain such independence and to remove yourself from parental control.

Instrumentalising the idiom of witchcraft in such a way also offers a possibility for children to challenge parents, public authority and the established order. Here, we touch on another, and less innocent, element in which the use of the idiom of witchcraft gives a lot of agency to children. This agency might perhaps be described as a victim's agency, but yet it is very powerful. Children may use their narratives, during the moments of public witnessing in the churches, for example, to settle certain scores with some adult relatives or neighbours. It is at moments like these that children are in a position to demonstrate the real power they possess. In their testimony they may and almost always will implicate adults who allegedly initiated them in the world of witchcraft: a market woman who offered some food to the child in order to link her to the nocturnal forces of evil, or a father, mother or other relative who offered a glass of water to the little friends of their son or daughter, but expected a nocturnal counter gift in human meat in return. In many cases, these public accusations have severe consequences for the adults whose names are mentioned in the children's testimonies. Frequently, it sets in motion a violent reaction of relatives or neighbours, and it may lead to the beating up, stoning, lynching, necklacing and burning of the accused adults. Often the latter find these accusations against them as bewildering and difficult to understand and interpret as they would be for most of us in the West. A couple of years ago, I interviewed Lukaya, a man in his mid-seventies, who had recently left his village to join his children and grandchildren in Kinshasa. Shortly after his arrival, five of his grandchildren were denounced as witches in a local Pentecostal church community. The children told the preacher that their grandfather was the one who had lured them into the second world. As a result of their revelation, Lukaya's house was burned down and he himself was only saved from a certain death by a Catholic parish priest of Belgian origin who accidentally passed by and had the courage to rescue him from the anger of the neighbourhood. Unfamiliar with the new forms of urban witchcraft, Lukaya was not only bewildered by the power and weight the words of his grandchildren carried, but also by the sheer fact that children may turn out to be witches.

This anecdote illustrates the spiritual insecurity that many adults feel they are currently undergoing. Like this old man, they have started to mistrust, and sometimes accuse and mistreat their own children, not necessarily because they are bad parents or cruel care-takers, but because they genuinely believe that they are in danger. Many adults live with the basic fear of being attacked by their children, while there is little or no possibility to defend oneself against these attacks.

Here we touch on yet another aspect: that of the role of law and legal protection in this whole debate. It may be noted that, with a few exceptions such as Cameroon (Geschiere, 2006), most countries in sub-Saharan Africa have a legal framework in which to accuse a person of witchcraft is seen as illegal and punishable (see for an example Hund, 2003 on the anti-witchcraft suppression act in South Africa). The law, however, does not punish witches, for it does not recognise their existence. What this entails is that, in a world in which the belief in the existence of witches and witchcraft is undiminished, officialdom, the state itself, is perceived to be on the witch's side. In popular understanding, it is the witch that is protected by the law, not the persons suffering from the witch's attacks. In Congo, lawmakers, politicians and other decision makers are currently discussing the possibilities of reforming the penal code in such a way that it offers more protection against forms of spiritual insecurity and attacks. The failure to come up with a reform against the perceived widespread proliferation of witchcraft so far leaves the state with a deficit, politically but also morally. As Ashforth (2005) has rightly pointed out for the South-African context, the state's incapacity to come up with a satisfactory response to witchcraft poses a number of very real problems concerning the credibility and authority of political institutions, practices of good governance and the regulation of the public sphere, and indeed the very nature of the democratic state itself.

Churches of Awakening and the Production of Witchcraft

The widespread feeling that the state is not capable of helping those in need of protection against all these new forms of spiritual insecurity has undoubtedly contributed to the growing success of a new brand of fundamentalist Christianity which is currently flourishing all over Africa and its various diasporas. Contrary to the state, the churches of awakening do offer remedies to protect oneself against occult attacks and the spiritual risks that one is constantly running in the interaction with the city. Their message is simple and straightforward, but therefore also extremely powerful and efficacious. In a world caught up in a battle between the forces of Good and Evil, an Armageddon in which demons have gathered in an all-out war against God (see the Book of Revelation, 16:16), the churches constantly offer the possibility to crusade against all the forces of evil, which are overcome with the help of the Holy Spirit and through prayer. Not only have they taken over the role of the state in defining what is good, rightful and lawful, but they have also acquired the monopoly on the correct ways to convert disorder into order.

In doing so, though, preachers are constantly faced with a dilemma well known to novelists. 'Happy families are all alike; every unhappy family is unhappy in its own way', wrote Tolstoy on the first page of *Anna Karenina*. In other words, to tell a good story one needs something to set it in motion: a divorce, adultery, a crime of passion… In their own way, preachers are constantly facing the same 'laws of the novel'. In order to spread the good word, they constantly draw attention to all kinds of manifestations of Evil that will then be overcome. By devoting a lot of attention to the figure of Satan, to demons and the struggle between Good and Evil, the fundamentalist Christian churches thus play a crucial role in the ceaseless production and increasing centrality of the figure of the witch in the collective imaginary of Congolese society. Paradoxically, therefore, the diabolisation of the figure of the witch in the discourse of these churches makes the witch itself more omnipresent in the social field. Therefore, the position of the churches in relation to evil, straightforward as it may seem at first sight, nevertheless produces contradictory tensions in the social field.

The churches' role with regard to the child witch phenomenon is an equally ambivalent one, which makes them both part of the witchcraft problem itself as well as of the local solution to this problem. On the one hand, the space of the churches is one of the most prominent sites in which the coincidence of the figure of the witch and the child is produced. During the masses and collective prayers, children are urged to make a public confession in order to reveal their true nature as a witch and confess the number of their victims. Rather than being a perversion, the naming of the witch often offers an opportunity to solve the crisis, as it has always done in more traditional settings. Before this public moment they have usually been sniffed out or recognised as witches by the church leaders and *pasteurs* during more private consultations. In these meetings more 'traditional' divinatory models are often blended in with the church discourse to create a ritualised moment of witch-finding. As a consequence of these witch identifications, however, international aid agencies and NGOs such as Save the Children, in their struggle against the marginalisation of children, accuse the church leaders and *pasteurs* of child abuse. These organisations usually treat the problem of witch-children in Kinshasa as a humanitarian problem of street children, while choosing to disregard totally the cultural implications of the witchcraft aspect. And yet, one could argue that the churches, in providing and authorising this type of diagnostic, open up a possible therapeutic space and offer an alternative for the violence and conflict that occurs in the family as the result of a witchcraft accusation. As noted before, the church leaders do not usually produce these accusations themselves, but merely confirm and thereby legitimate them. In doing so, the space of the 'healing' church enables to relocate and reformulate the sometimes extreme physical and psychological violence that the accused children have to undergo within their kin-group. As such, the child is removed from the threatening family context in which its place has become highly problematic, and is left in the care of a *pasteur*. The mere fact that the preacher is the sole person capable of exorcising the child and thus bringing about a change in the status of the child, makes him a key player in the whole process. Many preachers also insist on the necessity to reinsert the child in question into its family after the exorcism. Many churches therefore try to work together with the child's parents or caretaker during the therapeutic prayer sessions which take place after the moment of public witnessing, and which may go on for weeks or even months. Often though, it is the parents who refuse to collaborate, not because they do not care about their child but because they remain too afraid of the possible evil identity of the child in question. It is true that other caretakers, on the contrary, use the church groups as a dumping ground for children they want to dispose of, as the case of Ginette illustrated. Many preachers whom I interviewed complained about the fact that they take all the blame for acts that they do not produce or control. They insisted that it is often the children's relatives, not the preachers, who behave irresponsibly towards their children. Confronted with the fact that these relatives do not retrieve their children after the exorcism rituals have been performed, preachers, for lack of means, often have no other option but to release the child in question into the streets of Kinshasa's urban jungle.

Conclusion: On the Position of NGOs and Humanitarian Organisations

As I indicated, NGOs have oftentimes been very outspoken in their criticism of both preachers and parents, whom they have readily accused of child abuse and mistreatment of children. In the preceding pages I tried to demonstrate that such an interpretation, although easy to understand, without doubt offers a too simplistic and straightforward reading of the child witch phenomenon. It risks turning the main protagonists (child, parent, preacher) into too one-dimensional figures.

First of all, in my view most of the actions of NGOs and other organisations tend to focus too much on the child itself, without taking into account the reasons driving parents and other caretakers to act as they do. Recently, Cole and Durham (2007) drew our attention to the fact that treating children as a separate and isolated category might not be the most fruitful approach to understand changes occurring within that category. Rather, the category of childhood receives its meaning through its embeddedness in wider networks that are shaped and changed through very complex and highly dynamic relationships between different generations. By trying to comprehend the position of children in a wider context of families, age groups and intergenerational relations, it becomes clear that each of the three main actors involved in the drama of child witch accusations, that is, the child itself, the caretaker or relative responsible for that child, and the preacher, are in and of themselves complex figures, and need to be understood and approached as such. While the child is indeed a victim and at risk, it also has a victim's agency which, as the case of Lukaya illustrated, may be a very powerful one, with far ranging consequences. Children, therefore, are not only at risk, but may also constitute a real risk to those living with them. In Lukaya's case, the grandchildren's accusations nearly cost him his life.

This brings us to the other protagonists in the relationship. Although some parents or other relatives do indeed act irresponsibly by using the alibi of witchcraft to rid themselves of a child, most parents and caretakers are people who, in normal circumstances, care about their children, but who, due to the perceived risk of becoming bewitched, see no other alternative but to denounce their child.

Here too, it would be one-sided to treat these adults as constituting a risk for children, without taking into account the fact that they themselves feel persecuted, victimised and at risk. As long as the dimension of spiritual insecurity which, for a multitude of reasons, adults experience in relation to children in Congo today, is not properly taken into account, whatever solution one might come up with will be bound to fail. In fact, these organisations are perceived by many adults as behaving in exactly the same way as the state (see above), namely by siding with the aggressor rather than the victim. Many aid workers refuse to take witchcraft beliefs seriously, or are not capable of viewing them as anything other than a (cultural) 'invention' or the unfortunate result of a lack of education, of poverty and of other forms of social insecurity. Yet they should realise that stigmatising parents for being superstitious and 'backward' will not contribute to offering a solution. Moral indignation does not help parents and caretakers to counter the reality of what they experience as a real and genuine threat. In other words: NGOs should be urged to take seriously parents' anxieties about the occult worlds which they believe their children are inhabiting.

One final remark with regard to parents and caretakers is the following: Even if parents themselves doubt the veracity of accusations against their children, it often proves impossible for them to stop these allegations. To fight against the social pressure of the neighbourhood, for example, is often an uphill struggle, and one should not underestimate the forceful weapon that is rumour. Once one's neighbours start whispering that a child might be a witch, parents or other members of the children's support group can often do little to counter this rumour mill. In Kinshasa, doing so often means running the risk of being labelled a witch yourself, with all of the negative consequences that might entail. Actions intended to counter the course of witchcraft accusations should therefore always also involve the broader community

Finally, there is the preacher. Here as well, one should take care not to see preachers and church leaders as merely constituting a risk for children. As I pointed out above, their position is much more complicated, and they may play an important healing and mediating role. In my opinion, NGOs and aid workers often fail to take full advantage of preachers' crucial position within the whole process of the production of child witches.

References

Ashforth, A. (2005). *Witchcraft, Violence and Democracy in South Africa*. Chicago: University of Chicago Press.

Astill, J. (2003). 'DRC Casts Out its "Child Witches"', *The Observer*, 11 May.

Barry, A. (1998/1999). 'Marginalité et errance juveniles en milieu urbain. La place de l'aide psychologique dans les dispositifs de prise en charge des enfants de la rue', *Psychopathologie Africaine*, 24/2: 139-90.

'"Bewitched" Children are Forced to Bear Curse of Congo' (2003). *The Scotsman*, 26 January.

Bosongo, B. (1999). 'Les "enfants sorciers", bouc émissaire de la misère à Kinshasa', *Agence France Presse*, 13 October.

Boulierac, C. (2003). *Le mauvais sort des enfants dit sorciers en RDC*. Available online at: http://monuc.unmissions.org/.

Biehl, J. (2005). *Vita. Life in a Zone of Social Abandonment*. Berkeley: University of California Press.

Burdot, E. and E. van Hove (2004). *La nouvelle stratégie du diable*. Film.

'Child witches in Kinshasa'. (1999). *Newsnight*, BBC 2, 12 November.

Cole, J. and D. Durham (eds) (2007). *Generations and Globalization. Youth, Age, and Family in the New World Economy*. Bloomington/Indianapolis: Indiana University Press.

'Congo Orphans Accused of Sorcery, Cast into Mean Streets' (2006). Cable News Network (CNN), 4 October.

Davies, J-A. (2006). 'Torture of the Congo's Child "Sorcerers"', Reuters, 4 October.

—— (2004). 'Witch-Hunt: Julie-Ann Davies on the Torture of the Congo's Child "Sorcerers"'. *New Humanist*, 1 March.

De Boeck, F. (2006) 'Youth, Death and the Urban Imagination. A Case from Kinshasa', *Bulletin des Séances*, 52/2: 113-25.

—— (2005). 'The Divine Seed. Children, Gift and Witchcraft in the Democratic Republic of Congo', in A. Honwana and F. de Boeck (eds), *Makers and Breakers. Children and Youth in Postcolonial Africa*. Oxford: James Currey.

—— (2004). 'On Being Shege in Kinshasa: Children, the Occult and the Street', in T. Trefon (ed.) *Reinventing Order in the Congo. How People Respond to State Failure in Kinshasa*. London: Zed Books.

—— (2000). 'Le "deuxième monde" et les "enfants-sorciers" en République Démocratique du Congo', *Politique Africaine*, 80: 32-57. Available online at: www.arts.uwa.edu.au/MotsPluriels/MP2202fb.html.

—— and A. Honwana (2005). 'Introduction: Children and Youth in Africa. Agency, Identity and Place', in A. Honwana and F. de Boeck (eds), *Makers and Breakers. Children and Youth in Postcolonial Africa*. Oxford: James Currey.

—— and M.-F. Plissart (2004). *Kinshasa. Tales of the Invisible City*. Ghent/Tervuren: Ludion/Royal Museum of Central Africa.

De Herdt, T. (2004). 'L'évolution de la pauvreté monétaire à Kisenso entre 1997-2002: que pouvons-nous dire, ou vaut-il mieux se taire?', *Afrique et Développement*, 19: 211-53.

D'Haeyer, A. (2004). *Enfants sorciers, entre magie et misère*. Brussels: Labor.

'DRC: Children's Lives Torn by Accusations of Witchcraft' (2006). *The Times*, 21 November.

Dummet, M. (2003). 'DR Congo's Unhappy Child "Witches"', Report for BBC, 17 January.

Devey, M. (2007). 'Enfants sorciers: quand le 'réveil' devient cauchemar', *Afriqu'Echos*, 11 April.

Ekholm F., K. Biluka Nsakala Nenga and B. Nsakala Nsenga (2002). 'A Study of Children at Risk in Zaire, Uige and Luanda Provinces'. Unpublished preliminary report on child witches in Angola.

Fabian, J. (1990). *Power and Performance. Ethnographic Explorations Through Proverbial Wisdom and Theater in Shaba, Zaire*. Madison: The University of Wisconsin Press.

Foxcroft, G. (2007). 'Supporting Victims of Witchcraft Abuse and Street Children in Nigeria'. Paper. Article presented by Gary Foxcroft. Available online at: www.stepppingstonesnigeria.org.

Geschiere, P. (2006). 'Witchcraft and the Limits of the Law: Cameroon and South Africa', in J. Comaroff and J. Comaroff (eds), *Law and Disorder in the Postcolony*. Chicago: University of Chicago Press.

'Girl Tortured "for Being a Witch"'. 9 May 2005. [Online]. Available at: http://news.bbc.co.uk/1/hi/england/london/4530197.stm [accessed 10 September 2009].

'Mothers in Congo Give Birth to "Witches"'(2000). *Handelsblad*, 24 March.

Human Rights Watch (2006). *What Future? Street Children in the Democratic Republic of Congo*. Available online at: http://www.hrw.org/reports/2006/drc0406/

Hund, J. (ed.) (2003). *Witchcraft Violence and the Law in South Africa*. Pretoria: Protea Book House.

Miano, L. (2006). *Contours du jour qui vient*. Paris: Plon.

Molina, J.A. (n.d). 'The Invention of Child Witches in the Democratic Republic of Congo. Social Cleansing, Religious Commerce and the Difficulties of Being a Parent in an Urban Culture'. Summary of the research and experiences of Save the Children's 2003-2005 programme funded by USAID.

Oien, C. (2006). 'Transnational Networks of Care: Angolan Children in Fosterage in Portugal', *Ethnic and Racial Studies*, 29/6: 1104-17.

Oyeyemi, H. (2005). *The Icarus Girl*. London: Bloomsbury.

'La police kinoise fait la chasse aux "Shégués"' (Kinshasa Police Hunt Down Street Children) (2006). *Congo Indépendant*, 25 September.

Report on mass exorcisms of children in Kinshasa (2000). Agence Presse Associée (APA). March.

'"Sorcerers" Swell Ranks of Congo Street Children' (2006). Reuters, 4 October.

Stephens, S. (1995). 'Introduction: Children and the Politics of Culture in "Late Capitalism"', in S. Stephens (ed.), *Children and the Politics of Culture*. Princeton, NJ: Princeton University Press.

Stobart, E. (2006). 'Child Abuse Linked to Accusations of "Possession" and "Witchcraft"'. London: Department for Education and Skills Research Report RR750. Available online at: http://www.dcsf.gov.uk/research/programmeofresearch/projectinformation.cfm?projectid=14953&resultspage=1

Trovato, M. (2005). 'The So-Called Child Witch: The Creation of a Local Human Rights Story in the Democratic Republic of Congo'. Interview with filmmaker Angela Nicoara (from Internews-Rwanda). Available online at: http://www.brandeis.edu/ethics/

'"Witchcraft" an Excuse for Child Abuse in Angola' (2007). Afrol News/IRIN, 25 March.

Zajtman, A. (2006). 'DR Congo Children Held after Riot', Report for BBC, 24 September.

Chapter 12

Child Abuse Linked to Accusations of 'Possession' and 'Witchcraft'[1]

Eleanor Stobart

This report concerns the frequency and severity of child abuse linked to accusations of 'possession' and 'witchcraft'. It identifies key features common to these cases and draws conclusions. The report is based on desk research and discussions with social workers, school teachers, police officers, voluntary workers and others who had knowledge of aspects of the subject. An important feature has been collecting and examining reports of cases that occurred since January 2000, analysing the often limited information recorded and drawing conclusions from this material. The belief in 'possession' and 'witchcraft' is widespread. The UK is not alone in seeing cases of this nature; cases have been reported worldwide. The children discussed in this report came from a variety of backgrounds including African, South Asian and European. Seventy-four cases of abuse clearly linked to accusations of 'possession' and 'witchcraft' were identified. To safeguard against double-counting, only cases for which there were identifying factors were analysed. Therefore, this report only analyses 38 of these cases. It should be noted that prior to enquiries only 14 cases were clearly identified and new cases were being reported right up to the date of publication of this report.

The number of cases of child abuse linked to accusations of 'possession' and 'witchcraft' so far identified is small compared to the total number of children abused each year. In the year to 31 March 2005, 30,700 children were placed on child protection registers in England. There were 72,100 child protection enquiries in England in the year to 31 March 2004.The abuse in question occurs when an attempt is made to 'exorcise' the child. The abuse consists of severe beatings and other premeditated cruelties such as starving, burning and isolating the child. The perpetrators are usually carers – often not the natural parents – and the abuse

---

[1] This article is a slightly abridged version of a report delivered to the (then) DfeS in 2006 entitled 'Child Abuse Linked to Accusations of "Possession" and "Witchcraft"' by Eleanor Stobart. Research report RR 750 ISBN 1844787354 Department for Education and Skills. © Crown copyright material is reproduced with the permission of the Controller of HMSO and Queen's Printer for Scotland. Bibliographic data that was contained in footnotes has been collected at the end of the article in accordance with the style of this book. We are grateful to the DCSF for permission to let us print this version of the report. Copies of the original report can be obtained from the Department for Children, Schools and Families.

usually occurs in the household where the child lives. As a last resort the child may be abandoned overseas. Their further history is not known.

There appear to be common features between cases, for instance, a child being scapegoated, family structure and disability. By recognising these patterns and links, it may be possible to identify children at risk early and prevent cases from escalating. The recommendations address gathering better information about cases, drawing up guidance about handling cases, monitoring the movement of children and protecting children in places of worship.

In this report the total number of cases analysed is 38 and the total number of children involved is 47. This reflects the fact that five families have more than one child involved in the case. On some occasions, children do not always appear as statistics in the charts because so little is known about them. For example the exact age is not known of four of the children. In some cases, a social care service may have responded to state that they have a case that fits into this profile but as yet have not supplied all the required data (two children). In other cases, the referral is current and therefore little information is available – and even at the time of writing other cases are coming to light. Where it is thought significant, charts have a bar representing 'unknowns'; otherwise the charts only include known data.

The main feature about Figure 12.1 below is the number of cases identified in 2005. As this issue has been the focus of so much attention recently and this research actively looked for cases, it is unsurprising that more cases were found and are now being recognised. During the four months available for this report, 24 new cases were found. Cases are shown in the years in which they came to notice. It is often the case that when a particular type of abuse starts to be openly discussed and awareness is raised, more incidents will be recognised.

Figure 12.1 Cases identified per year (38 cases)

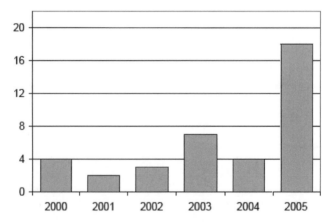

Victim's Age and Gender

In the cases seen, gender does not appear to play a significant role. Boys and girls are equally at risk from this abuse. However, the majority of children came in the 8-14 age range. It is impossible to judge whether the incidents of abuse stop after the age of 14. Equally, it may be that children find another way of dealing with the abuse – for example they may run away or they may be able to defend themselves. It could be that this research simply did not find any cases of children over 14 years old. What is known is that people of any age can be accused of 'witchcraft' or 'possession' so it is unlikely that abuse stops at 14 (Rees and Lee, 2005).

Figure 12.2   Victims' age (in years) and gender (43 cases)

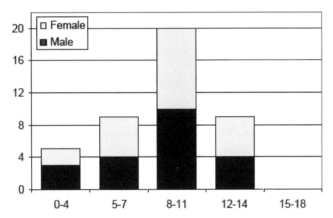

Identifying Agency

Schools appear to be the main source of referrals. There are possibly a number of reasons for this. Firstly, children who attend school regularly usually build a rapport with a teacher and may either give an indication of a problem at home or feel safe enough to disclose abuse. Also a teacher may recognise early signs of distress such as depression, withdrawal and general neglect. In contrast, the families in these cases are less likely to have a relationship of trust with police and social care. These agencies usually become involved when the situation has escalated. For many families, turning to the police or social care is a last resort. This raises concerns for children who arrive in the UK and are not enrolled at a GP surgery or in a school. This takes away important avenues to identify and prevent cases. It is perhaps also relevant that, as will be seen in Figure 12.3, it is not uncommon for a family who are abusing their child in this way to remove the child from school – again cutting him or her off from one of his or her main sources of protection. Children who were abused following accusations of 'possession' or 'witchcraft' showed behaviour consistent with distress. They frequently appear isolated, quiet, withdrawn and sad. For this reason, a significant number of them (20) came to attention via their teachers who noticed signs of neglect. Some of the children came to school hungry and brought no food with them. Others were described as unkempt and uncared for – with dirty, unlaundered clothes. Some children came to attention because of their injuries. Two children were excluded from school for aggressive behaviour and two came to attention for truanting.

Figure 12.3   Identifying Agency (36 cases)

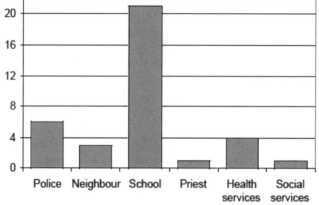

Cases by UK Region

The majority of cases in this report occurred in the London area. However, it should not be considered a London problem – previous research has concentrated on finding cases in London. To some extent this research has also focused on those known cases from London. During the course of this report, of the 24 new cases identified a quarter was from outside the London area.

Figure 12.4   Cases by UK region (38 cases)

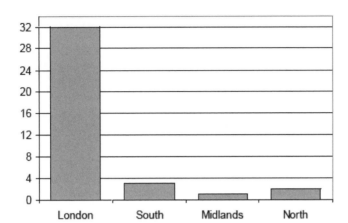

Origin or Background

The research tried to assess the nationality and background of both the victim and the parents or carers. This was extremely difficult as it was rare for the nationality of the parent or carer to be recorded in case files. From the information that was available it appears that children were with adults from the same background. Figure 12.5 shows the background of the children. While there is a significant cluster from the Democratic Republic of Congo, again this may reflect previous work on this community.

Figure 12.5   Origin/background (37 cases)

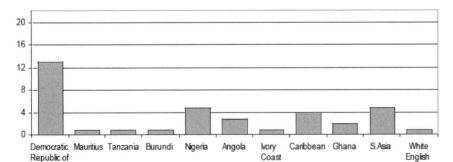

Period of UK Residency

There is a perception that abuse related to accusations of 'witchcraft' and 'possession' is more common amongst new immigrant communities. It is interesting to note that about half the children in the cases were born in the UK. The ages of those born in the UK range from 2-14 years with six being between 8 and 14 years.

Figure 12.6   Period of UK residency (in years) (30 cases)

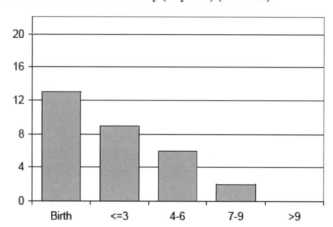

Religion

The research tried to establish the religion of the families involved but again this was difficult, as religion was not usually recorded in the case notes. Of those that were recorded, the majority described themselves as Christians. The case that is classified as 'mixed' indicates a particular carer who alternated between faiths. The number of families whose religion is not recorded means that it is not possible to make an assessment of the role of particular religions. All the cases that were not Christian were identified during the four-month period of this research. This may suggest that so far the emphasis has been on particular communities and so gathering more information may throw up cases across many religions.

Figure 12.7   Religion (38 cases)

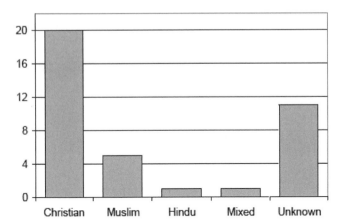

Place of Worship Involved

The term 'involvement' is used to show an identified connection between the carer and a place of worship, a connection that was reported as having an influence on the case, for example a request for an exorcism for a child, a religious leader diagnosing a child or fasting for him or her.

Figure 12.8   Place of worship involvement (38 cases)

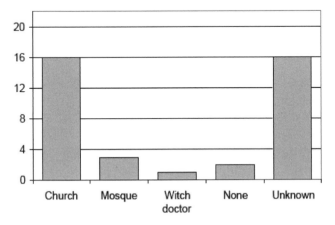

Family Structure

In many cases the relationship between the child and the carer was unclear because in many cultures the head female in the household is called 'mother' and the head male, 'father'; other adults may be called 'aunties' and 'uncles'. Further, the true relationship was not always clearly recorded. We were able to establish that in six cases the children lived with both their natural parents. In 19 cases there was a stepparent or carer in the household who was not related to the child. The category of 'other' includes a range of specified relationships such as children being cared for by siblings, uncles and guardians.[2]

Figure 12.9   Family structure (34 cases)

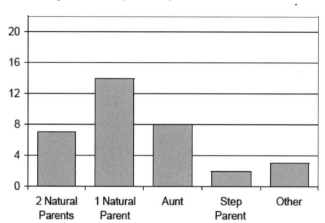

A Child with a Difference

A common feature between some of the cases was that the carers found it difficult to accept a child with certain characteristics or behaviour. They rationalised these traits as being a sign of 'witchcraft' or 'possession'. These traits included disability and illness, challenging behaviour, sleepwalking, wetting the bed and having bad dreams. Commonly these dreams are described as taking the shape of an animal and flying to other parts of the world to kill and eat people.[3]

---

[2]   The categories used in Figure 12.9 are those used in the public sector records and are not relationships that have been verified.

[3]   Some children exhibited various characteristics and behaviours and appear in the chart a number of times.

Figure 12.10 A child with a difference (22 cases)

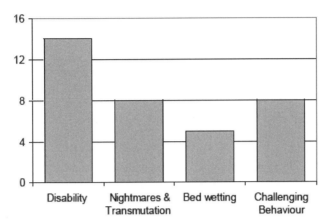

Accusation

Every child in this report had an accusation of 'evil' made against him or her although the precise language may vary. In addition, when a child is accused of 'possession' or 'witchcraft', it is commonly accompanied by a belief that they can 'infect' others with this 'evil'.[4]

Figure 12.11 Accusation (38 cases)

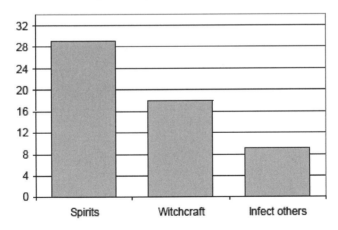

[4]   Some children received various accusations and appear in the chart a number of times.

Types of Abuse

There are various forms of abuse involved in ridding a child of an 'evil spirit'. In these cases, they ranged from neglect to severe physical abuse including beating and burning. The way in which the 'evil spirit' is removed may have different rationales and may vary according to the culture or religions of the family involved. Figure 12.12 shows the incidence of some of the forms of abuse. Neglect and beating feature prominently. Two more unusual actions that were regularly reported were – 'threat of abandonment' and 'wanting the child removed'. Nine carers asked social workers to take the child into care, others spoke of taking a child overseas for an exorcism, from which it was unclear whether the child would return. Some simply threatened to abandon the child overseas. Some children were not allowed to eat meals with the family and suffered long-term malnutrition, others had to prepare food for themselves. There were cases where children were made to fast for up to three days. Others were systematically starved. One of these children lost half its body weight. Two children were taken overseas and it is unknown whether they suffered other types of abuse.[5]

Figure 12.12 Types of abuse (36 cases)

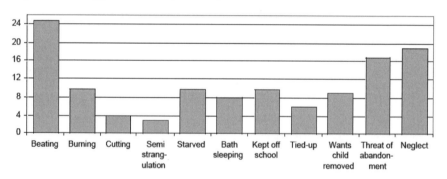

Outcomes

Eighteen children who had been abused following an accusation of 'witchcraft' or 'possession' were placed in long-term foster care. Two were placed in secure care. A further 23 of their siblings were also placed in foster care even though they had not been accused. Figure 12.13 includes the outcome for other siblings. Four children returned home with no further action taken and seven were returned

---

[5]   Some children suffered several forms of abuse and appear in the chart a number of times.

home and placed on the child protection register or under a supervision order. Ten children were taken overseas and nothing further is known.

Figure 12.13 Outcomes (71 cases)

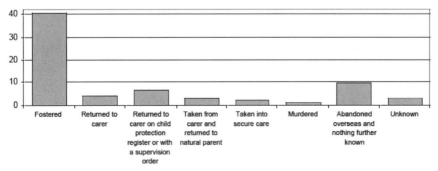

Findings

Given the constraints of the time available together with the scarcity and confidentiality of the facts, this chapter does not claim to be a full account of child abuse in England linked to accusations of 'possession' and 'exorcism' but simply the report of a first reconnaissance. Even so, there is sufficient information to hand to identify significant features of this form of child abuse and to set out the steps needed to begin to reduce the number and severity of the cases that occur.

Common Features Between Cases

Family Structure

One of the notable features surrounding family structure was the difficulty in understanding the relationship between the child and the carers. The family structure tended to be complex. Children lived with 'mothers', 'fathers', 'aunts', 'uncles', siblings and half siblings all in the same household – it was difficult to establish whether the carers were related to the child or whether it was a private fostering arrangement.[6] Carers often had partners who were transient or several partners – some appeared to be polygamous marriages.

---

⁶   A privately fostered child is one under 16 (or under 18 if disabled). The child receives care and accommodation continually for 28 days or more by someone who is not a parent, does not have legal parental responsibility and is not a close relative. The Children Act 2004 defines close relatives as parents, stepparents, grandparents, siblings, aunts or uncles.

The information about relationships was often conflicting. In some cases immigration status and benefits depended on the child being with a natural parent. Children therefore did not disclose the real relationship. In one case DNA was used to establish if the child and carer were related.

Research suggests that children become more vulnerable to accusations of 'possession' and 'witchcraft' if there is a change in family situation or there is no bond of affection between the carer and child. Carers may have developed a strong family relationship prior to the arrival of the child or the remaining natural parent may form a stronger bond with a new partner and their subsequent children. At least five of the carers were pregnant at the time of the abuse.

At least 25 of the children had siblings or half siblings in the household. In three cases, two children in the same family were accused of being 'possessed'. In all the other cases one child was singled out and accused.

Scapegoats

The change in family situation or a change of circumstances for the worse, may lead to the isolated, more vulnerable 'outsider' being blamed. The work of Tom Douglas (1995) on scapegoats as cited in *Working with Black African Children and Families* is relevant (Anane-Agyei, 2002).

The main factors influencing the selection of the 'scapegoat' are:

- The relative powerlessness of the child vis-à-vis the parents.
- The need to choose someone who was not performing any essential family role.
- The choice should be able to symbolise the conflict by, for example:
  - A lack of achievement, failure.
  - Acting independently and violating the family norms of loyalty.
  - The choice usually had suffered serious physical disease when young or had a striking physical abnormality.

A Child with a Difference

The reason why a particular child is singled out and accused of being 'possessed' or being a 'witch' is difficult to ascertain. Our desk research suggests that several factors combine to make a child more at risk. These include rationalising misfortune, a change of circumstances for the worse, a child with a 'difference' and a weak bond of affection between the carer and the child. It is human instinct to try to rationalise misfortune – whether it involves seeking a medical, scientific, religious, mystical or spiritual explanation. In the cases we have seen, rationalisation often takes the form of believing oneself to be cursed, to be the victim of black magic, vodou, witchcraft, obeah or believing that someone else is 'possessed by evil spirits'. When family troubles begin or are exacerbated – serious illness, financial troubles, unemployment and so on – people may look for anything that is new or 'different' as the cause of the problem. It may be a child who has recently joined the family or a child with a 'difference' that is blamed and becomes a scapegoat. Research[7] suggests that when a family experiencing problems has a child who exhibits a behaviour that the family views as problematic, difficult to understand or outside the family norms, this, combined with a change in family dynamics, may increase the risk of the family accusing the child of harbouring some 'evil' force such as 'witchcraft' or 'possession'. The behaviour that carers view as challenging includes rebelliousness, disobedience, independence, defiance and developing and establishing individuality. Many of the children were described by their carers as 'naughty'.

Disability

Children with a disability were also viewed as 'different' and their disability may be explained away as 'possession' or 'witchcraft'. We were able to establish that 14 of the children had some degree of disability, imperfection or blemish. This could be as mild as a stammer or a severe mental and physical disability. These were:

- Epilepsy (2)
- Stammer (2)
- Deafness (1)
- Learning disabilities (4)
- Autism (2)
- Mental health issues (4)
- Life limiting illness (2)

This suggests that carers might view any illness or disability as a sign of 'possession'. Interestingly, three of the children were described as exceptionally bright which could have been the reason for them standing out as 'different'.

Types of Abuse

There were a variety of different types of abuse. There was no evidence that the abuse had the regularity of a ritual.

---

[7]   Javier Aguilar Molina, 'Enfants Sorciers en République Démocratique de Congo', September 2005, Save the Children UK.

Beating

Twenty-four children reported being beaten, kicked, hit or punched. The arm of one child was broken deliberately. Carers often talked about this abuse as 'beating the devil out' of the child.

Burning

Ten children were burned – this involved scalding and burning with an implement. In four cases the children were burned with an iron. Although no carer gave an explanation for burning the child, our research suggested that extreme heat may burn the 'evil' out.

Cutting/Stabbing

In four cases children were stabbed – an explanation given for this was 'to create a way out' for the 'evil'.

Semi-Strangulation, Applying Pressure and Smothering

Three children reported being semi-strangled. Research suggests this is 'to squeeze the life out of the evil'.

Made to Fast and Starved

Ten children described being made to fast for various periods of time from 15 hours to three days. A further two children were starved – one lost half his or her body weight. One child fasted on his or her own initiative in the belief that would provide a cure. The rationale for fasting and starving a child was to weaken the 'evil spirit'.

Isolation

Isolation was reported in many cases. The rationale for this was to prevent the 'evil' from spreading to other people. This took the form of not allowing a child to eat with the family, to associate with the family, to share a room or have any physical contact with anyone. In one case the carers were so scared of the child they only touched him or her with a stick. Five children were removed from school in an attempt to isolate them further. This prevented them from seeking help. The level of neglect was described as severe in 19 cases.

Other Abuse

Other forms of abuse included being made to sleep in the bath (two children), being forced to have cold baths, being held under water, being tied or locked up (four children) and having chilli peppers (four children), salt (five children) or ginger (two children) applied to eyes and genitals[8] (this may be viewed as burning).

In one case a girl appeared to be 'groomed' for sexual exploitation. Four children were reported as hiding, storing or smearing their faeces. Two children were turned away from school for having faeces on his or her clothing. In two cases, siblings were encouraged to take part in the violence. In several cases siblings were not allowed to talk to the victim.

Outcomes

Police officers, social workers, teachers and others considered that children who are abused following an accusation of 'possession' suffer lasting damage in many areas of their lives. They suffer damage to their physical and mental health, education, ability to form relationships and self-esteem. The victims who are convinced that they are 'possessed' may require years of support. Some never recover. In short, their life chances are severely diminished.

When social care did decide to intervene, the child was usually removed from the household and placed in care. In only two of the cases did the carer object to the child being taken. In nine cases the carers specifically asked social [workers] to take the child into care. Eighteen of the children accused of being 'possessed' have been taken into long-term care. Twenty-three of their siblings were also taken into long-term foster care. In each of those 18 cases the professionals involved stated that there was a weak bond of affection between the carer and the child. In only one case has there been on-going contact between the carer and child since their separation. In a further ten cases the child was taken overseas and their whereabouts are unknown. Half of them went for a specific purpose such as 'traditional treatment' or an 'exorcism'; four of them are known to have been abandoned. Two attempted to seek help to return to the UK but were not British nationals.

Case Handling

Throughout the research of this report, it became apparent that there were variations in the way that public sector agencies handled these cases. The accusation of 'possession' or 'witchcraft' frequently went unrecognised or the child was thought

---

[8]   In some cultures applying chilli peppers to parts of the body is considered acceptable chastisement. Therefore the use of chilli peppers does not necessarily indicate that a child is a 'witch' or 'possessed'.

to be 'making it up'. A lack of understanding around the issue and sometimes failure to apply existing best practice led public sector professionals to act in a way that was not always in the best interests of the child. In one case, a child was returned home for family counselling even though the carer asked for the child to be removed. In another case, the social worker had never visited a child, even though it was known that the child had been taken to various places of worship for a 'cure' and there had been a threat to take the child overseas. One child was never spoken to alone. On another occasion a social worker left a child in the presence of his or her carer while the child was awaiting a medical examination following a severe physical assault by that carer. The child later withdrew all allegations and returned home. Schools were able to identify children suffering abuse at an early stage but in some cases the level of abuse did not reach social care threshold criteria for engagement. Children were left with or returned to carers with no further action. When cases are identified, there are still occasions when public sector agencies fail to implement multi-agency procedures, for example attending joint home visits, attending strategy meetings and maintaining good communication between agencies.

Migration

One case involved a white English family. All the other families were first or second generation migrants. It may be that the predominance of cases in this report involving first or second generation migrant families does not so much concern their cultural background but the additional stresses placed on families adjusting to migration. It is well documented that migrating families face particular difficulties. These include isolation from extended family, a sense of not belonging or feeling threatened, misunderstood and confused. The expectations associated with migration, such as the quality of life, levels of income and ability to help relatives overseas financially may not be fulfilled. Other stresses include continuing uncertainty around immigration status, being unable to work, living in inadequate housing and not receiving the recognition of status, value or worth that they held in their home country. Many major changes, particularly those resulting from migration, can cause significant stress to individuals especially those trying to manage conflicting identities. In some cases this can go so far as constituting an actual mental health problem (Carta, Bernal, Hardoy and Haro-Abad, 2005).

Mental Health

In 11 cases it was reported that there were concerns for the mental health of a carer. The illnesses involved included post-traumatic stress disorder, depression and schizophrenia.[9] One carer starved himself or herself to death for which the child was later blamed by the surviving carer. Three carers were sectioned under the Mental Health Act. The carer often genuinely believes the child has been completely taken over by the 'devil'. In the perpetrators' minds any abuse is not going to affect the child because the child is effectively not there anymore – any violence is directed at the devil. Although it is helpful to understand the context, this in no way excuses the abuse. Public sector professionals acknowledged that they had difficulty in understanding that some carers truly believed that a child could be 'possessed'. They had even more difficulty in understanding the belief that a child was so 'evil' that the carer's life might be in danger. Some may assume that those holding this belief must have a mental illness. Some carers were sectioned under the Mental Health Act while others were prosecuted.

Religious and Spiritual Beliefs

In all the cases reviewed the carers held the belief that the child was a 'witch' or 'possessed'. This belief is widespread in many cultures and religions. The scarce information available in case reports about the role of places of worship means that our findings in this area are limited. We did establish that five children alleged being beaten in a place of worship. Two children were taken to 'various' mosques but it was not clear what happened at the mosques. One child was diagnosed in a mosque. Two children were taken to church for an exorcism – the details of these were not available. A further child was diagnosed in a church. On one occasion a priest referred the case to child protection agencies. In three cases carers are known to have paid for help from places of worship or witchdoctors.[10] The vulnerability of these families may make them susceptible to exploitation. In 17 cases it was unknown whether a place of worship was involved. It is not clear whether this means the abuse occurred entirely independently of the involvement of the place of worship or simply that the question was not asked. We found that different terms are used in different religions. In Muslim cases the 'evil' may be referred to as 'possession by evil spirits', 'the Evil Eye' or '*jinns*' [see Chapter 6]. In the Hindu case the terms 'possession' and 'bad spirits' were used interchangeably. In the Christian cases a variety of terms were used including devils, snakes, voodou, curses, demons, evil spirits, and witches.

---

[9]   'Delivering Race Equality in Mental Health Care', 4 July 2005. Available online at: www.doh.gov.uk. See also speech by Rosie Winterton, Minister of State for Health, 3 November 2005 to EU Presidency at the launch of the EU green paper on Migrant Mental Health.

[10]   The label 'witchdoctor' can be applied to a variety of different healers and religious specialists. The common feature is usually that they operate as individual practitioners. [Ed.]

Movement of Children

Through the course of this report it has become apparent that children including unaccompanied minors can travel internationally and nationally with considerable ease in a way that is very difficult to monitor. This lack of monitoring can increase their vulnerability – few, if any, checks are made on any adults they are with, where they are to reside in the UK and whether they are registered in school or with the health service. It was also common for children to move schools regularly. Sometimes this appeared to be in connection with an investigation carried out by Children's Social Care. It was not clear whether this was a deliberate attempt by the carer to avoid close scrutiny.

Good Practice

During the course of researching this report some areas of good practice were identified. Some examples of this good practice include: early intervention.

Social care threshold criteria for engagement are often too high to pick up this type of abuse at an early stage. In practice this means that when a case comes to light early and the child is referred to social care, social care is not in a position to act. There are some non-governmental and faith based organisations who work with families who are struggling to adapt to life in the UK. These organisations give advice about a range of issues including child-rearing practices, illness, housing, immigration status and so on. Migrant families are more likely to turn to these organisations for support than to public sector agencies. They are more likely to discuss openly cultural and belief issues without fear of being misunderstood. These organisations often see struggling families at an early stage. At this early stage, it may be possible to change the carer's response to the child by helping them to view the issue in the wider context rather than simply as a problem of 'possession' or 'witchcraft'. These organisations can prevent cases escalating by making early referrals and interventions to public sector agencies. In London there is a non-governmental organisation with a network of therapists working in schools alongside children with behavioural problems. The children often disclose abuse and neglect and several have revealed accusations of 'possession' or 'witchcraft'. Some local authorities with diverse populations like Tower Hamlets, Southwark, Hackney, Haringey and Enfield are making efforts to find out more about their local non-governmental and faith based organisations and to work more closely with them on child protection.

Experience in France and Belgium

In some cases, assisting the family to resolve their problems diminishes the likelihood of the family blaming a child for the problems. Dr Ezembe from Afrique

Conseil in Paris cited an example of a family with problems concerning their visa. They had decided their stepdaughter, recently arrived from overseas, was a witch blocking their progress and had started to mistreat the girl. When Dr Ezembe's staff were able to solve the visa problem the family decided that the problem had not been the daughter at all but probably had been a jealous brother overseas and relations with the girl normalised quickly. A similar example from France concerns a case where the stepfather began mistreating a girl believing her to be a witch and the staff at Afrique Conseil arranged for the girl to go and stay with a third party for a while until the situation had calmed down and they had been able to help the stepfather find another way of looking at his problems. This reflects the Congolese family background of that case whereby it is very normal when relations are strained in a family to send the child away for 'a breathing space'. In the Western European context this extended family network to provide a break does not exist and for a child to be fostered or taken into care by social care is usually not viewed in this light but rather as a failure or a shame.

Child Protection in Places of Worship

The Churches' Child Protection Advisory Service (CCPAS) provides literature and training on all aspects of child protection including exorcism – termed 'praying for children'. CCPAS encourage and facilitate churches to undertake Criminal Record Bureau (CRB) checks on their staff. They publish a quarterly magazine called *Caring*, which looks exclusively at child protection issues within churches. They also provide DVDs, videos and training on child protection in churches. They recently held a conference with pastors from majority black churches. This was positively received as they 'felt they had been marginalised and excluded, partly because of the press publicity'.

The African Caribbean Evangelical Alliance (ACEA) in partnership with Churches Together in England (CTE) held a conference on black majority churches looking at a range of issues for their churches today including child protection and interaction with local authorities. ACEA also have a minority ethnic Christian affairs working group looking into this issue in partnership with a child protection non-governmental organisation and with local authority agencies. The ACEA, the Metropolitan Police Service, Local Authorities and the CCPAS held a conference with pastors from the community to address the issue of child protection in churches and specifically dealing with children accused of 'being possessed' or 'witches'. The ACEA also require churches wishing to be a member of their alliance to have child protection procedures in place and for church staff to have undergone CRB checks.

The Muslim Parliament organised an interfaith conference to consult on good practice in tackling child abuse and from this has drawn up and circulated guidance in conjunction with Kirklees Council for the Muslim community (Kirklees Metropolitan Council Education and Social Services, 2004).

Specialist Training and Support

Tower Hamlets has held a series of workshops and produced a handbook to assist social workers dealing with black African children and families. Hackney held a Serious Case Review of a case involving 'witchcraft' and 'possession'. The outcome was that they have changed their assessment criteria for families when this belief is a factor in the abuse. A French consultancy, Afrique Conseil also provide specialist training days for French social workers dealing with black African families. They complement this with parenting classes for recently arrived migrant families.

Conclusions

The number of cases of child abuse linked to accusations of 'possession' and 'witchcraft' are small compared to the total number of children known to be abused each year. There were difficulties identifying cases. The difficulties included lack of awareness, concerns around confidentiality, reluctance to share information and poor record keeping. The belief in 'possession by evil spirits' and 'witchcraft' is widespread. The belief is not confined to particular countries, cultures or religions nor is it confined to recent migrants. The abuse occurs when the carers attempt to 'exorcise' the child. There are various social reasons that make a child more vulnerable to an accusation of 'possession' or 'witchcraft'. These include family stress, a change in the family structure, disability, a child with a difference and a weak bond of affection between the carer and the child. The role of places of worship in these cases is unclear. The effect on the family and the victim are devastating. The children and their siblings invariably need long-term foster care. Police and social workers are not able to change the beliefs of carers. Schools and non-governmental organisations appear to be in the best position to identify abused children at an earlier stage. Children tend to come to the attention of police and social care after the abuse has escalated. Early intervention may prevent repetitive abuse. There are variations within public sector agencies in the way that cases are handled. Some professionals were more aware of the signs than others.

Recommendations

It is recommended that information about this type of child abuse should be collated centrally. This would provide a clear national picture of the scale and extent of the problem. This could be managed by DfES [now DCSF - Ed.] or police and should be maintained for at least three years. The information for each case in the record should be compiled in a standardised form that is easily retrievable for everyone that has a legitimate need for access. Contact details of professionals familiar with dealing with these cases could also be held centrally. They could then provide support to police officers, social workers, teachers and other professionals less familiar with handling this type of case.

Practice Guidance

DfES, social care, police, schools and immigration should combine in preparing 'good practice' guidelines for handling these cases. The guidance should include information on:

- Early intervention.
- Reporting cases.
- Liaison between public sector agencies, non-governmental organisations, faith based organisations and places of worship.
- Confidentiality and information sharing.
- Risk factors.
- How to handle cases.

Movement of Children

Better information about children moving in and out of the UK is required. The Immigration Service should work with public sector agencies to protect children at risk that pass through immigration controls.[11]

Working with Non-Governmental Organisations

Non-governmental organisations working with some of these families are effective but lack resources. In order to assist early intervention in cases, Local Authorities should develop links with these organisations with a view to offering support, training and funding.

Child Protection in Places of Worship

Places of worship need child protection procedures in place together with information about good practice in 'praying for', 'delivering' or 'exorcising' children. Local Safeguarding Children Boards (LSCBs) should identify places of worship within their area and build links with them in order to monitor effective child protection measures.

---

[11]   Metropolitan Police Authority, Operation 'Paladin Child', 12 July 2004.

References

Anane-Agyei, A. (2002). *Working with Black African Children and Families. A Report on Two One-Day Workshops Held in April and September 2001.* London: Learning Design Ltd.

Carta, M.G., M. Bernal, M.C. Hardoy and J.M. Haro-Abad (2005). 'Clinical Practice and Epidemiology: Report on Mental Health in Europe Working Group', *Mental Health Journal*, 1/13.

Douglas, T. (1995). *Scapegoats, Transferring Blame.* Routledge: New York.

Kirklees Metropolitan Council Education and Social Services (2004). *Safe Children Sound Learning – Guidance for Madressahs*.

Molina, J.M. (2005). 'Enfants sorciers en République Démocratique de Congo'. Report to Save the Children, September.

Rees, G. and J. Lee (2005). 'Safe and Sound, Still Running II', The Children's Society, October.

Winterton, R., Minister of State for Health (2005). 'Delivering Race Equality in Mental Health Care', speech 3 November to EU Presidency at the launch of the EU green paper on Migrant Mental Health and press releases 4 July. Available online at: www.doh.gov.uk.

Chapter 13

The Impact of Spirit Possession on the Child's Mental Health and Social Work Intervention[1]

Amma Anane-Agyei

Those of us in the field of Child Protection are only too aware that one of the many presenting problems now, certainly amongst social work cases, is that of children that are being perceived as possessed by spirits. As a practitioner, a specialist social worker and an expert witness, I am interested in what social workers do, or should do when they are confronted with these presenting phenomena. So I have produced a case study to take you through what happened, what should happen and what we should do when we are faced with these given phenomena.

Figure 13.1 Composition of the family

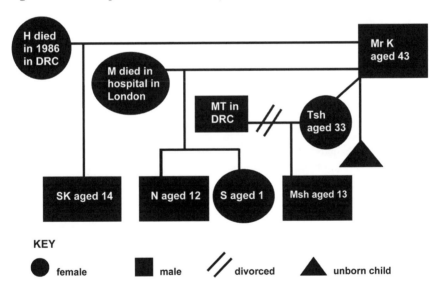

[1]   Much of the material in this chapter has already been published in my *Working with Black African Children and Families. A Report on Two One-Day Workshops Held in April and September 2001* (2002). Inform has my permission to use it and in particular to use the diagrams in it. In editing the presentation for publication I have included some material that I gave as answers to questions.

To start with take a look at Figure 13.1 and keep a focus on the children. That is our paramount consideration, that the children should be given the primary attention. We are particularly concerned with the boy Sebastian,[2] aged 14 at the time of these events.

In 1990 Mr Kavubu came to the UK alone from the Democratic Republic of Congo seeking political asylum. His first wife had died leaving one child, Sebastian. His second wife, their child Norbert, two years younger than Sebastian, and Sebastian joined him in 1991. In 1992 the second Mrs Kavubu gave birth to Suzanne in Whipps Cross Hospital; the baby survived but her mother died from complications after surgery. After this tragic incident, Mr Kavubu met Therese who had also come to this country seeking asylum, with her son from a previous marriage, Michel. Certainly in the environment where I grew up, when your first wife dies and your second wife dies, all the women in that village run away from you. But this guy happened to be in Britain so he was lucky. They married in 1993 and Mr Kavubu, Sebastian, Norbert and baby Suzanne moved in with Therese and Michel. Mr Kavubu was unemployed.

In the same year, 1993, Sebastian was perceived by the family as possessed by *kindoki* (the spirit of witchcraft) and believed to have caused the death of his father's previous two wives. I do not have the space to do more than give you a brief summary of what that means. In the Democratic Republic of Congo the title ancestor is not given to everyone. Only wise men and women who have earned the respect of their fellowmen are honoured with the title of ancestor after their death. The unwise, unkind and the bad ones are called *nkugu*. The spirit of the *nkugu* is *kindoki*, witchcraft, which is believed to be responsible for most deaths.

When an individual is perceived as possessed, it has a corresponding effect on the behaviour of the accused individual and he or she manifests the behaviour that both they and their family see as characteristic of someone possessed by *kindoki*, as was the case with Sebastian. The intruding spirits then have to be driven out of the individual by magico-religious formulae: noises, dancing, praying and sometimes by making incisions or cuts. In Sebastian's case his family claimed that they had not used incisions, although there were cuts all over his body; his injuries were caused, they said, by his throwing himself against the wall and on the floor when he was possessed by *kindoki*.

Sebastian was isolated. No member of the family interacted, communicated or played with him and he also believed that he was possessed and manifested the behavioural characteristics of an individual possessed by *kindoki*, as understood both by himself and his family. He had nightmares. He talked about being taken away by *kindoki* to the cemetery and about drinking blood from dead bodies. He talked about being the spiritual cause of the death of his father's two wives. He would get hysterical at times and throw himself against the wall and onto the floor, resulting in injuries to himself. His behaviour at school was similar.

Sebastian's problem was compounded, however, by a medical problem which Mr Kavubu felt needed treatment. Sebastian, he stated, complained of pains in

---

2   All the names in the case history are fictitious.

his genitals and when he was medically examined by the family he had neither testicles nor a proper scrotum. When I visited the boy, his father called him over and said 'Auntie Amma' (as I am often called) and before I knew where I was he pulled down the boy's trousers, saying 'Look there is nothing there, that is why I am saying this boy is possessed by *kindoki*.' In his country such an abnormality may be seen as evidence of being a witch.[3] Having been brought up myself in an area where the subject is not openly discussed, I went home after this event and checked with my husband what was normal male physique. (He thought I was either possessed or losing my mind!)

One night Sebastian went to his parents' room saying that the spirits were calling him to follow them. He was hysterical and threw himself against the wall and onto the floor, causing injuries. The family made a lot of noise, as these spirits needed to be removed from the possessed person and loud prayers are involved. They also poured water over him to free him. A neighbour became concerned and called the police and when they came they found Sebastian behind the door having cold water poured over him. They also noticed cuts and bruises on his body. So straight away a Police Protection order was taken, followed by an Emergency Protection Order. Sebastian was taken to hospital and admitted for observation. The other three siblings were all placed with a foster carer. Social Services were informed and an initial child protection conference was held; the decision was taken to put Sebastian on the Area Child Protection Register under all the categories one can think of. The case was then referred to what was then called the Specialist Child Protection Team and that is where I got involved in the case.

Now we can take a look at the family's support systems

Figure 13.2   The support network of the family

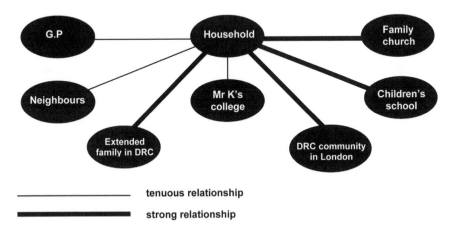

——————————   tenuous relationship

▬▬▬▬▬▬▬▬▬▬   strong relationship

---

[3]   This condition, undescended testicles, can be cured by a simple operation.

I like to use diagrams and from this one you can see clearly why the neighbour called the police. The family did not have a good relationship with the neighbour, although they did have a strong bond with an evangelical church and with their extended family in Africa. The neighbours called the police because they did not have a good relationship with the family, but in that case it actually served the interests of the child.

Let us look at the intervention. At the time the third wife was pregnant; she had been pregnant apparently for ten months and the doctors were running around looking for her, because she refused to have an induction of any kind as she thought that the baby would come when it was ready, so she hid from them. The anxiety level in the house was rising in a crescendo and Sebastian was then seen as possessed. Then there was the police intervention and the social services and the siblings taken into care. There had been conferences and then I took over.

As you may be aware, social work is largely a mental process though we are given a few physical tools to work with. The key things to look at are:

1. a general knowledge of child protection;
2. a particular knowledge of the family in question;
3. a knowledge of the informal, formal and social systems surrounding both the worker and the client. And the last one is:
4. a form of self-knowledge (see Mitchell, 1996: 1) This involves an understanding of one's own motives, irrational fears, obsessions and so on so that these do not interfere with the exercise of distinguishing the fact from the non-factual. So what we are being told here is that with all your knowledge and your skills, there is also yourself to deal with and that means that a certain sort of self-knowledge of your anxieties, your prejudices or anything that may stop you working effectively.

So where do we begin in terms of working with these children? Professor Nobles wrote (1973) that to understand this child you are to work with, you must understand the African philosophical view of self. He writes that it is: 'I am because we are and because we are there, I am.' Emphasising this view, he makes no real distinction between the self and others, they are in a sense one and the same. Self-identity is always a people's identity. Or what one can call an extended self. So it is not only the state of mind of the child but the state of mind of the family as well, because you cannot work with the boy in isolation. So while you are working with the boy you are working with the family. And we would work closely with the school and compare behaviour in both places.

However an accusation of *kindoki* does not only impact on the children's learning and behaviour in school, it impacts on the well-being of the child, the psychological health, the identity, the whole being of the child. And in many cases the children also see themselves as possessed. There is no short way to deconstructing the set mind of the child. So whereas I took his three siblings home to the family quite soon, I had to work with the boy and the family in my case history for a year before he could go home. Those of us who have been involved in cases showing various practices prejudicial to the African child would know that you must turn the parent's attention to the effect, the harmful effect, of whatever the phenomenon is that we are dealing with. Once the community understands the health and mental implications of the practice we move them along. So there is hope.

The art of social work is certainly one's ability to relate the theory, views and the skills to practice. I propose a method to do this. You ask the children, in a language they understand, to draw themselves in the middle of a page, as the self, and put around them everyone else and any object or thing they cannot do without and then pick the three most important to them. This shows a good deal about them. The detailed outcome can be seen in my book (Anane-Agyei, 2002). Here we just show Sebastian's drawing

Figure 13.3   Diagram to illustrate a child's perception of essentials

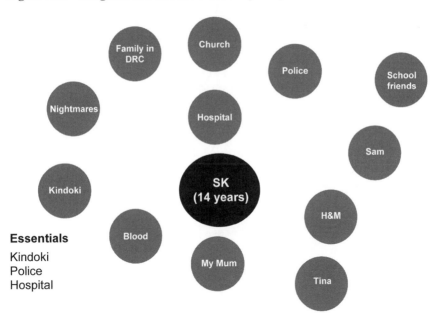

which makes clear his isolation from the others in his family and his awareness of his dependence on the authorities.

The thinking behind the second tool is from Andrew Billingsley (1968) who is an African American himself: 'to say a people have no culture is to say that they have no common history that has shaped and taught them. To deny the history of a people is to deny their humanity. I believe that the principle of maintaining a positive cultural and racial identity and their value in terms of an individual's mental and emotional well being should be firmly accepted in social work.' So in relating that to practice: when you talk of the culture, I mean the culture of the children, of the clients that we work with, who are the children. By culture I mean the totality of the children's way of life. So you must talk to the children about their culture, what they perceive as their culture of origin and whether or not they mean here in Britain; about the composition of their family, what they perceive as the composition of their family. They might for example have parents but those that they are in foster-care with are also their parents.

So, in my view, in working with these families therefore, there needs to be an acknowledgement, at the highest level, by people who have the power to change things, of the need for specialist skills and knowledge. Moreover the social workers should share their knowledge and skills with their clients. Social workers have to know the theological framework and where the family is coming from. There have been cases where social workers have been involved with families for years and the children have never heard about the children's part in the problems. These families have not got a clue about the power that the social services have, the reasons why they have the power to intervene and remove their children. Understanding the family is not going to work by itself, however; you have to be seen to be showing that you respect them, regardless of their poverty or whatever social level they are at. And sometimes you have to disclose things about yourself to make a connection with the family. I'm not talking about suddenly pouring all your problems out on them, but saying something that makes you human, in order to establish a relationship with the family. You must also acknowledge that state intervention is not common in their country of origin. You also have to be mindful that your first contact is very relevant because if you get it wrong, then you set yourself back a stage right at the beginning. For example you should identify the best time to visit the family because they work round the clock: some of them do early morning cleaning, or in the afternoons, at night – round the clock. And then you explore their expectations and you succeed if you are generous in your approach, but any pretence will be spotted.

References

Anane-Agyei, A. (2002). *Working with Black African Children and Families. A Report on Two One-Day Workshops Held in April and September 2001.* London: Learning Design Ltd.

Billingsley, A. (1968). *Black Families in White America.* Englewood Cliffs, NJ: Prentice Hall.

Ellis, J. (ed.) (1978). *West African Families in Britain.* Routledge: Kegan Paul.

Mitchell, R.C. (1996). 'The United Nations Convention on the Rights of the Child and Canadian Implementation Efforts for Indigenous Children and Youth', *Child and Family Social Work*, 1/4: 243-54.

Nobles, W. (1973). 'Psychological Research and the Black Self-Concept: A Critical Review', *Journal of Social Issues*, 22.

Chapter 14

'Project Violet': Addressing the Practice of Faith and/or Belief Based Ritualistic Related Abuse of Children

Robert Pull

Introduction

I was a Detective Inspector with the Metropolitan Police with 30 years police service and I retired in September 2006. Prior to retirement I was operational leader on Project Violet, a project set up by the Child Abuse Investigation Command (SCD5) as a response to 'the practice of faith and/or belief based ritualistic related abuse of children'. This type of abuse on a child may involve physical assault, mental cruelty, sexual assault or neglect by an adult because they believe their faith, religion or belief, demands such behaviour, actions or religious ritual. The exorcism of demons in a manner described above would constitute abuse.

In the five years before this, I worked in a multi-faith environment, building strategic links for the Metropolitan Police with Sikhs, Hindus, Muslims, Jews and Christians. When I left the police service I set up an organisation which is called Safe2Worship[1] which primarily assists the relatively new and emerging black majority Christian churches to develop child safeguarding policies and procedures in the UK. There is an intention to offer consultancy and training services to all faith communities.

The Forming of Project Violet

Project Violet was set up as a result of a number of issues; the first being the Victoria Climbié enquiry, where some police and social workers received severe criticism of their actions. Victoria Climbié was so severely abused that it was fatal. Prior to her murder she had actually been to a deliverance service at a church in London. The pastor of the church didn't recognise the marks and scars on her body as the result of serious assaults that had nothing to do with spirit possession. She was the victim of abuse and serious neglect by the guardians.

---

[1] For more information, see www.safe2worship.co.uk.

Another case that police currently believe to be related to ritual murder was that of a child named posthumously as 'Adam'. Adam's torso was discovered in the River Thames. It was subsequently discovered through forensic examination that the child might have come from Nigeria. Police have yet to discover the identity of the child. No one has been brought to justice for this murder. During the investigation the Metropolitan Police Serious Crime Group Commander Andy Baker[2] said 'We are looking at the possibility of a ritual murder.' The investigating officer described the murder as a *muti* killing. This entails the ritual murder of a person and utilising body parts to make potions or charms to bring good luck or remove curses for individuals. These two cases alone make it understandable as to why police have got an interest in spirit possession and in practices which cause injury not only to children but to adults as well.

The third and equally important case that became the catalyst for the formation of Project Violet was a case where two women and one man were convicted of child abuse. The victim in this case was a girl of eight[3] who came from Angola and had Congolese connections. She was living with a distant relative who at first claimed she was the girl's mother; DNA testing proved she was not. The child was accused of being a witch possessed by *kindoki*.[4] The adults took her to an independent Congolese church whose pastor confirmed the diagnosis.

The two women and the man had a responsibility to care for the child, but they proceeded to beat, stab and abuse her. They then put her into a laundry bag with the intention of throwing her off a second floor balcony, prior to drowning her in a nearby river. This was all because they believed she was possessed by an evil spirit. They changed their minds and let her live. They were convicted of various criminal offences and were sent to prison for many years.

The implications of the above should also be seen in the context of a wider global community. These are not solely issues concerning various African Communities. Over recent years the Metropolitan Police Service (MPS) had become aware of various activities which in this country are illegal and seen as offences committed against children. These include forced marriage, female genital mutilation, the immigration of children alone and various spiritual syncretic[5] practices including abusive forms of deliverance ministry or exorcism practised across many faith communities. Such offences are generally, but not exclusively, confined to African and Asian diaspora communities in the UK. A report for the MPS completed by

---

[2] Report by Dan McDougall, *The Scotsman*, 31 January 2002.

[3] She could not be identified because of a court order and was known throughout the trial as Child B.

[4] Translated into English this means 'witchcraft'. In Lingala, the trade language of eastern Congo, it may also be written *ndoki*.

[5] A blending of cultures, spiritual beliefs and practices.

Perdeep Gill[6] argued that there was anecdotal evidence to confirm the police concerns.

To complicate the picture there are issues of child trafficking from the African and Asian continents, economic migration of young children, illegal private fostering arrangements, and the emerging issue of children being sent from the UK to the parents' country of origin to facilitate deliverance ministry.

When Does the Practice of a Religious Belief or Faith Become Abusive?

Definition of Child Abuse[7]

Based on the premise of a 'child suffering or likely to suffer significant harm' the following constitutes child abuse in the UK.

Physical Abuse

Physical abuse may involve hitting, shaking, throwing, poisoning, burning or scalding, drowning, suffocating, or otherwise causing physical harm to a child. Physical harm may also be caused when a parent or carer fabricates the symptoms of, or deliberately induces illness in a child.

Sexual Abuse

Sexual abuse involves forcing or enticing a child or young person to take part in sexual activities, including prostitution, whether or not the child is aware of what is happening. The activities may involve physical contact, including penetrative sex (for example; rape or buggery, that is anal sex) or non-penetrative acts (oral sex). Such activities may include involving children in looking at, or in the production of, pornographic material or in watching sexual activities, or encouraging children to behave in sexually inappropriate ways.

---

[6]   The 'Community Partnership Project Report 2004–5', conducted by Perdeep Gill for Aditi Consultancy Services, commissioned by the Metropolitan Police was leaked to the media in June 2005 before its public release. A London newspaper subsequently published an article with a banner headline 'London churches sacrifice Children' and the Metropolitan Police Authority subsequently declined to publish the document in full.

[7]   Extract from 'Safe and Secure' a booklet produced by the Churches Child Protection Advisory Service in Partnership with the Metropolitan Police, February 2006. The definition relates to The Children Act 1989.

Neglect

Neglect is the persistent failure to meet a child's basic physical and/or psychological needs, likely to result in the serious impairment of the child's health or development. Neglect may occur during pregnancy as a result of the mother's taking drugs or drinking too much. Once a child is born, neglect may involve a parent or carer failing to provide adequate food, clothing or shelter including exclusion from home or abandonment, failing to protect a child from physical and emotional harm or danger, failure to ensure adequate supervision including the use of inadequate care-takers, or the failure to ensure access to appropriate medical care or treatment. It may also include neglect of, or unresponsiveness to, a child's basic emotional needs.

Emotional Abuse

Emotional abuse is the persistent emotional ill-treatment of a child such as to cause severe and persistent adverse effects on the child's emotional development. It may involve conveying to children that they are worthless or unloved, inadequate or valued only insofar as they meet the needs of another person. It may feature expectations imposed on children that are inappropriate for a child's age or developmental stage. These may include interactions that are beyond the child's developmental capability, as well as overprotection and limitation of exploration and learning, or preventing the child participating in normal social interaction. It may involve seeing or hearing the ill treatment of another. It may involve causing children to frequently feel frightened or in danger, or the exploitation or corruption of children. Some level of emotional abuse is involved in all types of ill-treatment of a child, though it may occur alone.

By this definition, abuse can still occur when consideration for a child's emotional well-being is not respected, even when children have not been harmed physically. This can easily happen, in prayer ministry involving children, in particular when it relates to a child partaking in deliverance services either as the subject or even the witness to the 'exorcism of evil spirits'. The key is to be found in the expression that a 'child is suffering or likely to suffer significant harm' is abuse.

Furthermore, to accuse and attempt to 'deliver' a child from being a witch or being possessed by *kindoki* may involve actions that affect all four parts of that definition. In particular emotional abuse may take place, where continually referring to the child as a witch is shown to cause significant harm to the child. Neglect may occur by encouraging a child or forcing them to fast. In one case[8] the child was forced to fast for seven days, not even allowed to drink water or clean his or her teeth. The ritual continued one week on, with one week off, for a number of months.

---

[8]   This case cannot be identified for legal reasons.

The physical and emotional abuse of the children reported to police included putting chilli peppers on genitals, whipping, stabbing and imprisoning. Such abuse is caused by some families being gripped by a total belief in evil spirits, and their lives being lived on this basis. This belief is sometimes encouraged by faith leaders.

In the light of all this, Project Violet developed as a means to address these complex cultural developments which are also criminal, and by doing this to try and prevent further atrocities. This also involved gathering information which would have an effect on prosecutions, and on the prevention and detection of future criminal acts of this sort.

Project Violet

Six priorities were to:

- Install a high level of confidence in partnership agencies and the wider community in the way the MPS responds to and deals with allegations of ritualistic belief-related child abuse.
- Initiate intelligence led, pro-active investigations to identify and judiciously deal with those involved in the practice of ritualistic belief-related child abuse.
- Co-ordinate and manage the progress and quality of each investigation.
- In partnership with faith communities, develop an effective education and prevention programme.
- Raise awareness by organising or hosting conferences on relevant themes and by delivering training directed at these issues.
- Agree a multi-agency media strategy.

Community Engagement

Whilst I worked as part of a team of four to achieve all of the strategic objectives, I had only a relatively short time to actually concentrate on engagement with faith communities and partnership activities. I chose to focus my efforts on Congolese communities where there were immediate concerns. This also involved working with social services, health, the Church, the Churches Child Protection Advisory Service and other child agencies in the statutory and voluntary sector.

My work was primarily to help in terms of training and education. However, by the very nature of my occupation at the time I was also involved in gathering information to assist prosecutions if required.

Such building of partnerships was exceptionally useful and forms a significant part of my current role as a community's consultant. The relationships I have within the independent, predominately black majority church communities across

London have been invaluable. I also discovered an extraordinary range of Christian theology, style of worship and belief.

Congolese Communities Engagement

In my experience the Congolese communities in London and the UK reflect that of the Democratic Republic of Congo. Their religious membership in the DRC is estimated as:

- Indigenous traditional beliefs: 11.5 per cent;
- Roman Catholic Christianity: 41 per cent;
- Protestant Christianity: 32 per cent;
- African Christianity: 13.5 per cent, nearly all of whom (13 per cent) are followers of Kimbanguism;
- Other Christian denominations: 1 per cent;
- Islam: 1.5 per cent.

There are small communities of Jews and Hindus. Atheism appears to be rare. The vast majority of Congolese citizens have a belief in witchcraft though the abuse of children accused of it is a relatively recent development.

I identified a particular group of Christian pastors who come from the Evangelical Pentecostal Congolese churches. Evidence suggested that this particular group were generally engaged with deliverance ministry with children, although they were not the only ones.

My investigations led me to engage with a small group of Congolese and Angolan pastors. In my dual role of police officer and trainee Christian Pastor, I met with them one evening in Tottenham, North London, and highlighted the issues of child abuse within Congolese communities. The meeting was conducted in English, French and to a lesser extent Lingala. As a result of this meeting an accountability umbrella group was formed which has now grown to over 180 pastors. Membership is formed from across the UK and is known as the 'Congolese Pastorship'.

In the past 18 months in partnership with the Metropolitan Police and CCPAS the Pastorship has:

- introduced child safeguarding policies and procedures;
- undergone child safeguarding training for 230 church leaders/workers;
- arranged a community conference with social services to encourage fostering and adoption within the Congolese Christian Community;
- become aligned with other UK church umbrella groups;
- attended a community meeting where they were the subject of criticism by families who had been accused of witchcraft.

As part of their organisational development they now wish to extend their influence in respect of child safeguarding beyond the UK such as the street children of Kinshasa.[9] There is also evidence that Congolese Protestant Evangelical Christian Communities are beginning to adopt the Pastorship model of accountability across various countries in Europe and USA.

In addition to my work with the Protestant Evangelical Christian Pastors I met and provided training for UK leaders of the Kimbanguist Church. Kimbanguists are followers of the late Simon Kimbangu who was an evangelist imprisoned by the Belgian authorities in the Congo accused of crimes against the state. After his death in prison and the eventual release of his corpse to his family, his casket was opened to reveal that his body had not decomposed. He had founded a religious movement closely aligned to Christianity but not universally accepted as Trinitarian.

Putting the Issues in Context

The Department for Education and Skills commissioned a report by the independent researcher Eleanor Stobart to measure the extent of abuse and provide recommendations. In her report Stobart stated in the executive summary[10]

> Seventy-four cases of abuse clearly linked to accusations of 'possession' and 'witchcraft' were identified. To safeguard against double-counting, only cases for which there were identifying factors were analysed. Therefore, this report only analyses thirty-eight of these cases. It should be noted that prior to enquiries only fourteen cases were clearly identified and new cases were being reported right up to the date of publication of this report. The number of cases of child abuse linked to accusations of 'possession' and 'witchcraft' so far identified is small compared to the total number of children abused each year. In the year to 31 March 2005, 30,700 children were placed on child protection registers in England. There were 72,100 child protection enquiries in England in the year to 31 March 2004.

This evidence allows us to better understand the numerical context of the cases we are dealing with. It is my contention that the extreme manner of abuse combined with the ethnicity of the alleged abusers has fuelled media attention. Government and agencies react to the press scrutiny. Whole communities then become stigmatised and marginalised. This is not in any way to condone the horrific crimes

---

[9] M. Waddington (2006).'"Child Witches", Child Soldiers, Child Poverty and Violence: Street Children DR Congo', gives a comprehensive overview of the issues affecting children and the challenges to be faced.

[10] E. Stobart (2006). 'Child Abuse Linked to Accusations of "Possession" and "Witchcraft"'. See Chapter 12 in this volume.

against children nor is it a comment on the widespread belief in witchcraft[11] which from my own observations and as evidenced by daily internet news reports, is endemic within various communities across the world.

Issues of belief in witchcraft and the syncretism of faith and culture goes beyond the Congo, but the model for engagement with the Congolese communities provides an insight into the complexities of engaging with emerging communities. It is also insufficient to concentrate purely on communities. During my watch, Project Violet also worked in partnership with, and on training for, staff in the statutory and voluntary sector. My team and I attended seminars and conferences providing advice to those involved in health, education, children's services, police and other child safeguarding agencies.

Beyond this work the team gathered information. As cases came to light enforcement was conducted through the arrest of some individuals. There were however no further prosecutions during my time with Project Violet. The lack of prosecutions and convictions in this area of criminality is in part because authorities have as yet not fully engaged with the communities nor are the issues fully understood by the statutory agencies. I do however submit that whilst it would be naive to suggest that the practices have ceased, there is compelling assumptions that the continued work with the Congolese Pastorship may have prevented the abuse of some children in the UK. There is also the possibility that this prevention strategy may prevent some abuse against street children in Kinshasa whose pastors have UK links.

Conclusion

In this short chapter, I have endeavoured to give a whistle-stop summary of some of the issues that arise on the subject of policing 'the practice of faith and/or belief based ritualistic related abuse of children'. It is by no means comprehensive and perhaps provokes more questions than it answers. By concentrating on the Congolese Christian community's response to my engagement with them, I hopefully have provided a model from which solutions for other communities may evolve.

I am not naïve enough to believe that every church within the umbrella group of the Congolese Pastorship will have a leader or leaders who comply with the new child safeguarding policies and procedures. After all, the UK indigenous mainstream churches are not immune from having abusers in their midst.[12] But I am sufficiently convinced as I continue to consult, advise and work with Congolese

---

[11]   The term witchcraft is used as the least misleading word to describe beliefs and practices within the context of this chapter.

[12]   The Revd Simon Thomas, aged 44, of Hythe, Hampshire, a married church minister, is facing a life sentence after pleading guilty to 35 counts of child abuse, including two charges of raping an 11-year-old boy. 'Minister is Guilty of Rape'. 29 June 2006. [Online].

pastors that there is a sea change of confidence within their congregations. Those leaders outside of the accountability group may in turn feel the pressure, perhaps by dwindling numbers and dare I say finance, to consider their theological positions and seek to be part of an accountability grouping.

Whilst enforcement must have a place as part of the solution, I argue that engagement, education and training of church leaders, workers and opinion formers, are by far the best and most effective means of safeguarding children from abuse in the context of exorcism and deliverance.

Beverly Hughes, the Children's Minister said 'These are relatively new communities in this country, they're relatively closed already and we can't actually be clear that we're safeguarding children properly unless we do open up conversations ...'[13] This statement effectively sums up the work that I have been engaged with, and I cannot emphasise enough the importance of community engagement.

References

Gill, P. (2005). *Community Partnership Project 2004-5*. London: Aditi Consultancy Services.

McDougall, D. (2002). Report in *The Scotsman*, 31 January.

'Minister is Guilty of Child Rape'. 29 June 2006. [Online]. Available at: http://news.bbc.co.uk/1/hi/england/hampshire/5129386stm [accessed: 24 August 2009].

Pearson, D. (ed.) (2006). *Safe and Secure*. Swanley: CCPAS/MPS Partnership.

Stobart, E. (2006). 'Child Abuse Linked to Accusations of "Possession" and "Witchcraft"'. London: Department for Education and Skills Research Report RR750. Available online at: http://www.dcsf.gov.uk/research/programmeofresearch/projectinformation.cfm?projectid=14953&resultspage=1

Waddington, M. (2006). '"Child Witches", Child Soldiers, Child Poverty and Violence: Street Children DR Congo'. London: All Party Government Report.

'Witch Trial Girl's "Mother" Found'. 1 July 2005. [Online]. Available at: http://news.bbc.co.uk/1/hi/uk/4670727.stm [accessed: 10 September 2009].

Available at: http://news.bbc.co.uk/1/hi/england/hampshire/5129386.stm [Accessed: 24 August 2009].

[13] BBC News Website report: 'Witch Trial Girl's "Mother" Found'. 1 July 2005. [Online]. Available at: http://news.bbc.co.uk/1/hi/uk/4670727.stm [accessed: 10 September 2009].

Acknowledgements

David Pearson (CCPAS).
Chris Bourlet (Superintendent, Metropolitan Police).
The Congolese Pastorship.
Jo Clark (Detective Constable, Metropolitan Police).
Jason Morgan (Detective Constable, Metropolitan Police).
Andrew Cameron (Police Sergeant, Metropolitan Police).
Safe2worship Partnership © 18 January 2007.

Chapter 15

The Christian Church and Child Protection – an Overview

David Pearson

This chapter takes a look at recent trends and influences within the church in the UK in the area of child protection. Due to the significant growth of independent Christian gatherings, it can be seen that 'church' in the twenty-first century comprises not only the traditional denominations but also faith groups, congregating in conventional church buildings and transient meeting places. As we will see these trends have raised new issues in terms of effective child protection, but whatever the tradition, it continues to be the case that every church has a vital role to play in safeguarding children.

It may be stating the obvious, but the Christian church is not one single organisation. Although many of its foundational beliefs are comparable, it is nevertheless made up of a multitude of diverse and different groups that operate across the whole spectrum of society. Bodies such as Churches Together in Britain and Ireland, the Free Church Federal Council, the Evangelical Alliance and the African Caribbean Evangelical Alliance operate as coalitions representing some of these individual groups, but none speak on behalf of all.

In addition, it is not uncommon for an independent church to be formed in somebody's front room today, be meeting in a warehouse tomorrow or perhaps cease to exist altogether. Such groups are often isolated from other churches and networks, and can be extremely difficult to locate in order to disseminate any sort of child protection message. The same sort of fragmentation exists in other faith groups.

Developing Child Protection Policies in Churches

Following publication of *Safe from Harm* (Home Office) in 1993, the older church denominations began developing formal child protection policies. Today most have designated child protection officers with varying degrees of child protection experience, responsibility and influence. The Church of England, for example, has a National Child Protection Adviser as well as a Bishop's Adviser for each Diocese. A similar arrangement operates within the Roman Catholic Church, but most other denominations have one named individual centrally. Many newer and independent churches (and some denominations) have adopted policies based on a Churches' Child Protection Advisory Services (CCPAS) model contained in our comprehensive child protection manual, Guidance to Churches, which over the years has had a strong influence on policy formation across the church and other faiths. Peter Brierley's study (2006)[1] discovered that 73 per cent of all church leaders knew about Guidance to Churches, whilst 25 per cent were using CCPAS as a main source of child protection information. From those who contact our helpline, it is clear that as churches develop such child protection policies they also grow in their ability to identify and respond to the needs of children at risk.

The Charity Commission requires churches and organisations working with children and young people to adopt child protection policies before granting registration, and they are often referred to CCPAS to aid this process. These requirements and insurance company expectations make it more likely these days that child protection policy issues will be addressed by churches sooner rather than later. CCPAS places a significant emphasis on the safe recruitment of workers, support, training and reporting procedures, in conformity with national policies, that, ironically, did not include churches until the CCPAS campaigned for their inclusion (see reference to *Working Together* below). This policy also includes 'whistle blowing' clauses enabling individuals to raise issues outside the church or organisation if the internal response has been inappropriate or insufficient. CCPAS also stresses the need to publicise policies, procedures and helpline numbers to all, including children.

The benefit of telephone help-lines should not be underestimated. ChildLine, the free telephone helpline established 20 years ago, has been recognised as an important resource for abused children, who may find it difficult to speak about their abuse. Similarly, Church representatives, children, victims and others can also be reluctant to contact the statutory services initially and find it easier to phone the CCPAS helpline. Receiving some 500 calls a week, CCPAS helps individuals to report concerns appropriately and, if needed, provide on-going support to those involved.

The Church as a Service Provider

Apart from schools, the church probably works with more children than any other organisation. The church therefore has a duty to ensure the protection of all children in its care including vulnerable children and young people, some of

---

[1]   Dr Peter Brierley works for Christian Research, which is responsible for the church attendance survey carried out bi-annually. This study commissioned by CCPAS, selected a substantial sample of churches in England to reflect the full spectrum of denominations, churchmanship (or leadership), geographical location (urban/rural) and congregational size. Information was sought separately from both the church leadership (the clergy) and those working directly with children and young people from 0-18 years. The results were published in January 2006 as 'Churches and Children 2005'.

whom will be victims of abuse or regarded as being 'in need' under section 17 of The Children Act 1989.

Churches also have a 'social service' function. In many communities, people turn to the church first for help, advice and support, especially when health and social care agencies are not able to meet a specific need. Black majority churches in particular have an excellent track record in this area. Help from churches is also available during evenings, weekends and bank holidays, when other agencies are closed.

It is a fact that some people approach churches for help due to a mistrust of the statutory agencies. This is particularly true of churches serving minority ethnic communities and those on the margins of society, inevitably including vulnerable children and their carers who have limited or no contact with formal agencies. CCPAS always emphasises the responsibility of church leaders to pass on any child protection concerns to the appropriate investigating authorities and also, where appropriate, encourages parents and young people to make contact directly. However, churches often provide much-needed day-to-day support from their own resources. It follows therefore that churches should consider themselves, and be considered, part of the local child protection network and maintain close links with statutory agencies.

The Role of CCPAS

An important strength of CCPAS is that although a Christian organisation, it has no allegiance to a particular denomination, church structure or faith group. This independence enables it to respond without compromise on behalf of children and survivors of abuse and, if necessary, challenge a church or faith group's decisions or practices. Although CCPAS is an important resource to the independent churches, statistically most of its work is in the established denominations because of their size. This includes support to denominational child protection officers in policy development, training and advice in particular cases. CCPAS also supports victims of abuse who may feel unable to go to their church or the local statutory services. It is important that CCPAS is able to mount such challenges and provide support independently, especially in light of some of the concerns outlined below.

'Closed' Churches and Groups

As in other communities, there are exclusive churches and sects that appear closed to the outside world. Such institutions raise particular concerns in identifying children at risk. They include:

- sects or groups which lack accountability and which are exclusive by nature and not related to the rest of the community;

- groups which promote a mistrust of secular authorities and a corresponding reluctance to work in partnership for the sake of children's welfare, especially those who believe that allegations of abuse should be dealt with internally;
- an imbalanced interpretation of Christian doctrine which is used to justify the subjugation of women and children, a denial or minimisation of their rights and, in some circumstances, the demonisation of such individuals;
- an over-emphasis on control of children which can be associated with harsh discipline;
- a lack of awareness of the risks to children based on naivety about people's good nature;
- dangerous assumptions such as *people in our community would not abuse children*, or that a display of repentance and granting of forgiveness following acts of abuse means that an adult no longer poses a risk to a child; and
- a lack of priority given to the protection of children and a reluctance on the part of some leaders to get to grips with the challenges of implementing sound child protection policies and practices.

CCPAS engages regularly with these groups, where it can, to seek a change of attitude and will often advise statutory agencies in relation to particular investigations.

Churches and Sex Offenders

From our work with statutory agencies CCPAS is aware that in some areas 50 per cent of known sex offenders attend a place of worship regularly. In many situations (but not all) it is possible to supervise offenders attending a church or faith group by setting clear boundaries as part of a written agreement. CCPAS has devised a model contract which, according to Peter Brierley's research (2003), some 83 per cent of churches in England are using where there are known offenders in the congregation. Such a contract is based on the provision of supervision and pastoral care to the offender; contact with the police, probation and any other agencies involved; and linking with any Multi Agency Public Protection Arrangements (MAPPA) involvement.

Faith and Abuse

The relationship between beliefs and abuse is one that cannot be ignored. For example, an Anglican lay reader (also a GP) who recently attended one of our conferences said that the procedures for dealing with an allegation of child sexual abuse were '*non Christian ...and sneaking to the authorities*', and quoted bible references (out of context) to support his argument. There are also cultural differences that complicate the issues. Some of these are:

- an over-emphasis (in British eyes) on control of children which can be associated with what British people would consider harsh discipline and which might constitute the (British) legal offence of abuse;
- the mistaken view that the British authorities wish to prevent them bringing up their children in the way their own culture prescribes;
- loyalty to the community that treats the possibility of abuse as a slur which must be combated, not considered as a warning that will help them to be prepared;
- a lack of priority given to the protection of children and a reluctance on the part of some leaders to get to grips with the challenges of implementing sound child protection policies and practices.

Whilst it is not generally the role of safeguarding agencies to judge culture or belief, clearly there are some beliefs and practices that have to be challenged. Recently CCPAS provided a day's child protection training in London for 230 Congolese pastors that addressed concerns raised in the case of 'Child B'. This event was unique in that the leaders had not previously met together as they were from different groupings and individual church fellowships. One result, therefore, was a commitment given on the day to working together as a Pastorate to respond not only to the issues of child protection, but other community concerns too. The organisation which came into being (the Congolese Pastorate) is now being developed across Europe and in the Congo. Representatives of this new grouping have spoken about the issues at various events since then, including at training programmes put on by Africans Unite Against Child Abuse (AFRUCA).

There was quite a mixed group at the training session, with the majority of pastors concerned about the issues and appearing quite genuinely to want to know the legal boundaries in relation to issues like child discipline and so on, but also wanting to address the more serious issues highlighted in the case of 'Child B'. Present also were individuals from the community who were under investigation at that time by the Police, and it was quite clear that we were addressing a few individuals who were well aware of the issues!

A strong point for me that came from the whole day was the need for basic education in regard to the care and upbringing of children as we see it in Britain. A particularly poignant moment involved a mother describing how she had been having difficulties with her child in the Congo. She went to a church leader and asked for prayer for deliverance. Later the woman and her family came to the UK and she was told that the child had autism and he was sent to a special school. By now he was in his teens and as a result of particular problems she approached 'my wise Congolese pastor' (her words) for deliverance prayer, and he told her that her child did not have a witch or demon, but raging hormones. He explained how her son was like any teenager, but given his disability, was unable to express his feelings. The pastor gave her, in effect, a behaviour management programme to follow which worked! This was warmly received by the audience.

This case can be related to one of Eleanor Stobart's findings in her research on children accused of witchcraft, for the DfES (Stobart, 2006 and Chapter 12 of this volume). Children with disabilities were significantly often the victims in cases she located. This emphasises the need for parents and others to be helped in understanding parenting issues, and particularly the problems faced by children with special needs and those struggling with the effects of having come from a war-torn land (where who knows to what they were exposed) to the UK and having to adapt to a totally different culture.[2] Certainly my contact with this community would suggest that they feel very isolated and marginalised in the UK and that they have been under attack. It is not helped by the fact that many are not familiar with English. Since then, together with DI Bob Pull of the Metropolitan Police, we have also been involved in other training events and meetings with other African groups, for example Nigerian Pastors.[3]

The community generally does not have confidence in Children's Services or the Police; indeed they really do not know who they are and what their role is. We initially seek to establish a relationship based on a shared faith (in God). As a result they will often talk more openly with us as fellow believers and they will feel that we will understand where they are coming from. Whilst it is not our role to question beliefs (unless there are safeguarding issues), we will present alternative ways of looking at issues and help leaders to appreciate and meet the expectations in the UK, providing a bridge to statutory and voluntary agencies. The publication, *Safe and Secure*, (CCPAS) contains clear child protection guidance within a faith context. We are uncompromising in what we say about our responsibilities to safeguard children and to report any concerns about possible abuse. This is understood and respected. As a result, CCPAS is in a better position to tackle these issues than a statutory body, though it is vitally important that agencies do not apply different thresholds in these circumstances.

Should Churches be Regulated?

In a final submission of Phase 1 of the Inquiry into Victoria Climbié's death, her parents' Counsel, Margot Boye, called for statutory regulations for churches. She told the Inquiry:

> Having heard the evidence from several churches, it cannot be left to the churches to take on a welfare and childcare role... If some sort of statutory regulation is not looked at there can be little doubt that some churches and

---

[2]   See F. de Boeck (Chapter 11 in this volume) and also his book *Kinshasa. Tales of the Invisible City* written with Marie-Francoise Plissart (2004).

[3]   Robert Pull, see Chapter 14 in this volume.

religious institutions will continue to act in a manner that is totally at odds with the child's welfare.

CCPAS does not believe that this proposal is workable or that it is necessary. In the past, statutory procedures have not saved children such as Victoria Climbié or others who have suffered abuse and died. The majority of churches now understand the principles of their role in terms of child protection. The challenge is ensuring implementation.

However, this does not negate the need for the Government to set clear standards for *all agencies*, including faith groups. The DfES consultation paper *Working Together* hardly mentioned churches or faith groups. Since my presentation at Inform's conference, the DfES has recognised the need to include them and *Working Together* now does so.

Conclusion

The role of the church in our communities should not be underestimated, as for many people it provides a service in much the same way as statutory services. This means that while churches should not be singled out for statutory measures and regulation, they should be considered and included in legislation in much the same way as other statutory services. The traditional, mainstream Christian churches have managed to incorporate child protection successfully in most instances. However, there are still challenges for organisations such as CCPAS and the Government in terms of ensuring that harmful practices are identified and confronted in a sensitive and informed manner.

References

De Boeck, F. and M.-F. Plissart (2004). *Kinshasa. Tales of the Invisible City*. Ghent/Tervuren: Ludion/Royal Museum of Central Africa.

Brierley, P. (2006). 'Churches and Children 2005'. Swanley: CCPAS.

—— (2003). *UK Christian Handbook: Religious Trends No. 3*. 2001 (2000/2003 edition). London: Christian Research.

Further Reading

These readings have been recommended by contributors, but have not been referred to explicitly in their articles, so that they do not appear in the list of references at the end of each article.

Adler, M. (1986) (revised edition). *Drawing Down the Moon: Witches, Druids, Goddess-Worshippers and Other Pagans in America Today*. Boston: Beacon Press.

Bado-Fralick, N. (2005). *Coming to the Edge of the Circle: A Wiccan Initiation Ritual*. Oxford: Oxford University Press.

Brown, K.M. (2001). *Mama Lola: A Vodou Priestess in Brooklyn*. Updated and Expanded Edition. (Comparative Studies in Religion and Society; 4) Berkeley/ Los Angeles: University of California Press.

Brunet, A., D.W. Holowka and J.R. Laurence (2001). 'Dissociation', in J. Michael, M.J. Aminoff and R.B. Daroff (eds), *Encyclopedia of Neurological Sciences*. San Diego: Academic Press.

Crowley, V. (1996) (revised edition). *Wicca: The Old Religion in the New Millennium*. London: Aquarian Press.

Dayan, J. (1995). *Haiti, History, and the Gods*. Berkeley: University of California Press.

Desmangles, L. (1992). *The Faces of Gods: Vodou and Roman Catholicism in Haiti*. New York: University of North Carolina Press.

Friesen, J.G. (1991). *Uncovering the Mystery of MPD; Its Shocking Origins ... Its Surprising Cure*. San Bernardino: Here's Life Publications.

Leacock, S. and R. Leacock (1975). *Spirits of the Deep*. New York: Anchor Books.

Lurhmann, T. (1988). *Persuasions of the Witch's Craft: Ritual Magic and Witchcraft in Present-Day England*. Oxford: Blackwell Press.

McAlister, E. (1992/3). 'Sacred Stories from the Haitian Diaspora: A Collective Biography of Seven Vodou Priestess in New York City', *Journal of Caribbean Studies*, 9/1 and 2 (1992/1993): 11-27.

Melton, J.G. (ed.) (2001). *Encyclopedia of Occultism and Parapsychology* (2 vols). Detroit: Gale.

Milner, N. (2000). 'Giving the Devil His Due Process: Exorcism in the Church of England', *Journal of Contemporary Religion*, 15/2: 247-72.

Pearson, J., H. Roberts and G. Samuel (eds) (1998). *Nature Religion Today: Paganism in the Modern World*. Edinburgh: Edinburgh University Press.

Schmidt, B.E. (2008). *Caribbean Diaspora in USA: Diversity of Caribbean Religions in New York City*. Aldershot: Ashgate.

Singleton, A. (2001). 'No Sympathy for the Devil: Narratives about Evil', *Journal of Contemporary Religion*, 15/2: 177-91.

Thomas, K. (1973). *Religion and the Decline of Magic*. Harmondsworth: Penguin.

Whitwell, F.D. and M.G. Barker (1980). '"Possession" in Psychiatric Patients in Britain', *British Journal of Medical Psychology*, 53: 287-95.

Young, A. (1975). 'Why Amhara Get "Kureynya": Sickness and Possession in an Ethiopian "Zar" Cult, *American Ethnologist*, 2/3: 567-84.

Yu, C. and R. Guisso (eds) (1988). *Shamanism: The Spirit World of Korea*. Berkeley: Asian Humanities Press.

Index

Africa 7, 10, 14-15, 17-18, 20, 23-4, 30-31,
    85, 103, 111-12, 115, 118-26,
    132-3, 137, 140, 144, 151, 170,
    176-7, 180-81, 194
    Angola 17-18, 30, 117, 126, 133, 138n,
      142, 180, 184
    Benin, Republic of 92n, 93, 109
    Cameroon 118-19, 144
    Democratic Republic of Congo ix, 7, 9,
      23, 33, 115, 121-22, 129-47, 155,
      169, 174, 180, 183-6, 193
      Kinshasa 7-8, 10n, 115, 120-25,
        129-47, 185-6
    Ghana 23
    Kenya 31
    Morocco 31, 33
    Nigeria xiii, 2n, 30, 92n, 109, 113, 121,
      126, 133n, 180, 194
      Aladura 30
    North Africa 80
    Somalia 80
    South Africa 4
      Soweto 139
    Uganda 118
African-Caribbean/Afro-Caribbean 6, 17n,
    20, 28, 30, 91, 97, 103
African and Caribbean Evangelical
    Alliance 17n, 169, 189
African Initiated Churches/African
    Independent Churches 7, 15n, 17,
    21, 25, 101, 120-21, 125, 184
Africans Unite Against Child Abuse
    (AFRUCA) 193
Afrique Conseil 168-70
Alan, E. 62n-63n
altered state of consciousness 29, 46, 107
America 1-2, 5, 14, 21, 24, 44-6, 49-53, 71,
    91, 94, 133
    New York 28, 91-2, 97-100
American Medical Association 55

American Psychiatric Association 50-51,
    55
amulet 30, 44, 82-4
Anane-Agyei, A. ix, 9, 162, 173
angel 3, 79-80, 82, 105
Anglican, *see* Church of England
Angola, *see under* Africa
Ashforth, A. 139, 144
Asia 17n, 77-8, 82n, 124, 151, 180-81
    Bangladesh 6, 28, 30-31, 77-89, 120,
      124
      Sylhet 77-8, 81-3
    Pakistan 21, 31, 77-8, 80, 84
Asian Times, The 84-5
Assemblies of God 5, 28, 61-75

Bandoki 130, 137
Bangladesh, *see under* Asia
Bangwa 118-19, *see also under* Africa,
    Cameroon
Barker, E. ix, xv, 1
Barry, A. 143
Basham, D. 71-3
Belgium 122, 130n, 168-9
Benin, Republic of, *see under* Africa
Berg, D. 16
Berg, M. 16
bhut, see ghost
Bible 1n, 5, 28, 63, 66, 67, 68n, 70, 71, 73,
    109, 111, 137, 193
Billingsley, A. 177
Boeck de, F. ix, 7-8, 115, 120-22, 125-6,
    129
bori, see possession
Boureau, A. 39
Bourguignon, E. vii, 29, 46
Brain, R. 118-20
Brazil 14, 29, 30, 92n
Brick Lane, *see under* London
Brierley, P. 17n, 190, 192